TEACHER EVALUATION THAT WORKS!!

THE EDUCATIONAL, LEGAL, PUBLIC RELATIONS (POLITICAL) AND SOCIAL–EMOTIONAL (E.L.P.S.) STANDARDS AND PROCESSES OF EFFECTIVE SUPERVISION AND EVALUATION

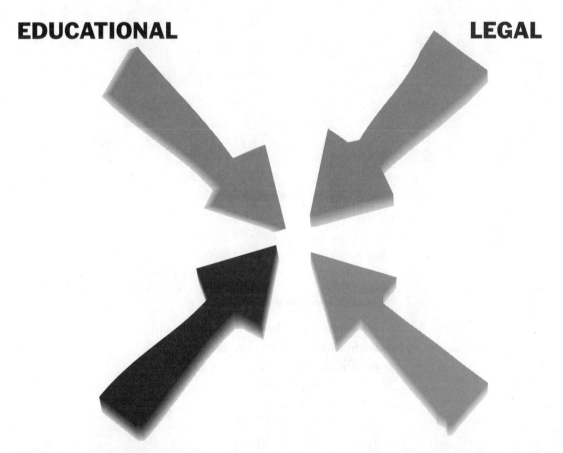

EDUCATIONAL

LEGAL

PUBLIC RELATIONS (Political)

SOCIAL–EMOTIONAL

BY WILLIAM B. RIBAS

For Anna and William,
and all the outstanding teachers and principals
who have touched their lives.

Ribas Publications
9 Sherman Way,
Westwood, MA 02090
Fax: 781-551-9120
ISBN 0-9715089-0-9

THANK YOU

My thanks to the following people for their help with various sections of this book.

James Walsh, Superintendent of Schools in Brookline, MA, and Associate Professor of Educational Administration at Simmons College, and the Brookline School Committee for consistently supporting the development of the E.L.P.S. program over the past seven years.

Philip Katz, Brookline Educators Association President, and David Weinstein, Gretchen Albertini and Bill Hibert, Brookline Educators Association Grievance Committee Chairs for Brookline, MA, for their suggestions on various documents and procedures developed over the past six years.

Dorine Levasseur, Massachusetts Teachers Association Consultant, for her descriptions of "Duty of Fair Representation" and the "Weingarten Right."

Martin Sleeper and Susan Moran, Principals in Brookline, MA; Mike Frantz, Secondary Curriculum Coordinator for Mathematics in Brookline, MA; Mark Springer, Principal of the Mason-Rice School in Newton, MA, and Robin Welch, Principal of the Woodrow Wilson School in Framingham, MA; Ina Hart Thompson, Brookline Educators Association Grievance Team; Sandra Spooner, Executive Director of Research for Better Teaching; Bill Simmons, Principal in the Oneida, NY, Public Schools; Kelly McCausland, Director of Human Resources for the Lexington, MA, Public Schools and Vice President of the Massachusetts Association of School Personnel Administrators; and Don McCallion, Director of Human Resources for the Framingham, MA, Public Schools and past President of the Massachusetts Association for Personnel Administrators, for reading various parts of the book and providing helpful editorial comments.

Robert Fraser, Attorney at the law firm of Stoneman, Chandler and Miller, for the initial translations from "legalese" into lay terms which are the basis for the sections of the book on *due process, just cause* and *progressive discipline.*

Claire Jackson, Superintendent of the Sharon, MA, Public Schools, for assisting with the connections between supervision and evaluation and curriculum implementation.

Carol Gregory, Principal of the Thurston Middle School in Westwood, MA, and Jonathon Saphier, President of Research for Better Teaching, for their work connecting the Brookline Principles of Effective Teaching with the language of *The Skillful Teacher.*

A special thanks also to Jonathon Saphier whose work in the area of supervision and evaluation has been an inspiration to me since my first exposure to it in 1986. Jon has also been very generous with sharing his substantial expertise as a published author when reading drafts of the book.

Gretchen Underwood and Charles Webb, Deans at Brookline High School; Emily Ostrower, Principal, Cambridge, MA, Public Schools; Mary Matthews and Chris Whitbeck, K–8 Curriculum Coordinators, and Carol Schraft, Barbara Shea, John Dempsey and Milly Katzman, Elementary and Middle School Principals in Brookline, MA, for their assistance with case studies and sample documents.

Jennifer Dopazo, Assistant Town Counsel, Brookline, MA, for her help in writing "An Evaluator's Guide to Gathering and Verifying Evidence."

The Lexington and Brookline, MA, Public Schools for permission to use their excellent supervision and evaluation documents as samples for the readers.

Anna and William Ribas for giving their Dad many quiet weekend hours so that he could devote time to writing this book.

Bill Ribas
December 2001

TABLE OF CONTENTS

Chapter 3

The Educational and Social–Emotional Skills and Knowledge
Needed to Be an Effective Supervisor and Evaluator

Ensuring Inter-rater Reliability and Permanent, Positive Change
in Your District's Supervision and Evaluation System 275

   Please Don't Make Me Train the Administrators! 277

      Keep Them Interested 278

      Creating Training Groups 278

      Changing the Groups When Confronted With a Negative Dynamic 279

      Assigning Tasks to Group Members 280

      Getting Started 281

      Why Am I Here? (Think, Pair, Share) 281

      Sample Introductory Activity 282

      Procedures 283

      Handouts 283

      Inter-rater Reliability Activity 1: Climbing the E.L.P.S. 284

      Steps of the Lesson 284

   Increasing Inter-rater Reliability Using Your
   District's Performance and Curriculum Standards 285

      Inter-rater Reliability Activity 2: High-Performing Teachers and
      the District's Teacher Performance Standards 286

      Inter-rater Reliability Activity 3: Recommendations for Improvement Are
      Hard to Hear! or Saying the "Hard-to-Say Stuff" Verbally and in Writing! 286

   Assigning Homework 288

      Inter-rater Reliability Activity 4: Low-Performing Teachers and the
      District's Teacher Performance Standards 289

      Inter-rater Reliability Activity 5: The Way We Want Supervision and
      Evaluation to Happen Versus the Way It Really Happens 290

INTRODUCTION

One of the most important tools districts possess for improving the quality of education for all students is the supervision and evaluation process. It is a district's primary method of quality control and educational improvement. It is one of the few processes that impacts every teacher, thereby affecting the education of every student in the district.

[handwritten note: — really?]

Creating a system for successfully supervising and evaluating the entire teaching staff of a school district is a daunting task. The reason for this is that an effective system-wide program can be achieved only if the administrators, teachers and the teachers' association understand and attend to the educational, legal, public relations (political) and social–emotional dimensions (E.L.P.S.) of supervision and evaluation. Historically, the expertise, time and money needed to provide adequate training for such a program has forced most districts to focus at best on only one or two of these dimensions. Consequently, evaluators are often frustrated with the supervision and evaluation process because they lack the understanding, training and support in the dimensions not addressed.

[handwritten note: — ugh.]

This book provides districts with the tools to systematically *and cost effectively* assess and revise their supervision and evaluation programs so they successfully address the E.L.P.S. The book incorporates my own experiences and those of my colleagues during my twenty-two years as a teacher association officer, administrator association officer, teacher, guidance counselor, curriculum coordinator, vice-principal, principal, director of pupil services, assistant superintendent for personnel (a.k.a. human resources) and as a consultant to school districts assisting with the development of effective supervision and evaluation. During the years in which I worked as vice principal, principal and director of pupil personnel services, I personally conducted over 150 evaluations of teachers, guidance counselors, school psychologists, speech and language therapists and a myriad of support staff. In my years as an assistant superintendent for personnel, I directly supervised over 75 supervisors and evaluators who were responsible for evaluating over 1400 teachers and other school professionals. In my years as a consultant, I have trained over 300 administrators in eight districts of three different states.

> Every example in this book is taken from an actual teacher's evaluation. The evaluation documents, the sample evaluations, the case studies and all the examples are from teachers' evaluations completed by administrators I trained or supervised.

I wrote this book as a practical guide that focuses primarily on proven techniques that are used effectively in school districts. Every example in this book is taken from an actual teacher's evaluation. The evaluation documents, the sample evaluations, the case studies and all the examples are from teachers' evaluations completed by administrators I trained or supervised. The book relies on theory and research, with the support of proven successful practice.

An example of this inclusion of practical experience is that most authors on this topic draw a clear distinction between supervision and evaluation. They treat these concepts as connected but exclusive activities. I believe this separation has some value as an academic framework. However, for the evaluator in the real world of staff supervision and evaluation, these two concepts are virtually inseparable. For example, every evaluator in the course of his/her career will make decisions about whether an observed ineffective teacher behavior is indicative of the teacher's performance or just an aberration. If the evaluator concludes, based on his/her comprehensive knowledge of this teacher, that the activity is a distinct, one-time error, the evaluator may discuss the issue in a supervisory or even collegial manner without formally documenting the activity. If the future shows the issue is indeed a one-time error then the discussion concludes the supervision–evaluation interaction related to this incident. However, if the future shows that the teacher's behavior was an early incident indicative of a change in the teacher's pattern of behavior a yet undetected pattern of behavior, the evaluator will have to reach back to the first incident and the discussion and make it part of the teacher's evaluation history. Every supervisory, collegial or other piece of information the evaluator possesses about the teacher is part of the total body of information the evaluator uses, either consciously or subconsciously, to make his/her final judgments about the teacher's performance.

I agree with the theoreticians that in most evaluator–evaluatee relationships there are (or should be) innumerable interactions aimed at improving teacher performance but are not formally documented. I also agree with the theoreticians that there are specific interactions such as classroom observations, evaluation conferences and the review of professional development plans that are formally documented. In the final analysis, however, if the evaluator is to truly give a 360-degree assessment of a teacher's performance, everything the evaluator sees, hears, tastes and feels must impact the judgments the evaluator makes about the teacher's performance when it comes time to write a summative evaluation. Therefore, throughout this book, I speak of supervision and evaluation as a single activity that is divided into formative and summative activities.

THE EDUCATIONAL, LEGAL, PUBLIC RELATIONS (POLITICAL) AND SOCIAL–EMOTIONAL PROCESSES AND STANDARDS OF SUPERVISION AND EVALUATION

Districts with successful supervision and evaluation programs recognize that each of the four dimensions has processes and standards that must be adhered to. *Webster's New Riverside University Dictionary* defines a process as "a series of actions or functions that achieves a result." (Soukhanov, 1988, p. 938) It defines a standard as "an accepted measure of comparison for quantitative or qualitative value." (Soukhanov, p. 1113) Chapter 1 gives a brief overview of the processes and standards involved in supervision and evaluation.

SOURCE

Soukhanov A. H. (Ed.). (1988). *New Riverside university dictionary.* Boston: Houghton Mifflin Company.

Chapter 1

Ascending the E.L.P.S. (Educational, Legal, Public Relations [Political] and Social–Emotional) Toward Excellent Supervision and Evaluation

E-The Educational Process and Standards

The primary goal of supervision and evaluation is educational improvement. Most districts' supervision and evaluation systems are designed to improve students' achievement and attitudes by enhancing teachers' professional performance and fulfillment. Recent education reform initiatives in Massachusetts, New Jersey, New York, Tennessee, Vermont, Maryland, Kentucky, Texas, Virginia and other states have focused on the development of standards for teachers' and students' performance that can be used as the objective basis for evaluating teaching. In many states the

Department of Education has developed standards for instruction, curriculum and assessment of student achievement that are consistent with the standards recommended by the various national organizations in each curriculum area (e.g., National Council for the Teaching of Mathematics, National Board for Professional Teaching Standards). Other states have required individual districts to develop standards of instruction, curriculum and assessment.

> Historically, the problem with most training programs in supervision and evaluation is that they enhance the evaluator's skills only in the educational component and ignore all or most of the other three dimensions.

Public education's move toward articulated written standards has significantly enhanced districts' ability to objectively evaluate teaching.

The supervision and evaluation process works with teachers **formatively** to improve their performance on the standards of instruction, with the goal of improving students' performance on the district's curriculum standards. It also **summatively** assesses each teacher's performance as measured against the district's articulated standards for curriculum and instruction. The educational process and standards are the most important of the four E.L.P.S. dimensions. However, the educational dimension of supervision and evaluation can be successfully implemented only if evaluators effectively attend to the legal, public relations (political) and social–emotional processes and standards as well. Historically, the problem with most training programs in supervision and evaluation is that they enhance the evaluator's skills only in the educational component and ignore all or most of the other three dimensions.

L-The Legal Process and Standards

Every state has laws that require the evaluation of all public school teachers. The labor laws and contracts governing teacher and administrator evaluation in most states and districts use the legal standard *just cause* to indicate the level of *due process* required for personnel actions that impact teachers who have tenure (*professional teacher status* in Massachusetts). The procedures set forth in districts' teacher evaluation documents are designed to be consistent with the just cause standard for due process. Fortunately, in most of the relationships between evaluators and teachers, the primary focus is on the educational and at times the social–emotional processes. However, one evaluation of a low-performing teacher can take as much of the evaluator's time as six to ten evaluations of high-performing teachers. Therefore, it is important that evaluators understand the legal standards for the procedures they use. If evaluators wait to learn about just cause until one of their evaluations is challenged for due process flaws, it will be too late to effectively use that knowledge.

A procedurally flawed evaluation can legally negate hundreds of hours of an evaluator's effective and educationally sound work. Chapter 5 includes further explanation of the due process standard of just cause as it impacts teacher supervision and evaluation.

Another legal standard related to the evaluation of a low-performing teacher is the *duty of fair representation*. Teachers' associations are legally bound to provide a *reasonable level* of representation to their members. An association that does not provide this level of representation leaves itself open to being sued by the teacher for failure to meet its duty of fair representation. The key words related to the test of fair representation are *reasonable level* of representation. Most associations provide a reasonable level to protect themselves and their members, but will not provide representation beyond that point for a poorly performing teacher who has received reasonable notice, support and time to improve, and yet has still failed to be consistently successful in meeting the district's standards. Many teachers' associations in the new millennium are committed to quality teaching and understand the political advantage in avoiding a reputation for "protecting bad teachers." (See the following discussion and that in chapter 4.) Chapter 5 contains an explanation of duty of fair representation written in part by a Massachusetts Teachers Association field representative well versed in matters of labor law. Chapter 5 also looks at the legal concepts of gathering direct and indirect evidence, harassment (gender, sexual, racial, disability or personal) of teachers and other labor law concepts that impact the supervision and evaluation process.

P-THE PUBLIC RELATIONS (POLITICAL) PROCESS AND STANDARDS

Increasingly, administrators, school committee members, teachers and teachers' associations are becoming aware that performance evaluation contributes significantly to the public's perception of schools. Quality performance evaluation is an important part of the evidence public schools can use to demonstrate to the lay public that we have quality control in public education. It is one of the strongest defenses against the movement toward voucher programs, for-profit schools and charter schools. If the public believes schools can effectively maintain a high level of instruction and student achievement, they will have the confidence that public schools can successfully complete their mission. When the public feels an institution like public education cannot monitor itself, it tends to abandon the institution. It instructs its legislators to change it dramatically or to create alternative options for students, such as voucher programs and charter schools. A growing number of states have enacted just such legislation over the last six years.

School boards, administrators, teachers and teachers' associations are sure to understand the danger to public education indicated by polls that show this unsettling new trend. For the first time, *the majority of adults* in America (51%) and *public school* parents in America (56%) favor the use of public money to pay all or part of a school-age child's tuition to any public, private or church related school (Gallup & Rose, 1999). It is incumbent upon those who understand this connection to educate those who do not yet understand it. All educators must recognize that the future of public schools is dependent upon demonstrating to the public our joint commitment to ensuring that all children receive teaching that is competitive in quality and cost with the other options. Chapter 4 takes an in-depth look at the effect that supervision and evaluation has on the public relations and political processes and standards that impact the long term viability of public schools.

S-The Social–Emotional Process and Standards

To quote Dr. James Walsh, retired superintendent of the public schools of Brookline, Massachusetts, and a former deputy superintendent of the Boston Public Schools, "Leadership is more psychology than anything else." Of course, this quotation overly simplifies leadership, which is in reality a series of complex processes that can be assessed by measurable standards. However, it does underscore how important it is for leaders to pay careful attention to the emotional impact of their interactions on a subordinate's performance. The process of being evaluated is a significant social–emotional event for many people. Our career persona is an important component of our self-image and integral to our ability to provide for ourselves and the people we care about. A threat to our career, real or perceived, often sends us into the fight-or-flight response, thereby making evaluation an extremely emotional activity. The emotions intensify exponentially when the message to the teacher is, "Your performance is less than satisfactory." One need only recall Psychology 101 and Abraham Maslow's hierarchy of needs (Maslow, 1943, pp. 370–396) to understand why job performance evaluation is such an emotionally-charged issue.

Teacher Social–Emotional Processes and Standards

In the majority of the interactions between evaluators and teachers, the primary E.L.P.S. dimension in play is the educational. In the cases of teachers with performance issues, their personal support network and ownership of the problem (components of the social–emotional dimension) become essential for the teachers' ultimate success. In chapters 4 and 5, this book takes a more in-depth look at the social–emotional impact on low-performing teachers and the role of evaluators and the teachers' association in dealing with that impact. Figure 1 on page 10 illustrates the various people and processes that impact the social–emotional state of a teacher during the supervision and evaluation process.

EVALUATOR SOCIAL–EMOTIONAL PROCESSES AND STANDARDS

Evaluators also experience difficult social–emotional situations and stress related to their work with teachers during the supervision and evaluation process. Most schools and departments are designed so the evaluator (e.g., principal or department head) is the sole evaluator of a group of professionals in a department or school. This isolation can lead to loneliness and self-doubt for evaluators. Asking teachers to change their behavior is difficult for them to hear. This makes it hard for the evaluator to explain the required change in a way the teacher can accept. When the request is put in the form of an observation write-up

> When an administrator is working intensely with a low-performing teacher, loneliness and self-doubt increase exponentially.

or final evaluation report, this interaction becomes significantly more difficult for the teacher to accept and the evaluator to deliver. Evaluators spend a great deal of time (often awake in the middle of the night) trying to find the right words for delivering the message that change is needed. Chapters 2, 3, 4 and 5 provide guidance for evaluators to assist them with the delivery of these difficult oral and written messages.

Figure 2 on page 11 illustrates the various people and processes that support the social–emotional state of an evaluator during the supervision and evaluation process.

When an administrator is working intensely with a low-performing teacher, loneliness and self-doubt increase exponentially. It is a typical human reaction for the teacher's colleagues to be emotionally supportive of their colleague. Even when staff members privately support the administrator's work with the teacher, very few ever indicate this position to the teacher, other teachers or the administrator. In some instances the low-performing teacher publicly berates the administrator to other staff members. Some colleagues join the administrator bashing, but most respond with silence or active listening. These responses are taken by the teacher as concurrence with his/her complaints about the evaluator. In this lonely and stressful situation, the evaluator can be prone to second guessing whether he/she is being too direct or not direct enough with the teacher.

Dr. Arturo Delgado, conducted research in 250 school districts in California which identified the top ten roadblocks to administrators giving constructive written and oral recommendations about performances that needed improvement. Nine of those roadblocks were social–emotional (Delgado, 1999).

Social–Emotional Components and Processes
Teacher

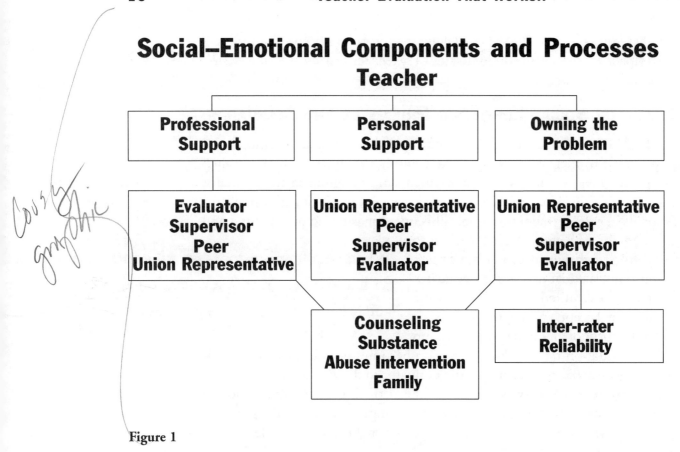

Professional Support	Personal Support	Owning the Problem
Evaluator Supervisor Peer Union Representative	Union Representative Peer Supervisor Evaluator	Union Representative Peer Supervisor Evaluator
	Counseling Substance Abuse Intervention Family	Inter-rater Reliability

Figure 1

   This book is designed to address these social–emotional issues in several ways. First, it enables a district to develop and maintain a high level of consistency (inter-rater reliability) among evaluators. Raising inter-rater reliability in the implementation of processes and standards decreases the feeling among some staff that performance evaluations are subjective rather than objective assessment, thereby increasing morale in general. Second, it increases the sense of support evaluators feel when all the evaluators in a district adhere to similar standards.

   Third, trained evaluators and an effectively-monitored evaluation system create an environment where most teachers trust the validity of the process and trust their evaluators' ability to objectively evaluate their performance. It enhances administrators' trust in the teachers' association to work with them on addressing issues of low performance. An effective system helps eliminate the dynamic in which low-performing teachers feel "bullied" by the evaluation process (or evaluator), causing them to make negative statements about the evaluator to other teachers and community members. It also removes the tendency for evaluators to feel "bullied" by the teachers' association and make statements to teachers, other administrators and the public about the association's role in blocking administrators' ability to require high standards of performance.

Social–Emotional Components and Processes
Evaluator

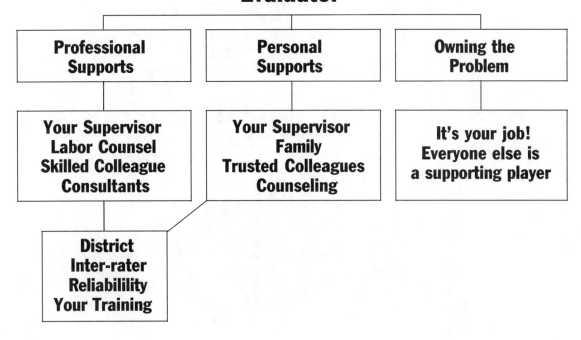

Figure 2

CONQUERING THE E.L.P.S.

An evaluation system that effectively attends to all of the E.L.P.S. helps administrators to be more effective instructional leaders, decreases litigation related to addressing low performance, improves staff morale and increases the public's belief that the entire school district (school board, administrators, teachers and the teachers' association/union) is committed to ensuring that every student receives a quality education.

This book provides teachers, school board members, district administrators, university faculty who train teachers and administrators and the lay public with an understanding of the complex, multifaceted supervision and evaluation process.

Figure 3 (page 12) illustrates the various components of the E.L.P.S. It at first appears more daunting than climbing the Alps. However, as you read on, you will see that this book breaks each dimension into its components. The E.L.P.S. enables districts to develop successful programs of professional development for evaluators.

Supervision and Evaluation

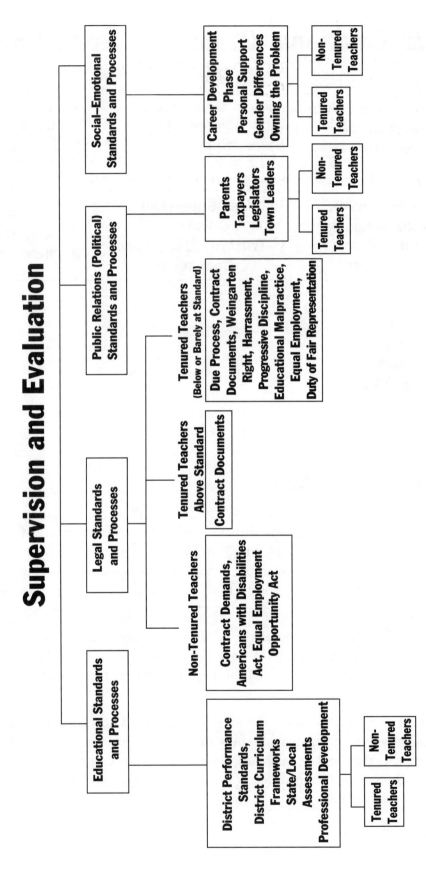

Figure 3

SOURCES

Delgado, A. (1999, October). *Factors that lead to internal conflict that influence elementary school principals when rating less than satisfactory teachers on formal teacher evaluations.* Dissertation research presented at the American Association of School Personnel Administrators Annual Conference, Ann Arbor, MI.

Gallup, A. & Rose, L. (1999, September). The 30th annual *Phi Delta Kappan*/Gallup Poll of the public's attitudes toward the public schools. *Phi Delta Kappan,* 41–56.

Chapter 2

DISTRICT-LEVEL SYSTEMS FOR TRAINING, COACHING AND ASSESSING AN EFFECTIVE PROGRAM OF SUPERVISION AND EVALUATION

This chapter focuses on the district-level systems that must be in place to support a successful program of supervision and evaluation. Such a program can be implemented only when supervisors and evaluators have been adequately trained in the E.L.P.S. standards and processes of this important education improvement activity. It is the interaction of these four standards and processes that makes supervision and evaluation inseparable activities in the real world.

The *educational standards* are primarily supervised and evaluated using a process that includes observing a teacher while he/she is teaching, conferencing with that teacher and writing about the teaching that was observed. This process is often referred to as **clinical supervision and evaluation.** In early years of clinical supervision and evaluation, teaching was often viewed as a set of rote skills that can be implemented successfully with a minimal amount of professional judgment by the teachers. The evaluator, in theory, could observe a lesson and make judgments solely on whether the teacher demonstrated certain skills. In recent years, educators' recognition of the complexity of classroom and out-of-classroom interactions has focused importance on a teacher's judgment in deciding when, how and to what extent to utilize specific teaching techniques. The work of Jonathon Saphier, Arthur Costa, Robert Garmston, Carl Glickman and others has focused our attention on the importance of teacher judgment and the need for evaluators to coach teachers in ways that improve teachers' ability to make these judgments.

Most states have laws that require the clinical supervision and evaluation of all teachers and administrators. A number of states also require that districts provide ongoing training in this area for their administrators. In addition, university graduate programs in administration and state certification regulations for administrators require training in clinical supervision and evaluation. This leads many administrators to receive preliminary training as part of their pre-service preparation. Unfortunately, this training is rarely comprehensive enough and is never sufficiently specific to an individual district's needs to enable evaluators to be effective. This chapter provides a framework that districts can use to provide the training and support needed for effective district-wide supervision and evaluation.

> Effective evaluators must know the *educational standards and processes* and be able to analyze a teacher's ability to use them, talk effectively with teachers about their implementation of them and write clearly and concisely about them. Evaluators must also be able to use a wide variety of information sources in addition to classroom observations to make accurate assessments.

The first step in improving a district's supervision and evaluation program is to require that all the supervisors and evaluators in the district attend refresher training in effective classroom instructional practices and the clinical supervision and evaluation of these practices (whether or not they have been trained prior to their employment in the district). This training should be designed to teach and/or refresh evaluators' understanding of the following five components of clinical supervision and evaluation. Effective evaluators must know the *educational standards and processes* and be able to analyze a teacher's ability to use them, talk effectively with teachers about their implementation of them and write clearly and concisely about them. Evaluators must also be able to use a wide variety of information sources in addition to classroom observations to make accurate assessments.

Component 1—Knowing the Educational Standards and Processes: Supervision and evaluation training should provide evaluators with an understanding of the components of successful classroom instruction. As in medicine, law and other professions, the knowledge base related to successful classroom teaching is constantly growing and improving. The evaluator need not be an expert on all classroom instructional techniques, but must possess sufficient knowledge about classroom teaching to be an effective supervisor and evaluator.

Component 2—Analyzing the Implementation of the Educational Standards and Processes: The second concept evaluators need to master is the ability to recognize and then analyze the components of successful instruction through classroom observation. The variety of techniques used in successful classroom instruction can vary depending upon grade and subject. The observer needs to understand and be able to detect and label a large repertoire of teaching techniques. This is essential if the evaluator is to assess whether or not the techniques used by the teacher are appropriate for the situation to which they have been applied and to detect missed opportunities. Knowing how to teach and knowing how to observe and analyze teaching are two different skills.

The type of classroom observation can vary as well. Evaluators must build their comfort and competence with all types of observation. The most well known is the single class period observation. This continues to be an effective and important means of observation. However, it is also imperative that evaluators use other types of observations as well. These can include a series of short (five to ten minute) observations[1], extended observations that can last a couple of hours or more and clustered observations that observe the same subject area or same instructional technique over two or more consecutive days.

Component 3—Talking With Teachers About the Educational Standards and Processes: The third supervision and evaluation concept evaluators need to master is the ability to effectively conference with the teacher about the classroom observation in a way that causes serious reflection by the teacher and causes positive change in his/her teaching. Knowing effective teaching and knowing how to analyze teaching is only helpful to students if the supervisor/evaluator knows how to discuss observations with the teacher in an effective manner. These conversations should also include the core practices that are expected of all the district's administrators and those practices specific to the district's standards and procedures. Effective supervision and evaluation conferences require that the evaluator understand the *social–emotional* dynamics that exist between a supervisee and supervisor during the evaluation interaction. Later on in this chapter, I will discuss more about effective conferencing techniques that attend to these dynamics.

---

[1] For more information on conducting multiple brief observations the reader will want to read the article written by Boston Public Schools principal and Harvard presenter Kim Marshall noted in the sources at the end of this chapter.

Component 4—Documenting a Teacher's Implementation of the Educational Standards and Processes: The training should clearly explain and frequently reinforce to administrators the message that supervision and evaluation in a standards-based program must be summative as well as formative.

Summative supervision and evaluation is a process designed to measure the level of success of teachers as compared to their district's curriculum and performance standards.

Formative supervision and evaluation is a positive, supportive and collaborative process designed to improve student performance and attitude by increasing the effectiveness and attitudes of a district's teachers.

Effective formative and summative evaluation requires that the evaluator document all the evidence and judgments made about a teacher's performance on the *educational standards and processes.* Clear and concise documentation is the only way to ensure that all parties have a common understanding of the evaluator's summative judgments about the teacher's performance. To the novice evaluator, this seems like common sense. Experienced evaluators know that people can often respond very differently to recommendations and admonishments once they are put in writing. Writing what we say and saying what we write is easier said then done. The written word raises far more *emotions* than the spoken word when it becomes a permanent record of a teacher's performance.

> Writing what we say and saying what we write is easier said then done. The written word raises far more *emotions* than the spoken word when it becomes a permanent record of a teacher's performance.

Component 5—Using Sources of Information in Addition to Classroom Observations: A common misperception among many evaluators is the belief that the only source of data they can use in summative evaluations is that gathered in classroom observations. Chapter 3 provides a comprehensive (but not all-inclusive) list of data sources other than classroom observations.

Chapters 2 and 3 contain documents which help evaluators use the common language, instruction standards, curriculum standards and procedures required to effectively recognize, analyze, discuss and write about the *educational standards and processes* that affect the majority of teachers evaluated. Chapter 7 contains examples of the supervision and evaluation documents used in two districts to achieve this goal. Those documents and the documents in this chapter were originally developed for use with Massachusetts Department of Education standards and procedures. However, since the Massachusetts standards are similar to those used in most states and those used by the National Board for Professional Teaching Standards as published in *What Teachers Should Be Able to Do* (National Board for Professional Teaching Standards, 1994), the documents can be easily adapted for use in any state or with any district's curriculum and evaluation standards and procedures.

The next section of this chapter provides guidelines for selecting a training program and a trainer.

WHO SHOULD TRAIN THE EVALUATORS IN YOUR DISTRICT IN SUPERVISION AND EVALUATION?

A few districts have qualified staff to train their own administrators, however, most districts find they need outside expertise to develop effective training for their administrators. Rarely do districts have a person on staff with the time or expertise to develop a comprehensive program that incorporates the four E.L.P.S. dimensions of supervision and evaluation.

> All districts have written procedures with a core of similar components. However, all have written procedures which have been used in a context of past practice that is unique to that district. Therefore no generic supervision and evaluation training program can be effective as a "one size fits all."

Specialists in the area of supervision are often used to either train administrators directly or to develop a training program that is carried out by a local administrator. Districts can obtain supervision and evaluation training from several sources. There are regional and national professional development companies that will provide on-site training for individual districts or training at a regional site for groups of administrators from several districts. All colleges and universities offering graduate programs in educational administration have faculty with backgrounds in clinical supervision and evaluation. These faculty will often provide training. Administrators who specialize in supervision and evaluation (often from larger school districts) may teach these skills in other districts. The Department of Education in your state or your state affiliates of the national professional organizations for school board members, superintendents, secondary school principals, elementary school principals and personnel administrators may provide the names of trainers.

It is important that districts carefully research and interview any trainer or organization that is under consideration. The quality of training varies greatly among programs and presenters.

Districts may use the following questions to determine the quality and breadth of the service an outside expert offers.

1. What are the trainer's qualifications in supervision and evaluation? Does the trainer have practical as well as academic and theoretical knowledge and experience about supervision and evaluation?

2. What do the trainer's other clients think about his/her work?

3. Can the trainer adapt his/her presentation to your district's language, standards and processes for curriculum, instruction and student assessment? I have reviewed dozens of district supervision and evaluation processes and standards over the past twelve years. All districts have written procedures with a core of similar components. However, all have written procedures which have been used in a context of past practice that is unique to that district. Therefore no generic supervision and evaluation training program can be effective as a "one size fits all." Some of the generic practices must be adjusted to account for the procedures, past practices and the evaluation loads that differ from one district to another. The trainer must project a sense of confidence among the administrators being trained that he/she understands the complexities of this difficult process when it is applied within the context of running a particular school or department.

4. Does the trainer know how to maximize the evaluators' use of the district's present evaluation processes and standards? Activities that contain written assessment and oral discussion of the following questions are one way to achieve this.

    a. What information in your evaluation documents and contract language do evaluators need to know?
    b. Why is it important for evaluators to know the information you identified?
    c. What other questions or comments do you have about your district's evaluation procedures (processes) and performance standards?
    d. What problems have you encountered when using your district's evaluation procedures (processes) and standards?
    e. What solutions have you found that resolved (partially or completely) the issues identified by your colleagues related to using your district's evaluation documents?

5. Is the trainer's presentation sufficiently motivational so that the administrators being trained will be interested to learn the information?

    We all have attended workshops and courses taught by brilliant people who practically put us to sleep or set us off thinking about issues back at the office which are totally unrelated to their topics. Supervisors and evaluators are busy people with many pressing personal and professional demands on their attention. Like a classroom teacher, the presenter needs excellent instructional skills to capture and keep the participants' interest. There are also some additional techniques a trainer of administrators should use in addition to those used by a classroom teacher. The following is a list of "should do's" for trainers of your administrators.

a. Have a clear understanding of the content he/she wishes the participants to master by the end of the program.

b. Be realistic about how much the participants can absorb in the time available. It is better to teach a few techniques comprehensively than to give a great deal of information that cannot be readily implemented after the workshop.

c. Have as much background information as possible about the participants, their level of knowledge about teacher supervision and evaluation and the contract procedures and standards they use in their districts.

d. Teach participants at least one practice in each session that they can apply immediately in their jobs, without a significant amount of preparation work.

e. Present the information in a way that maximizes retention of the learning by teaching to all four learning styles. In her book *The 4 MAT System: Teaching to Learning Styles and Right/Left Mode Techniques,* Bernice McCarthy (1981) describes the dominant learning styles of people who are primarily motivated by personal meaning, facts, how things work or self-discovery.

f. Create training activities that enable the participants to practice the new techniques in a variety of scenarios. These activities will enable the participant to use the information learned in the training to solve problems when they arise in the future even if the situations are not similar to those presented in the training.

g. When you give homework between sessions, make sure the assignment has direct application to their jobs. The best assignments are those that ask the participant to do something he/she normally does anyway, but also apply a new skill(s) taught by the trainer.

h. Use the Characteristics of Effective Evaluators self-assessment and the other techniques noted in chapter 2 to assess how much of the information and how many of the techniques taught in the training are applied over time in the participants' daily operation of their buildings/departments.

     i.   Structure reteaching as needed, based on the assessment program described later in this chapter.

6. Does the program provide administrators with a solid foundation in current instructional practices, assessment practices and a common language for discussing these practices? (See examples in the sample documents in chapter 7.)

7. Does the program teach administrators techniques for observing and/or verifying and analyzing classroom observations and evidence collected by other means?

8. Does the program teach administrators to effectively conference with teachers about their practices in ways that create positive change in those practices?

9. Does the program teach administrators to write clearly and concisely about performance by supporting conclusions with a variety of types of observed and/or verified evidence? (See the explanation of claims, evidence, interpretations and judgments (Saphier, 1993) in chapter 3 and the explanation of evidence in chapter 5.)

10. Does the training program teach and coach the evaluators in the legal, public relations (political) and social–emotional standards and processes that dominate the supervision and evaluation process when working with a low-performing teacher?

    These standards and processes are subordinate during the supervision and evaluation of good and excellent teachers. They can become dominant during the supervision and evaluation of low-performing teachers. The complex and unique nature of evaluating low-performing teachers has led to my devoting all of chapter 5 to the standards and processes for working with low performing teachers. Chapter 8 contains a sample of a lesson I use when training administrators to assess their knowledge of these four dimensions (pages 282–285).

11. Does the program teach administrators the difference between formative and summative supervision and evaluation and how to teach this difference to their staffs?

12. Can and will the trainer teach the superintendent or other appropriate central administrator to establish systems to coach, assess and support the continued effective implementation of supervision and evaluation skills by the district's evaluators and central staff after the training period has passed?

The next section of this chapter discusses the role of the central administration (superintendents, assistant superintendents, curriculum directors) in monitoring and supporting supervision and evaluation in their districts.

As you read on you will see that maintaining an effective program of supervision and evaluation requires a continuous process of teaching, coaching, assessing evaluator performance and reteaching the E.L.P.S. processes and standards? (See figure 4 on page 24.) Because effective supervision and evaluation requires this cyclical process, it is best if districts have someone available in-house to coach, assess and reteach. Or they should schedule the trainer to work with an in-house senior administrator to coach, assess and reteach the evaluators and to coordinate the central office functions such as labor relations, staff development, new teacher induction, etc. Many districts have invested a great deal of time and expense into a period of effective training by outside consultants only to see its impact diminish and even disappear over time because of the lack of continuous coaching, assessing and reteaching. The following case study is an actual example of this dynamic.

THE ARCHAEOLOGICAL DIG

Two districts in which I consulted (I will call them Districts A and B) exemplify the problem that arises when there is not a system within the district to support the supervision and evaluation program after the training consultant leaves the district. During the late 70s and early 80s, the districts trained all of their administrators and a large percentage of their teachers in a very effective model of supervision and evaluation and effective instructional practices. By the mid 80s both districts had trained all of their staff. District A changed to a maintenance training model that trained administrators and teachers new to the district in off-site courses taught by the consultant in other districts that were adopting the model. District B also sent its new administrators to off-site training sessions. However, District B had a teacher trained by the consultant to instruct new and experienced teachers on-site. Financial issues and senior administrative changes in the early 90s caused both districts to stop sending new staff to the off-site training. As a result, District A provided no training in the program for new teachers and administrators for five years. District B provided no training for administrators, but its specially trained teacher maintained the course for teachers each year.

I was hired by District A in 1996 and by District B in 1998 to reactivate training for administrators. Knowing the history of these two districts, I mistakenly assumed I could refresh the administrators' skills in the supervision and evaluation of classroom practice and build upon the previous years of training in which the two districts had already invested significant time and money. I soon learned that virtually none of the previous administrator training was operating in either district. It took an archaeological dig to find the remnants of the program in documents that were practically unused, although they were required by contract, and in the practices of a couple of the administrators who had maintained the skills on their own. In District A the teacher practices also were no longer in effect. However, in District B, the in-district trainer model established in the early 90s was still effectively training all second year teachers. (It was determined that first year teachers had too much on their plates to receive the training in that year.)

I was able to reteach the training for both districts in the skills of evaluating classroom practice. I now am able to focus the administrator training on other skills, such as working effectively with low-performing teachers and using sources of information other than classroom observations. I work actively with the senior administrators creating an "in district trainer" model to ensure that the model in Figure 4 continues to flourish after I leave the district.

Evaluator Training and Support Cycle

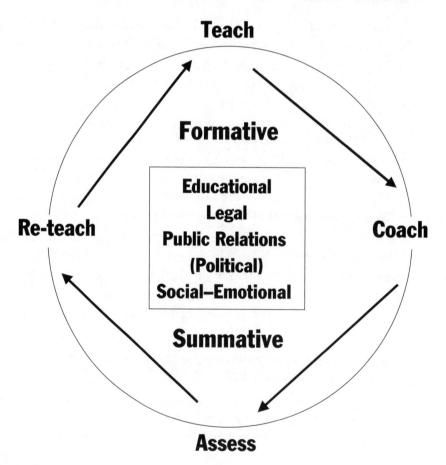

Figure 4

WHAT IS THE ROLE OF SUPERINTENDENTS AND SENIOR ADMINISTRATORS BEYOND PROVIDING EVALUATORS WITH TRAINING (TEACHING) AND COACHING IN SUPERVISION AND EVALUATION?

In the previous section, I alluded to the fact that many districts make the mistake of assuming that the school board and senior administration's job is completed once they have provided the funding and time for the evaluators to receive training in the skills of classroom supervision and evaluation. However, effective supervision and evaluation requires continuous planning, monitoring and support on the part of the superintendent and other senior level administrators. Figure 5 (on the next page) shows the responsibilities of the eight senior level administrators in one district. The lines between the boxes represent the lines of communication needed for an effective program of supervision and evaluation. As you can see, the larger the district, the more complicated and challenging it is to maintain an adequate flow of communication. In this district the grid below is sent to all administrators at the start of each school year. In so doing, senior administrators are reminded of their roles, and evaluators are reminded where to go for the coaching and support they need.

> A building-level evaluator involved in a difficult evaluation situation will usually make one call for help. If the only response received is that he/she is then directed to call another person, the evaluator might not make the second call. If directed to call a third person, it is unlikely the third call will ever be made.

A building-level evaluator involved in a difficult evaluation situation will usually make one call for help. If the only response received is that he/she is then directed to call another person, the evaluator might not make the second call. If directed to call a third person, it is unlikely the third call will ever be made. As you will see on page 29, there is a long list of roadblocks that keep evaluators from addressing difficult evaluation issues. Senior administration should not add *"frustration with getting assistance for difficult evaluation situations"* to the list.

As a consultant and trainer to districts, I often find that developing clear lines of support, such as the ones developed in the district shown in figure 5, one of the most important ways of improving district-wide performance of supervision and evaluation.

It is a rare building-level evaluator who possesses all the *E.L.P.S. expertise* required to work effectively with a difficult evaluation.

Identifying the Role the Various Central Office Administrators Play in Supporting Building-Level Administrators

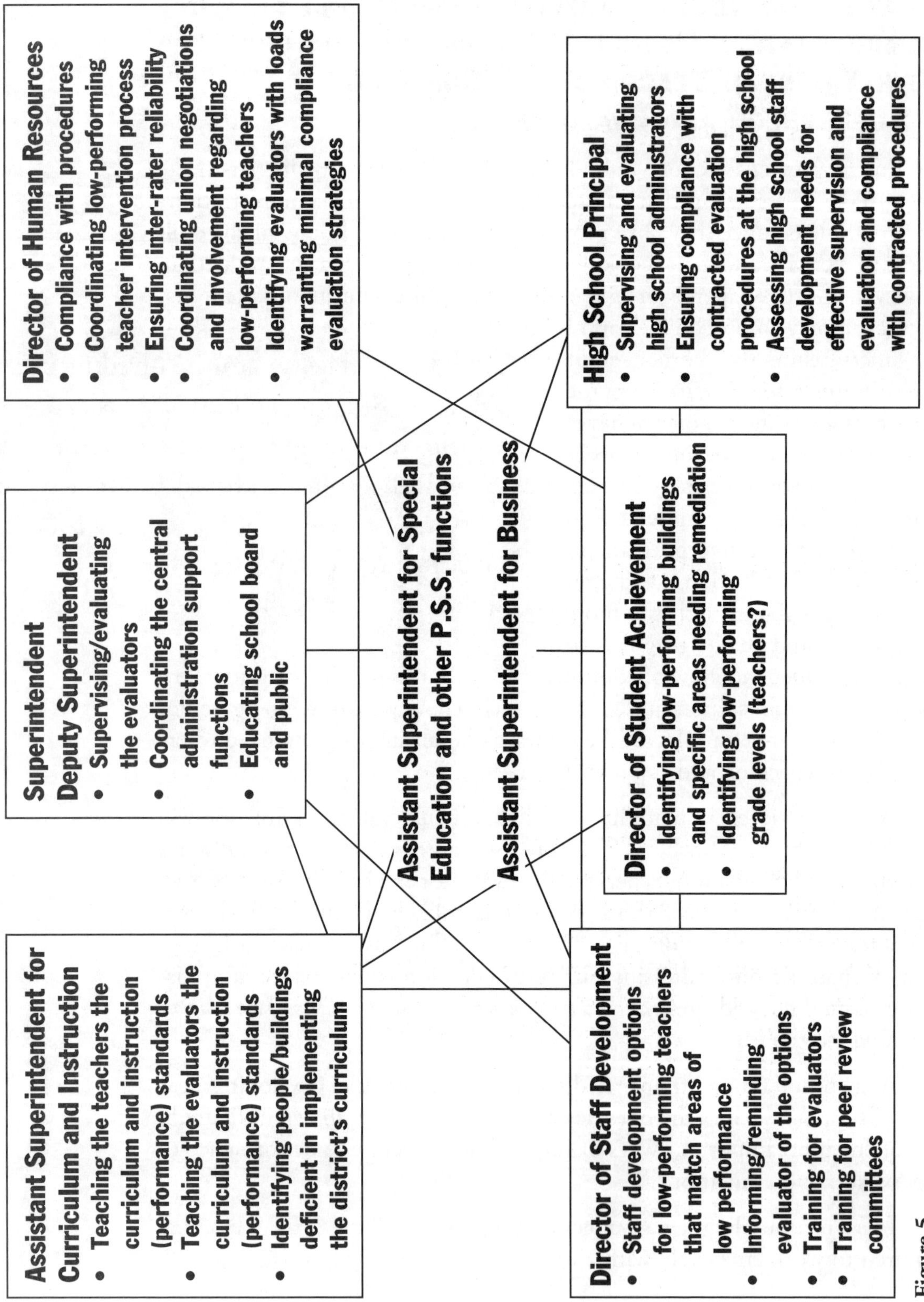

Director of Human Resources
- Compliance with procedures
- Coordinating low-performing teacher intervention process
- Ensuring inter-rater reliability
- Coordinating union negotiations and involvement regarding low-performing teachers
- Identifying evaluators with loads warranting minimal compliance evaluation strategies

High School Principal
- Supervising and evaluating high school administrators
- Ensuring compliance with contracted evaluation procedures at the high school
- Assessing high school staff development needs for effective supervision and evaluation and compliance with contracted procedures

Superintendent
Deputy Superintendent
- Supervising/evaluating the evaluators
- Coordinating the central administration support functions
- Educating school board and public

Assistant Superintendent for Special Education and other P.S.S. functions

Assistant Superintendent for Business

Director of Student Achievement
- Identifying low-performing buildings and specific areas needing remediation
- Identifying low-performing grade levels (teachers?)

Assistant Superintendent for Curriculum and Instruction
- Teaching the teachers the curriculum and instruction (performance) standards
- Teaching the evaluators the curriculum and instruction (performance) standards
- Identifying people/buildings deficient in implementing the district's curriculum

Director of Staff Development
- Staff development options for low-performing teachers that match areas of low performance
- Informing/reminding evaluator of the options
- Training for evaluators
- Training for peer review committees

Figure 5

You will note in Figure 5 that that the role of special education and other special services is addressed with a question mark. In many districts, the unique and varied responsibilities of these positions results in the need for as many as three sets of administrators having shared responsibility for evaluating and/or supervising these professionals. Often the evaluator and supervisor are clearly defined on paper. (See the document in chapter 7 for an example of clearly defined evaluation responsibilities for special services professionals starting on page 234.) However, in practice, the complex communications needed between and among the system-wide special services department administrators, the building administrators and the system-wide regular education administrators breaks down. This communications failure often leads to three different notions of the identity and methods of the supervisor and evaluators of special services practitioners. The result is that professionals such as physical therapists, occupational therapists, vision specialists, hearing specialists, psychologists and, even at times, special education teachers are ineffectively supervised and evaluated[2] or not evaluated at all. This problem is illustrated in the following case from a district in which I worked.

WHO DROPPED THE BALL?

In this district the assistant superintendent for special services retired. The district hired a consultant to conduct a yearlong evaluation of the department prior to hiring a new assistant superintendent. Among the recommendations, the consultant suggested that the evaluation responsibility for special education teachers in the elementary schools be moved from the special education administrators to the building principals. The consultant left when he completed his report and a new assistant superintendent for special services was hired. The special education administrators immediately followed the recommendation of the consultant and stopped evaluating the special education teachers. In addition, since the report did not mention speech therapists, occupational therapists or physical therapists, the special education administrators assumed they should no longer evaluate these people as well. The special education administrators were very happy to give up the *legal, public relations (political) and social–emotional* issues that summative evaluators face but continue to function solely as formative supervisors. The intention of the consultant, it was later clarified (though not written in the report), was that the special education administrators should continue to evaluate the speech, occupational therapy and physical therapy staff.

---

2 Starting on page 234 of chapter 7, is an excellent example of a district's performance standards designed for non-classroom teaching positions such as school nurses, psychologists, counselors, speech therapists, librarians and occupational therapists.

The principals, on the other hand, either didn't know they were responsible for picking up the special education teachers' evaluations or they "forgot." As a result, no special education teacher, speech therapist, occupational therapist or physical therapist was evaluated *for four years!*

Even in districts with a clear understanding of who evaluates whom, conflicts arise when there is more than one supervisor and/or evaluator. These conflicts can only be resolved with the assistance of the central administrator responsible for system-wide supervision and evaluation. Some of the longest and most contentious (and personally the most *emotional*) evaluation meetings I've run have involved neither the teacher who was being evaluated nor the union. The purpose of these meetings was to get two administrators to acknowledge and understand their differing responsibilities and perceptions of a single teacher's evaluation. This understanding is an essential step before the two or three administrators are able to work effectively with this teacher. Below are some guidelines for ensuring two supervisors/evaluators work effectively with a single teacher.

1. Discuss the evaluation with the teacher's other supervisor(s) before the start of the evaluation and periodically during the course of the evaluation so you send the same message to the teacher. This regular communication among supervisors will avoid confusing and overwhelming the teacher.

2. Come to agreement with the other supervisor(s) on the priorities and goals of the evaluation.

3. Use your partner(s)'s areas of strength.

4. Support each other through the periods of *aggression* often connected when giving a teacher summative areas for improvement. There will be times when the teacher will lash out at the person giving these recommendations.

IS YOUR SENIOR ADMINISTRATION "USER FRIENDLY" FOR THE EVALUATORS?

Evaluations are time-consuming for teacher evaluators. They are also socially and emotionally difficult, particularly when it comes to giving summative standards-based feedback in your conferences and write-ups. Dr. Arturo Delgado, superintendent of the San Bernardino Unified School District in California, researched the reasons why evaluators have a difficult time giving honest, summative feedback to teachers about areas that need improvement. Having surveyed evaluators in 250 California school districts, Dr. Delgado identified the top ten roadblocks to honest feedback, ordered below by the frequency stated by the respondents (Delgado, 1997, p. 64). The first is the most frequently cited roadblock.

1. I don't have a whole lot of confidence in the employee evaluation process.

2. I'm afraid of losing the employee's trust.

3. I'm afraid of hurting employee morale.

4. I don't like dealing with difficult people.

5. I've had too many negative experiences with employees when it comes to evaluations.

6. The employee has shown recent improvement.

7. I don't want a confrontation with the union over this.

8. I just don't have the time.

9. I hate to post a bad evaluation on the employee's permanent file.

10. I don't want to call the attention of the district office to my problems.

Most of the top ten concerns expressed by the administrators were about the *social–emotional* impacts on the evaluator, the teacher being evaluated and/or the staff that result from giving summative, standards-based feedback. When you couple these concerns with the frustrations that can occur as a result of the complex communications and multiple functions noted in figure 5, it is easy to see why many building-level administrators avoid tackling tough evaluation issues in their buildings or departments unless they have a senior administration that is "user-friendly." It is important that the senior administration streamline the building administrators' access to the functions noted in figure 5, making it easy for administrators to receive technical and emotional support when involved in difficult evaluation situations.

There should be a clearly articulated explanation of to whom the building or department administrator goes for the various supports he/she may need. Few districts have defined this line of support clearly for its evaluators. As a result, the evaluators feel they must deal with difficult evaluations alone, or the evaluators are quickly frustrated when they call someone in the senior administration for support and are shuffled to another office because neither central administrator sees the support requested as part of his/her job or resource allocation.

ASSESSING AND RETEACHING THE IMPLEMENTATION OF SUPERVISION AND EVALUATION IN YOUR DISTRICT

Someone in the district *must be responsible* to see that there is teaching, coaching, assessment and reteaching of evaluation work *by the evaluators.* Effective district-wide supervision and evaluation requires that someone ensure district-wide compliance, effective formative and summative work and consistent implementation of standards and processes by the evaluators. Depending on the size of the district, this responsibility is carried out by the superintendent or an assistant superintendent. Below are seven steps this person can take to ensure effective supervision and evaluation.

> Effective district-wide supervision and evaluation requires that someone insure district wide compliance, effective formative and summative work and consistent implementation of standards and processes by the evaluators.

Step 1: The Characteristics of Excellent Evaluators assessment (on page 41) should be given to all evaluators at the beginning of each year. A second copy should be sent to evaluators at the midpoint of the school year, when they are beginning to write their final evaluation reports for the year. Throughout the year, the central administrator responsible for supervision and evaluation needs to check in with evaluators to assess their progress on the standards addressed in this assessment.

The Characteristics of Excellent Evaluators contains criteria that superintendents can use to assess and evaluate the evaluators' implementation of the skills they need to be effective. It is a set of standards against which an evaluator's work can be measured. The sample district evaluation documents in chapter 7 use the Massachusetts standards. However, since these standards were based on the work in other states and the standards set by national professional organizations (e.g., The National Council for the Teaching of Mathematics Standards, the National Board for Professional Teacher Standards) the Characteristics of Excellent Evaluators can be adapted easily for use with the standards for curriculum and instruction in most states and districts in the United States.

Step 2: The written evaluations completed by teacher evaluators need to be reviewed for compliance with the Characteristics of Excellent Evaluators and the district's administrator performance criteria on supervision and evaluation and also to maintain inter-rater reliability. All the evaluations need not be read, however, an adequate sample should be reviewed. In one district with 50 evaluators and over 700 teachers, about 25% of all the evaluations (90 out of 360) are reviewed by the assistant superintendent for personnel and the superintendent to determine the extent to which the Characteristics of Excellent Evaluators have been met. Individual evaluators receive written and/or oral feedback with recommendations and commendations. The written feedback comes in the form of evaluation memos using claims, value judgments, and interpretations that connect the performance on the specific "characteristic" to its impact on the teacher evaluated and the evidence. Attached to each memo is the Characteristics of Excellent Evaluators, so the evaluator can easily refer to the standards. The attachment of this document also serves as one more reminder to the evaluators to review these standards.

Step 3: Evaluators should be observed in conferences with teachers and, where appropriate, with teachers' association representatives and second evaluators.

Step 4: Each year, evaluators should be surveyed to determine what supports will assist them in better meeting the standards in the upcoming year. The type of survey can vary depending on the size of the district. In some districts where I consult, the entire administrative staff is less than ten people. In those districts, we administer the Characteristics of Excellent Evaluators at a meeting of all evaluators as a self-assessment to spark the evaluators' thinking about the information, training and supports that would be most helpful to them. The evaluators are then asked to list their thoughts on the following three statements:

1. What I know about supervision and evaluation.

2. What I want to know about supervision and evaluation.

3. What I need to know about supervision and evaluation.

In mid size districts (approximately twenty to sixty administrators and evaluators) the administrators and evaluators complete the Characteristics of Excellent Evaluators as a self-assessment to stimulate their thinking about the information and training they need. A written survey such as the following one is administered to all administrators and evaluators and returned to the administrator responsible for supervision and evaluation in the district. The survey is designed so the results can be easily tallied by a clerical employee and the results given to a senior administrator. The clerical person need only sum up the numbers circled for each item. The higher the sum of the numbers, the greater the need for training in that area. This information enables senior administrators to maintain a user friendly support system for evaluators by providing the training and information evaluators want and need to be effective. It also provides senior administrators with useful information about which evaluators are accessing which resources and how well those resource people and programs are supporting the building-level evaluators.

Step 5: The teachers' association should be informed about current research in effective supervision and evaluation, the school committee's and superintendent's philosophies of supervision and evaluation and the training evaluators are receiving to ensure effective supervision and evaluation. Inviting the association leadership to complete the Characteristics of Excellent Evaluators and the following surveys is often a good ice-breaker around which to structure the discussion about research, philosophy and training related to supervision and evaluation. This of course assumes the district's teachers' association has a commitment to high teacher performance as well as a commitment to meeting its duty to ensure teachers' rights are not violated. (See chapter 4 for more discussion on this topic.)

Step 6: Once the teachers' association has sufficient information from step 5 to give informed feedback, it should be asked to make recommendations for improvements in the implementation of the evaluation process. Most teachers' associations hear a different perspective on the performance of evaluators and the evaluation process from their members than the one that is usually available to the senior administration. Asking the association to frame its feedback with the same objectivity it expects in teachers' evaluations will increase the validity of that feedback.

Step 7: Ask teachers how supervision and evaluation works in their schools or departments. One school district asks all teachers to fill out a twenty-nine question evaluation checklist with comments on their direct supervisors. (This step pertains to a *Teacher's Assessment ...* of his/her evaluator on page 37.)

EVALUATOR SURVEY OF POTENTIAL AREAS FOR TRAINING AND SUPPORT FOR THE DISTRICT'S TEACHER SUPERVISORS AND EVALUATORS

Name of respondent _____

Position _____ Date _____

Below are listed a number of areas related to the effective implementation of supervision and evaluation in the Sample Public Schools.

1 I have sufficient knowledge and training in this area to do what is indicated and have little or no need for further information or training on this topic.

2 I want to know more about this area and would benefit from more information and training on this topic.

3 I need to know more about this area to effectively complete this competency. This is one of my priority topics for training.

Please circle the number of the statement that *best represents* how you would rate your present knowledge and your need for additional information and training in each of these areas.

A) 1 2 3 Write **classroom observations** that clearly identify the teaching "moves" I observed (a.k.a. make claims) in language that is consistently used throughout the Sample Public Schools

B) 1 2 3 Write **classroom observations** that make clear value judgments about the claims

C) 1 2 3 Write **classroom observations** with interpretations that connect a teacher's behavior to its impact on student learning, development and the building's and/or department's culture

D) 1 2 3 Write **classroom observations** that contain objective evidence to support the claims, interpretations and judgments made by the evaluator

E) 1 2 3 Write **classroom observations** that use the language of the Sample Public School's performance standards wherever appropriate

F) 1 2 3 Write **final evaluation reports** that contain clear claims and judgments about each of the performance standards in language consistent with the Sample performance standards

G) 1　2　③　Write **final evaluation reports** with interpretations that connect teacher's performance on each of the standards to its impact on student learning, development and the building's and/or department's culture

(You will note that performance standard VII in the Brookline document in chapter 7 addresses in more detail the expectations for teachers related to activities that take place when they are not with students.)

H) 1　2　3　Write **final evaluation reports** that contain objective evidence to support the claims, interpretations and judgments

I) 1　2　3　Write **final evaluation reports** that use the language of Sample's performance standards wherever appropriate

J) 1　②　3　Pre-and post-conference in ways that effectively create positive change in a teacher's performance

K) 1　2　3　Understand the differences between peer review, peer evaluation, peer supervision and peer coaching in improving a teacher's performance *(See chapter 3 for more information on this topic.)*

L) 1　2　③　Use time-saving tips *(See chapter 3 for more information on this topic.)*

M)①　2　3　Work constructively with the teachers' association/union on issues related to supervision and evaluation

N) 1　②　3　Assess and determine the most effective way to implement Sample's supervision and evaluation documents and contract language

O) 1　②　3　Self-edit observations, memos and evaluations to ensure continuous improvement in the quality of my evaluation documents

P) ①　2　3　Work with a partner to peer-edit observations, memos and evaluations to ensure continuous improvement in the quality of my evaluation documents

Q) 1　2　3　Use effective techniques and time-efficient methods for teaching sample lessons *(See chapter 3 for more information on this topic.)*

R) 1　2　3　Explain the ongoing interaction of the educational, legal, public relations (political) and social–emotional standards and processes of supervision and evaluation

S) 1　2　3　Use a standards-based approach in our district's supervision and evaluation

T) 1　2　3　Understand the numerous types of evidence that are available to evaluators in addition to formal observations *(See chapter 5 for more information on this topic.)*

U) 1 2 3 Know which of my supervisors I should go to for information, coaching and/or support with the **Sample Public Schools' standards for curriculum and instruction**

V) 1 2 3 Know which of my supervisors I should go to for information, coaching and/or support concerning **the legal standards and processes** of teacher evaluation

W) 1 2 3

_____

_____

_____

Comments:

_____

_____

_____

Low-Performing Teachers

X) 1 2 3 Understand the impact of the law and work within the law during low-performing teacher evaluations: including the legal concepts *due process, just cause, duty of fair representation, rules of evidence, harassment* and *the Weingarten right*

Y) 1 2 3 Understand the impact of the law and work within the law during low-performing teacher evaluations as it relates to classes of people with legal protections from discrimination for gender, race, religion, age and sexual orientation

Z) 1 2 3 Effectively observe, verify, document and record direct and indirect forms of evidence other than classroom observations

AA) 1 2 3 Use the team approach to support evaluators and reduce the road blocks to effective evaluations of low-performing teachers

BB) 1 2 3 Effectively work with a second evaluator and/or supervisor during a low-performing teacher evaluation

CC) 1 2 3 Write and implement improvement plans for low-performing teachers

DD) 1 2 3 Appropriately use the steps of progressive discipline when disciplining staff members

EE) 1 2 3   Appropriately investigate claims of misconduct by staff

FF) 1 2 3   Appropriately document each step in progressive discipline using district performance standards, policies and universally accepted appropriate practice

GG) 1 2 3   Write progressive discipline notes and documents such as expectation clarification memos, memos after oral reprimands and written reprimands that contain clear claims and judgments about teacher performance, objective evidence to support the claims, and interpretations that connect teacher behavior to its impact on students and the building and/or department

> Go back and review your answers to "U" and "V" above in the context of work with a low-performing teacher to be sure your answer has not changed.

HH) 1 2 3   Understand the impact of the law and work within the law *during progressive discipline* situations: including the legal concepts *due process, just cause, duty of fair representation, rules of evidence, harassment* and *the Weingarten right*

II) 1 2 3   Understand the impact of the law and work within the law *during progressive discipline* situations as it relates to classes of people with legal protections from discrimination for gender, race, religion, age and sexual orientation

JJ) 1 2 3   Effectively conference with teachers about low performance and discipline issues

KK) 1 2 3   Know who to go to for specific supports (legal and otherwise) and coaching during a progressive discipline situation

LL) 1 2 3

_____

_____

_____

Comments:

_____

_____

_____

A sample survey related directly to the supervisors' work as supervisors and evaluators can be found below.

TEACHER'S ASSESSMENT OF HIS/HER EVALUATOR'S PERFORMANCE AS A SUPERVISOR AND EVALUATOR

Teacher's name: _____ Date: _____

Supervisor assessed below: _____

This survey is designed to help assess your supervisor's work as a supervisor and evaluator. It is based on research related to the practices used by effective supervisors and evaluators. Please fill out one survey for your evaluator. If you wish, you may also fill one out for any other person who functions as your supervisor.

Please circle the number that best matches your response to the comments below.

1= Always **2**=Often **3**=Rarely **4**=Never

A) 1 2 3 4 My supervisor compliments me for good work with specific praise that enables me to understand the impact of my successful actions on students, other staff, parents and/or the community.

B) 1 2 3 4 My supervisor provides me with suggestions for improvement related to my performance.

C) 1 2 3 4 My supervisor's suggestions are connected to the district's performance standards.

D) 1 2 3 4 My supervisor's suggestions are stated in a way that helps me understand the impact on students, other staff, parents and/or the community.

E) 1 2 3 4 My supervisor assists me in developing the skills to consistently evaluate my own performance.

F) 1 2 3 4 When I talk with my supervisor, I feel I can have an honest exchange of ideas.

G) 1 2 3 4 My supervisor makes his/her expectations clear.

H) 1 2 3 4 When I am dealing with a problem, my supervisor asks questions that help me understand the issues and assess options.

I) 1 2 3 4 My supervisor gives me frequent and useful data so I can assess how he/she believes I'm doing as a teacher.

J) 1 2 3 4   My supervisor encourages my initiative and innovation within the parameters of the district's and school's expectations.

K) 1 2 3 4   My supervisor assists me in solving difficulties in interpersonal relationships with colleagues.

L) 1 2 3 4   My supervisor assists me in solving difficulties in interpersonal relationships with students.

M) 1 2 3 4   My supervisor assists me in solving difficulties in interpersonal relationships with parents.

N) 1 2 3 4   My supervisor assists me with interpersonal relationships as described in K, L and M in a way that helps me improve the skills I need to better solve difficulties in the future.

O) 1 2 3 4   I find my supervisor easy to approach and talk with.

Please make any additional comments related to the statements above in the space below.

Comments: _____

_____

_____

_____

Describe one skill your supervisor demonstrates particularly well as a supervisor and evaluator and the impact it has on your performance as a teacher.

Skill: _____

_____

_____

_____

Describe one skill your supervisor should improve in his/her practice as a supervisor and evaluator and the impact it would have on your performance as a teacher.

Skill: _____

_____

_____

_____

All of the *evidence* obtained in steps 1–7 is reviewed and used to plan evaluators' training. This evidence will determine which concepts need to be taught, coached, retaught and/or if new concepts need to be taught during the subsequent year.

One District's Experience With Teaching, Coaching, Assessing and Reteaching the Concepts of Effective Supervision and Evaluation

The case below is an example of a district in which the senior administration used step 2 of the preceding survey and the evaluator change cycle noted earlier in the chapter to ensure the evaluators used the supervision and evaluation process to assess district-wide implementation of a change in the curriculum.

A district implemented a new set of curriculum standards. Although the district's first teacher performance standard was Currency in the Curriculum, a review of the evaluations for that year indicated that very few of the evaluators assessed teachers' implementation of the Currency in the Curriculum standard. Interviews with several evaluators indicated they were having difficulty incorporating statements about the teachers' use of the standard into their evaluations.

To address this issue, the superintendent, assistant superintendent for curriculum and instruction (who was responsible for developing and implementing the curriculum) and the assistant superintendent for personnel (who was responsible for the training and assessing of administrators in the area of supervision and evaluation) met during the following summer. They planned a workshop for principals and other evaluators that taught the evaluators strategies for incorporating the curriculum standards into their evaluations using the Currency in the Curriculum standard. In chapter 2 you will find examples of evaluations that successfully incorporate this district's curriculum standards (called learning expectations in the district's documents) into evaluations. These examples were part of the workshop given to evaluators at the start of the second school year.

The assistant superintendent for curriculum and instruction and the assistant superintendent for personnel made themselves available throughout the year to coach and reteach evaluators in this new skill. During the following year, the superintendent and assistant superintendent for personnel's review of evaluations indicated a significant improvement in these areas. The number of evaluations incorporating the curriculum standards *increased* from 10% during the first year to over 70% in the second year. This assessment led to reteaching those administrators who had not yet incorporated the assessment of the curriculum standards in their evaluations and to the additional coaching of others.

In the fall of the third year, evaluators and the assistant superintendent for personnel were taught by the assistant superintendent for curriculum and instruction to evaluate teachers' lesson planning using the backward design model advocated by McTighe and Wiggins in their book, *Understanding by Design* (1999). Both assistant superintendents made themselves available through the fall to coach evaluators in the implementation of the new model. Evaluations were again read in the spring to assess compliance and effectiveness. The column with references to the performance standards (see the examples in chapter 7) was revised to include connections to McTighe and Wiggin's book. As you can see, continued improvement required that the teaching, coaching, assessment and reteaching cycle shown earlier in this chapter continued on a regular basis.

As mentioned earlier, the following Characteristics of Effective Evaluators is used by the individual evaluator as a self-assessment tool. However, it can be revised for use by the senior administration to assess the performance of individual evaluators. An example of the document revised for this purpose can be found after the self-assessment form below. Characteristics of Excellent Evaluators, coupled with the preceding teacher survey, can provide an administrator with a substantial amount of information about his/her performance as a supervisor and evaluator.

CHARACTERISTICS OF EXCELLENT EVALUATORS: EVALUATOR SELF-ASSESSMENT

Date I completed this self-assessment: _____

The following exercise will be very helpful to you as a periodic self-assessment of your work as a supervisor and evaluator. Before each statement, circle the number that best describes your performance on the criteria. Total the numbers and save the sheet for comparison from year to year. You will note there is also space after each item for any useful reminders you may wish to make for yourself.

4 = 90 to 100% of the time   **1** = 25% to 49% of the time

3 = 75 to 89% of the time   **0** = less than 25% of the time

2 = 50% to 75% of the time

Evaluator: _____

A) 0 1 2 3 4 Ensures that all news that is hard to hear is delivered in conversation with the teacher prior to giving it to the teacher in writing in an observation report, annual evaluation report or other document

B) 0 1 2 3 4   Writes claims/judgments, evidence (and interpretations where appropriate) about all the district's performance standards in the final evaluation (called principles of effective teaching[3] in the samples in chapter 7 of this book)

Chapter 3 gives an in-depth explanation of claims, evidence, interpretations and judgments.

C) 0 1 2 3 4   Writes claims/judgments, evidence (and interpretations where appropriate) in observation write-ups

D) 0 1 2 3 4   Writes **evidence** about claims, interpretations and judgments in language that is observable, verifiable and/or measurable in observation write-ups and final evaluation reports

E) 0 1 2 3 4   Makes judgments in language consistent with the district's statements of judgment; for example, if the district requires the final evaluation be marked with the judgment statements **unsatisfactory, satisfactory or exemplary,** the evaluator should use these statements whenever appropriate in the judgments made in the observation write-ups and final summative evaluations

F) 0 1 2 3 4   Uses the district's performance standards and the language of effective instructional practices to describe teachers' behaviors; see chapter 7 for an example of a district's document that connects each of the performance standards to a book of effective instructional practices, The Skillful Teacher[4] (Saphier & Gower, 1997), used in that district as a basis for common discussion on effective instructional practices

[3] The principles of effective teaching (PETs) are standards of instruction based on the Massachusetts Department of Education's recommended performance standards.

[4] *The Skillful Teacher* (Saphier & Gower, 1997) is a book that describes successful instructional practices. Many administrators use it in the supervision and evaluation training they receive, and it expands the repertoire of instructional strategies used to assess the PETs.

G) 0 1 2 3 4 Uses curriculum performance standards (Principle of Effective Teaching I in sample documents found in chapter 7) to focus on the implementation of the district's curriculum standards

H) 0 1 2 3 4 Applies the district's performance standards at levels consistent with system-wide standards (inter-rater reliability)

I) 0 1 2 3 4 Recognizes and commends examples of successful practice

J) 0 1 2 3 4 Identifies areas for improvement and offers recommendations within the text and/or in the summary of all observation write-ups and annual reports (after discussed in conversation with the teacher as noted in number 1 above)

K) 0 1 2 3 4 Where appropriate, connects examples of successful or unsuccessful practice and recommendations for improvement with a description of the impact they will have on enhancing students' performance and/or development

L) 0 1 2 3 4 Meets all contracted time lines for all teachers scheduled to be evaluated—*if you are less than 100% on this item, your first goal should be getting to 100%.*

M) 0 1 2 3 4 Writes narratives in a way that enables a third party reading the evaluations to determine the varying levels of success among teachers in the school/department

N) 0 1 2 3 4 Chooses a final "check off" (see sample of the Annual Report of Teacher Effectiveness form found in chapter 7 of this book) that is consistent with the narrative and delineates varying levels of success among the teachers in the school/department. Some districts have a check off that delineates a variety of levels while others only indicate satisfactory (successful) or unsatisfactory (unsuccessful). Other districts have no check off area and rely on the narratives to be written in a way that clearly delineates varying levels of success.

O) 0 1 2 3 4   Includes an improvement or enhanced goals plan for those teachers who need more than a typical level of remediation; Follows the correct practices for implementing these plans, as described in the explanation of improvement plans in the sample plans found in chapter 5

P) 0 1 2 3 4   Uses a variety of forms of direct and indirect evidence in addition to classroom observations to support interpretations and judgments

Q) 0 1 2 3 4   Uses model lessons to promote a culture that is open to honest feedback about areas for improvement

R) 0 1 2 3 4   Knows where to find and how to use the district's resources and supports such as curriculum information, instructional strategies *(educational)* and *legal* advice when he/she is involved in a difficult evaluation

S) 0 1 2 3 4   Uses the performance standards to assess changes in the teacher's practice that are consistent with the district's initiatives

The statements below are applied to the evaluation of a low-performing teacher and in every case must be followed 100% of the time.

T) 0 1 2 3 4   Has completed enough observations and subsequent write-ups to provide sufficient evidence that a teacher's performance is not satisfactory on a particular standard

U) 0 1 2 3 4   Has sufficiently documented direct and/or indirect evidence to support a judgment that a teacher does not meet or falls below a particular standard

V) 0 1 2 3 4   Adequately investigates and calls to the attention of the teacher any complaints by parents, students, staff, etc., that are used as part of the evaluation evidence

W) 0 1 2 3 4   Follows the contracted/evaluation procedure regarding teachers' signatures/initials on written documents used in the evaluation

X) 0 1 2 3 4   Keeps evaluator's supervisor informed about supervision and evaluation work with low-performing teachers, particularly any teacher to be found unsatisfactory

Comments: _____

_____

_____

GENERAL COMMENTS, NOTES AND REMINDERS FOR IMPROVING SUPERVISION AND EVALUATION PRACTICES

In the example below, the wording of several items in the Characteristics of Excellent Evaluators has been slightly revised for use by those central administrators in charge of evaluation programs as an instrument to provide feedback to the evaluators. I have included three items as an example from an assistant superintendent who used the previous document to evaluate the work of the district's evaluators. The wording in italics is the central administrators' feedback to the evaluator.

In those districts in which the document is used to assess the work of evaluators, the directions are modified as in the example on page 46.

Characteristics of Excellent Evaluators:
Evaluating the Evaluators

Evaluator assessed _____

Date this assessment was completed _____

Administrator completing this assessment _____

    The following criteria are used as an annual assessment of an administrator's work as a supervisor and evaluator. Circle the number before each statement that best describes the administrator's performance on the criteria. There is space after each item for any claims, evidence, interpretations and/or judgments you may wish to make.

        4 = 90 to 100% of the time   **1** = 25% to 49% of the time

        3 = 75 to 89% of the time   **0** = less than 25% of the time

        2 = 50% to 75% of the time

The evaluator:

D) 0 1 2 3 4   Writes **evidence** about claims, interpretations and judgments in language that is observable, verifiable and/or measurable in observation write-ups and final evaluation reports

You have included very good claims with judgments that clearly state the value you placed on the identified move. Your interpretations do a fine job of identifying for us the impact on the students. In those judgments that indicated a need for improvement, it would be good to give more evidence. In the next to last paragraph you support a judgment of poor pacing with one student's question about the assignment. I'm sure there was other evidence (e. g., puzzled looks on students' faces, failure of students to write the assignments in their assignment notebooks or failure to check the next day to see how many completed the assignment correctly) that would support this judgment.

F) 0 1 2 3 4   Uses the district's performance standards and the language of effective instructional practices to describe teachers' behaviors

You frequently used the language of effective instructional practices such as time on task, appropriate questioning techniques, purpose of the lesson and others. This is the language used to describe these moves in the Sample Public Schools performance standards. Using the language of the performance standards reinforces a common language for successful teaching in the building and the district. Great job on this criterion!

K) 0 1 2 3 4   Where appropriate, connects examples of successful or unsuccessful practice and recommendations for improvement with a description of the impact they will have on enhancing students' performance and/or development

After your recommendation about eating the Kiwi fruit, you go on to describe very well the impact on students. "If you allowed the students to eat the Kiwi at that moment they could have described how it tasted in addition to what it looked like and how it felt." You state in the third paragraph, "As students entered their classrooms . . . This is an example of Ms. Smith maximizing the time allotted to this activity. We know that more time for learning means more learning so we know the impact on the students.

I suggest you also make these connections to student learning in the other areas you commend. For example on page 2 you state, "This is an example of Ms. Smith using good questioning techniques." It would be helpful for you to add a sentence or two about the impact of good questioning techniques on increasing students' ability to use deductive and inductive thinking, etc.

Sources

Curriculum frameworks. (1995). Malden, MA: Massachusetts Department of Education.

Delgado, A. (1999, October). *Factors that lead to internal conflict that influence elementary school principals when rating less than satisfactory teachers on formal teacher evaluation.* Dissertation research presented at the American Association of School Personnel Administrators Annual Conference, Ann Arbor, MI.

Marshall, K. (1996, January). How I confronted HSPS (Hyperactive Superficial Principal Syndrome) and began to deal with the heart of the matter. *Phi Delta Kappan,* 336–345.

Maslow. A. (1943). A theory of human motivation. *Psychological Review,* 370–396.

McCarthy, B. (1981). *The 4 MAT system: teaching to learning styles and right/left mode techniques,* (2nd ed.) Excel Inc.

McTighe, J. & Wiggins, G. (1999). *Understanding by design.* Alexandria, VA: Association of Supervision and Curriculum Development.

Principles of effective teaching. (1995). Malden, MA: Massachusetts Department of Education.

Ribas, W. (2000, April). Ascending the ELPS to excellence in your district's teacher evaluation. *Phi Delta Kappan,* 585–589.

Rutherford, P. (1998). *Instruction for all students.* Alexandria, VA: Just ASK Publications.

Saphier, J. (1993). *How to make supervision and evaluation really work.* Carlisle, MA: Research for Better Teaching.

Saphier, J. & Gower, R. (1997). *The skillful teacher.* Carlisle, MA: Research for Better Teaching.

What teachers should be able to do. (1994). Washington D.C.: National Board for Professional Teaching Standards.

Chapter 3

THE EDUCATIONAL AND SOCIAL–EMOTIONAL SKILLS AND KNOWLEDGE NEEDED TO BE AN EFFECTIVE SUPERVISOR AND EVALUATOR

ANALYZING OBSERVATIONS AND OTHER INFORMATION IN TERMS OF CLAIMS, EVIDENCE, INTERPRETATIONS, JUDGMENTS AND THE DISTRICT'S PERFORMANCE STANDARDS

This chapter looks closely at the process of observing, documenting and conferencing about teacher performance. It expands the traditional discussion about data sources to include a number of sources beyond the classroom observation. The first section examines the terms *claims, evidence, interpretations* and *judgments* (C.E.I.J.) as they apply to classroom observations.

Jonathon Saphier, a noted author and teacher on the subject of supervision and evaluation, describes the component parts of an observation write-up and discussion as follows. The explanations in italics are this author's attempts to further define the terms and to connect the terms to standards-based evaluation.

"A **claim** is a generalization about a person's teaching. For example, 'He is very alert to management problems that could block class momentum.'" (Saphier & Gower, 1997)

It is important that districts use a common language to discuss teaching. A claim is a label placed by the evaluator on a particular teaching move. Districts need to adopt a common language and train their evaluators to use it in their evaluation write-ups and conferences. The language used by evaluators should be consistent with that used in their district's performance and curriculum standards. For example, Dr. Saphier uses the term "momentum" which comes from his book, The Skillful Teacher *(Saphier & Gower). In chapter 7 you will find the performance standards from a district that uses language from* The Skillful Teacher *to create a common basis for discussing teaching.*

"**Evidence** is a literal description of something the observer heard or saw to support the claim, such as 'Walking past Stephen, he passed him a pencil without pausing and continued the discussion of double jeopardy.'"[1] (Saphier & Gower)

Interpretations explain why the evidence does, indeed, support the claim. Interpretations typically start with "thus" and "therefore" statements; they contain an inference such as "As a result of this behavior, what the teacher accomplished was . . . and here's why." To put it another way, interpretations tell what a teacher or the incident accomplished or intended to accomplish. They are often worded to reflect the impact on the student. For example, " . . . thus he got Stephen started with note taking without skipping a beat in the discussion." All pieces of evidence do not require interpretations in write-ups, but some really do. (Saphier, 1993)

Whenever possible, the interpretation should indicate the impact on students' behavior, performance and/or attitude. For some standards, such as standard VII in the Brookline document in chapter 7, the interpretation should be worded in terms of its impact on school climate or culture.

Judgments let the reader know what the observer thought of the observed event. "This was an excellent way to reengage Stephen." Sometimes judgments are built into the syntax of a claim and a separate judgmental sentence is unnecessary as in the claim sentence above. (Saphier, 1993)

Judgments are the value the evaluator places on the teacher's choice of teaching move and the teacher's level of expertise in executing the move. Judgments contain words such as satisfactory, exemplary, unsatisfactory, successful, unsuccessful, good, excellent, effective and outstanding. It is important in a standards-based

---

[1] Chapter 5 contains a comprehensive explanation of the types of evidence including hearsay, circumstantial and direct.

evaluation system that, wherever possible, evaluators use the same terms that are used in the final year-end evaluation report. This is particularly important in the evaluation of a low-performing teacher. In example 4 on page 56 you will note that the final statement tells the teacher whether the evaluator judged the activity as satisfactory or less than satisfactory. This language is consistent with the final evaluation report language in the Brookline document in chapter 7.

The order of presenting the four concepts above in a classroom observation write-up is less important than making the evaluation clear to the teacher and others who need to read it. It is also not important that the components be clearly delineated in separate statements, provided all the concepts are covered. The sample evaluation on page 57 has several of these components combined into one or two sentences to make an effective write-up.

What is most important is that the write-up shows the two major components. The first being the **subjective** components. Claims, interpretations and judgments are based on the evaluator's conclusions of what he/she actually observes, verifies or, in cases of indirect evidence, can reasonably infer from the accumulated evidence or the observation.

The second of the major components is the evidence. This is the **objective** description of the actual behavior or information observed or verified by the evaluator. There is a great deal of information that can be derived from watching and analyzing the students' actions as well as the teacher's actions in a classroom observation. Early childhood educators have known this for years. More recently, evaluators of elementary, middle school and high school teachers are increasing their observation of students during classroom observations as a way of analyzing the teacher's year-long impact on the students.

Evidence supports the claims and judgments and, perhaps more importantly, shows the teacher that the supervisor–evaluator cares enough to take the time to learn the specifics of what the teacher is doing. Chapter 5 contains a comprehensive explanation about the differences between observed and verified evidence (direct) and indirect evidence (circumstantial and hearsay) in the data-gathering process. For most teacher evaluations, the majority of the evidence cited is direct evidence gathered in classroom observations. Some examples of sources for evidence other than classroom observations are listed in the next section. This list is followed by examples of paragraphs from actual classroom write-ups which were done using the C.E.I.J. format as it relates to a district's performance standards. The standards used are in the sample evaluation documents found in chapter 7.

SOURCES OF OBSERVABLE AND/OR VERIFIABLE EVIDENCE (DIRECT) AND HEARSAY AND/OR CIRCUMSTANTIAL EVIDENCE (INDIRECT) OTHER THAN CLASSROOM OBSERVATIONS

The following are just a few of the many ways we obtain evidence that is observable, verifiable or circumstantial information. It is important that evaluators use as many avenues as possible to obtain the data on which their judgments are based. Examples of how to gather and document this data can be found in chapter 5.

1. Observing teacher-to-student interactions in non-classroom settings such as the playground, cafeteria, corridor, assemblies, before school, after school, etc.

2. Tracking cumulative indirect evidence about the teacher and student interactions in class and other settings obtained from the reports of staff, students and parents

3. Observing the teacher's interactions with colleagues at meetings and in other settings

4. Tracking the cumulative indirect evidence about the teacher's interactions with colleagues at meetings and in other settings obtained from the reports of colleagues

5. Reviewing groups of corrected student work and the teacher's grade book to assess the timeliness of the teacher's responses, appropriateness of those responses and effectiveness of recording of those responses

6. Reviewing the teacher-developed student assessments and how the students performed on those assessments

7. Observing the teacher's interactions with parents individually (e.g., three-way conferences with the parent, teacher and evaluator)

8. Tracking the cumulative indirect evidence about the teacher's interactions with parents individually obtained from the staff's and parent's reports from those who attended the conference when the administrator did not

9. Observing the teacher's interactions with parents in group presentations, such as curriculum night presentations

10. Tracking indirect evidence in reports received from parents and colleagues of the teacher's interactions with parents in group presentations, such as curriculum night presentations

11. Reviewing the teacher's correspondence with staff, parents and students

12. Touring the classroom with the teacher while he/she describes the reasons for the classroom set-up and displays

13. The information provided by the teacher in answer to pre- and post-observation conference questions (see the section on questions to create change later in this chapter) and/or other conversations

14. Tracking cumulative indirect evidence obtained from high school class registration numbers (including drops and adds), which can be further substantiated by interviewing students who request drops about the reasons for their requests

15. Tracking the cumulative indirect evidence obtained from parents' request letters related to elementary class placements (including requests to remove students from a classroom after the school year has started); this evidence can be further substantiated by interviewing students and/or parents who request that their child be removed from a class after the school year begins about the reasons for their requests

16. Reviewing students' performance on criterion-referenced and norm-referenced tests over a period of several years

    It is important to note that the formal use of norm-referenced and criterion-referenced student performance data in individual teacher's evaluations is still rare and controversial. Supervisors and evaluators should be cautious about the use of these data as conclusive evidence of excellent or poor performance (Holloway, 2000, p. 84). Tennessee is one of a very few states with a process for using student data from standardized tests as a measure of an individual teacher's performance. There continues to be significant research and debate about what is known as the Tennessee value-added assessment system (Archer, 1999, p. 26).

17. Students' performance as demonstrated by reviewing and assessing teacher developed portfolios known as "Demonstrated Student Achievement Portfolios such as those used in the Baltimore Peformance Based System" (Koppich, 2001, p. 29)

EXCERPTS FROM SAMPLE WRITE-UPS THAT INCLUDE SUBJECTIVE CONCLUSIONS SUPPORTED BY OBSERVABLE AND/OR VERIFIABLE DATA

Below are actual examples from teacher evaluation reports that use evidence in classroom observations to support the evaluators' subjective conclusions (claims, interpretations, judgments). The names have been changed to maintain confidentiality. The performance standard (principle of effective teaching or PET) and curriculum standard (learning expectation) are noted in italics. The claim/judgment has been underlined and the evidence is marked in **bold** print. Example 1 has been revised by this author to demonstrate the C.E.I.J. components in order (with claim and judgment together in the first sentence). Example 2 is how it actually appeared in the write-up with the components spread about.

Example 1

Mr. Morgan used appropriate and effective questioning techniques (PET IV C).

The class started with the students telling Mr. Morgan all the questions they had about density. Mr. Morgan wrote these questions on a chart paper.

"What does a rowboat do when it gets swamped with water in a lake? Explain why."

"What happens when a stick falls in the water? Explain why."

"What happens when a nail falls in the water? Explain why."

When the list was completed, Mr. Morgan worked with the students to determine which questions could be answered only with experimentation and which questions could be answered without experimentation.

As a result, students learned to use inductive and deductive reasoning to synthesize the information they had learned at the beginning of the unit. They learned to delineate between that information which could be found through background reading and the information that could only be obtained through experimentation.

Example 2

Mr. Morgan used appropriate questioning techniques (PET IV C). **The class started with the students telling Mr. Morgan all the questions they had about density. Mr. Morgan wrote these questions on a chart paper (see attached list of questions). When the students were out of questions,**

Mr. Morgan asked some open-ended questions that stimulated additional student questions.

"What does a rowboat do when it gets swamped with water in a lake? Explain why."

"What happens when a stick falls in the water? Explain why."

"What happens when a nail falls in the water? Explain why."

When the list was completed, Mr. Morgan worked with the students to determine which questions could be answered only with experimentation and which questions could be answered without experimentation (*Eighth Grade Science Learning Expectation I A*).

Example 3

Mr. Morgan's lesson ensured that students maintained appropriate standards of behavior, mutual respect and safety (*PET III B*). **The classroom procedures were clearly posted on a chart at the front of the room. These included the safety procedures for lab time.** Mr. Morgan reviewed the procedures at the start of the class. **"We will be using Bunsen burners and chemicals today. It is important that no one leaves their seat without permission when the burners are lit. Goggles must be used at all times and the test tubes should only be handled with the test tube holders. Who can review for me the emergency fire procedures if there is an accident?" John reviewed the fire expectations. Mr. M. asked if there were any questions on the expectations.** As a result, the students were able to work throughout the lab period without incident, using the appropriate safety procedures (*Eighth Grade Science Learning Expectation I B*).

It is usually recommended that evaluators arrange their write-ups by standard rather than in chronological order. However, there certainly are times when a write-up is better done in chronological order. You will note in example 4 below that the evaluator has carefully noted the time throughout the lesson and recorded the lesson chronologically. This was done to highlight the **efficiency** or **inefficiency**[2] of the teaching. Example 4 is a write-up for a low-performing teacher who had significant issues related to incompetency and inefficiency. She refused to acknowledge these issues. Chronological

---

2 Inefficiency has been defined by arbitrators as "not producing the effect intended or desired within a reasonable amount of time, whether or not a teacher has the knowledge or capability." (Lexington, Massachusetts, Public Schools, American Arbitration Association, 1995), and as "students not on task, teacher not monitoring work, not following lesson plans, inaccurate and incomplete record keeping have all been accepted as evidence of inefficiency in teaching . . . " (Little Rock, Arkansas, School District, American Arbitration Association, 1994)

write-ups such as this one objectively demonstrated the inefficiency in her teaching and forced her to recognize its existence.

Example 4

The start of this lesson was unsatisfactory. The room was not physically ready. **You were not present before the students began to enter,** and it did not begin within an appropriate time (*PET IIIA*).

Four students came into the classroom through the double doors by 9:01 and took their bags to the lab area instead of leaving them in the lobby area. You came in seconds later as the four of them left your classroom without permission. As others began to arrive, the lollipop-selling controversy became an issue. A student said that Mr. (the evaluator) gave her permission to sell the lollipops. That was not true, but you took four minutes checking it out and making sure students wrapped up the lollipops.

The room was in disarray. Some of it was from the day before (salt on a lab table). Some of it was from homeroom. Students' chairs were helter-skelter or, in one case, on top of the lab table. Lab tables were not orderly. The counters near the windows were in disarray with papers and materials from the astronomy unit, which has been over for at least three weeks.

At 9:05 things were beginning to calm down. You began to address the class at 9:07. Your first comments were "John, get in your seat. You have a seat." Jarmal interrupted with "How come there is salt on the table?" John chimed in with "Mrs. E., what is the stuff on the table?" "Why do you put stuff on the table?"

At 9:08 you began to explain, "What I have today is a short . . . At least you and a partner should have a pencil. I will pass out this sheet . . . Then go on to complete it for homework . . . So you have to do this whole packet." Jarmal interrupted again, "How come you didn't clean up the salt?" You responded, "I left it up to students." Jarmal made another comment, "Oh, so I have to clean it up?"

Meanwhile, David was walking around the room cleaning the tables.

At 9:10 you said, "Okay, the first activity . . . " and began the explanation of the first activity.

The physical condition of the class, the students' interruptions and your late arrival in the room resulted in the loss of five to six minutes of valuable instructional time and a less than satisfactory learning environment at the start of the lesson.

SAMPLE OBSERVATION WRITE-UP THAT INCLUDES SUBJECTIVE CONCLUSIONS (CLAIMS, INTERPRETATIONS AND JUDGMENTS) SUPPORTED BY OBSERVABLE AND/OR VERIFIABLE DATA

The following observation write-up integrates subjective conclusions with the evidence used to support these conclusions. As stated earlier, some evaluators are most comfortable using the C.E.I.J. format in order. Others use an integrated style such as the one below. The following write-up has many of the four C.E.I.J. components identified, but others are not. *This write-up is much longer than is typically necessary for a high-performing teacher. It was chosen to provide multiple examples for the reader to see and try.* Read this write-up and answer the following questions.

1. Can you identify other claims, evidence, interpretations and/or judgments not identified by the author?

2. Can you determine the impact of the various teaching moves on the students' performance?

3. As a reader did you find this style of write-up easy to read and understand? If yes, why? If not, why not?

4. Did you agree with the author's labels in the author's notes? If yes, why? If not, why not?

5. Mary is an excellent teacher and the evaluator frequently affirms her good work. However, please list those places in the evaluation in which the evaluator provided suggestions and/or questions designed to foster Mary's further growth.

Sample Observation Write-up of a High-Performing Teacher

Sample School
Classroom Observation: Mary Ong's 8th grade
Date and time: 12/15/01, 1:00 to 1:50
Observer: Joan Switt, Assistant Principal

Mary, this was an excellent lesson. It was original in its conception, well researched in its content, sensitively designed for the middle school student and impeccably executed (**judgment**).

Your objectives were clear (**claim/judgment**). By familiarizing themselves with the Boston Massacre, students will be able to interpret primary source documents, share their findings with classmates and work toward consensus (**interpretation**). To accomplish this you created a "Boston Massacre Trial" packet, which included primary source documents researched by you and a series of questions students were to answer about the documents. These documents, which captured the testimony of a variety of people involved in the Boston Massacre, were very well chosen (**judgment**). They were readable and understandable, and they represented a variety of viewpoints. They even possessed realistic subtleties of speech, showing some "speakers" to be better educated than others. I even detected varying levels of emotionality (**evidence/judgment**). By identifying the names of those who gave testimony at the trial, the massacre became more personal and personalized. All this added to the authenticity of your students' experience, helping to make the Boston Massacre seem more present, more real and more alive for them, thus increasing their motivation (**interpretation**). Further, by engaging them as jurors for the Boston Massacre Trial, you transported them in time (**claim/interpretation**). As your directions so very well stated (**claim/judgment**): "The year is 1770. An altercation has just taken place on King Street in Boston between the English soldiers stationed there and the colonial citizens of Boston. As a result of this, five colonists died and six were wounded. You have been assigned to the jury of the trial of Captain Thomas Preston, the leader of the English soldiers, and the other soldiers there. Your job will be to decide who is at fault for this incident" (**evidence**). Using this context, you structured a fabulous experience for your students, which expanded their knowledge of a slice of American history, developed their critical thinking skills and encouraged them to practice the fine art of compromise (**claim/interpretation/judgment**).

By having them read these primary sources for homework the preceding night, which you succinctly captured in a little less than three pages (which seemed about right for 7th graders), and by having them answer four questions about what they read, you helped structure the work they were to do as jurors in class the next day (**claim/interpretation/judgment/some evidence**). Within the constraints of the forty minute classroom period, you were able to accomplish what you set out to do with them (**claim**). You were ready with established jury groups and a Boston Massacre Jury Sheet for each student. Their job was to use their packets and homework from the preceding night, and "as a group discuss whether you think each of the following people or groups of people are guilty of the Boston Massacre." This well laid out graphic organizer listed five key players whose guilt they were to consider: Captain Thomas Preston, the first soldier who fired, the mob, the Sons of Liberty and King George III. While the directions were clearly stated on the sheet, it was your instructions to the class that clarified precisely what they were to do. "You will be assigned to a jury. I made these groups up in advance. Using the Boston Massacre Trial packet and the homework you did last night, you will discuss each of these people/groups listed on the sheet and systematically determine their guilt in this massacre, citing evidence for your position. Everyone needs a chance to speak . . . Take notes about each person, decide the percent of guilt, if they deserve a punishment and then choose a spokesperson, who will summarize what you as a jury decide." You stressed the importance of supporting all decisions with evidence. "Should I put this person in jail?" This is the kind of hard question that gets discussed in jury rooms. You pointed out that the students will need to have reasons to make this kind of decision. You added, "The hard part about being a juror is that you don't get to ask questions about the evidence. The only information you have to go on is what you have from class yesterday and your packet. After you assign guilt, come up with a punishment that you think would fit" (**evidence**).

Connecting this trial to the theme around which all of your lessons are built this year, you reminded students that their work as jurors is about looking at a variety of *perspectives*. You shared that the groups from the previous period had different findings of guilt and that's fine as long as you can support your positions with evidence" (**claim/evidence**). In this way you successfully defined the bigger picture for this activity, putting it in a wider context, while grounding it through the experience of other classmates (**interpretation/judgment**).

Students immediately engaged with this material. There was evidence of genuine passion as students argued the culpability of each of the five defendants. You moved from table to table, prodding some juries to move forward toward consensus: "It's important to listen to everyone's opinions and then come up with one idea for all of you." Adding in response to one student, "No, this is not 'Survivor.' You can't vote someone out" (**evidence**). In this way you stressed the importance that everyone's viewpoint counts even as they are to come together in a single voice. In another group Kevin felt it was the King who was the most guilty, but he said he'd be afraid to assign a punishment for fear of retribution. Even as you acknowledged this concern, "Yes, it could put you in danger," your further response to him provided some foreshadowing, as you suggested the King's wrath was definitely something to be concerned about and that this was a problem for the colonists. This exchange showed the degree to which students became their roles. Your conversations with students in each of these groups exemplify the ways you connect with your students as they move through their activity, encouraging them, prodding them to move forward and to think (**claim/interpretation/judgment with some evidence**).

When it was time for students to stop, representatives from each group shared their verdicts, complete with evidence and punishments (**evidence**). I was impressed with their responses (**judgment**). All made the King most culpable. While some wanted to behead him, at least one was afraid to do anything out of fear of reprisals. Ryanne was adamant that "The mob was innocent because they were just trying to express their anger because of what the king did to them." Furthermore, she added, "The mob only had snowballs and ice to use against the soldiers who had guns." Jesse suggested that perhaps that man in the black suit, who seemed to be the instigator of the battle, was really a member of the Sons of Liberty, perhaps Samuel Adams, thereby exonerating poor Captain Preston. At this point you promised to tell them whom *that man* was when they come to class on Monday (**evidence**). This both foreshadowed what was to come, but for me, also made me very curious to know the answer (**claim/interpretation**). These summaries, shared with the class, exemplify the level of higher order thinking students engaged in around this activity (**judgment**).

As a final cap-off of this experience, students were to gather the information and ideas from these discussions and conclusions to write a two paragraph essay of at least five sentences each, a Think Piece, as you called it, as follows: "One paragraph should tell why the person you think is to blame and another paragraph should tell why other people are not guilty." To further clarify these directions you gave them an example of how you wanted them to think about this. "You've heard a lot of people indicate they didn't like the King. The Patriots didn't like the King either. Be thoughtful with the Think Piece. Say why the King is guilty. If you believe the mob is innocent, explain why. Don't just say they are angry. Say why they are angry. Base all of your positions on evidence." In this way, once again, you insisted upon supportive proof to bolster their positions. One student wondered if it was all right "to change your opinion after today." You used that question as an opportunity to further encourage students to think and mull over the evidence. "You can change your decision between now and the time you write your essay. This means you're thinking about it, and that you listened to some of the other opinions here. It's important to look at the evidence in different ways" (**evidence**). This Think Piece will be an excellent assessment tool to determine the ability of students to see this historical event from a variety of perspectives and to use evidence to support their positions (**claim/interpretation/judgment**).

This observation wouldn't be complete if I didn't comment on your stellar classroom management skills. None of this would have gone as well as it did had you not been able to capture students' attention and move them through this so effectively (**claim/judgment**). Students know as soon as they enter your classroom that they are to take out their assignment notebooks and write down their homework. Wasting no time, you went on to say, "Once you have the homework written down, take out your homework from last night, including the transcript to the trial you read and the answer to your questions. Everyone will be in a jury today. Before I put you into a jury, you will need a sheet to fill out, the Boston Massacre Jury Sheet." With that you handed out the graphic organizer they were to use to structure their work as jurors. As soon as you heard a voice, you responded, "There shouldn't be any talking." And there wasn't. When you assigned students to their juries, you were quite clear, again managing the group beautifully. You established four juries in advance, calling out the names of the jurors, while walking to each table the jury members were to sit at. Students remained seated at your direction until you finished, and then you said, "Don't move yet, but does everyone know where to go? Make sure to bring your binder with your packet. Now go into your juries quietly, get to your chairs, and then look to me for more instructions" (**evidence**). With such explicit directions, you fully forestalled any possibility of pandemonium or chaos, which could otherwise ensue as the class reshuffled into their groups. Instead students moved to their assigned places and sat quietly to hear what you wanted them to do next (**claim/interpretation/judgment**).

Throughout the activity, you kept a watchful eye on the time for students, telling them how much time they had to begin with, and then how many more minutes they had left at specified intervals as they were deliberating (**claim**). You also moved them swiftly to summarize their positions to the class, forcing them to be succinct, so every jury would get a chance to share their verdict before the class period ended. When the noise level in the room began to rise as the juries deliberated passionately, you turned the lights off, which got them to quiet down immediately (**evidence**). This protected you from having to raise your voice over theirs (**interpretation**). It then gave you the opportunity to say, "The groups are getting heated because some of you are agreeing and some are disagreeing." By acknowledging their voice levels were high because of their passion about their discussion, it made it more palatable for them to hear your command that they needed to "keep their voices down" and instead "practice their library voices."

I loved this lesson, Mary. It was a joy to watch (**judgment**).

_____	_____
Teacher's signature	date
_____	_____
Observer's signature	date

Teacher's signature indicates the teacher received the observation. It does not indicate agreement.

Teacher's comments: _____

_____

_____

_____

SAMPLE END-OF-YEAR REPORT THAT INCLUDES SUBJECTIVE CONCLUSIONS (CLAIMS, INTERPRETATIONS AND JUDGMENTS) SUPPORTED BY OBSERVABLE AND/OR VERIFIABLE DATA

The following end-of-year report integrates subjective conclusions with the evidence used to support these conclusions. Read this report and answer the following questions:

1. Is there more evidence that can be used to support the conclusions? If so, what evidence would be helpful in doing this?

2. As a reader did you find this style of write-up easy to read and understand? If yes, why? If not, why not?

3. Did you agree with the author's labels noted in the author's notes? If yes, why? If not, why not?

4. Francine is an excellent teacher and the evaluator frequently affirms her good work. However, please list those places in the evaluation which provide suggestions and/or questions designed to foster Francine's further growth.

5. Can you identify other claims, evidence, interpretations or judgments not identified by the author?

6. Can you determine the impact of the various teaching moves on the students' performance?

Sample of a Third-Year Teacher:
Annual Report of Teacher Effectiveness 2000–2001

Teacher: <u>Francine Fourth</u>   School: <u>Sample</u>   Grade/Subject: <u>4</u>

   I.   Currency of Curriculum

   II. Effective Planning and Assessment of Curriculum and Instruction

   III. Effective Management of Classroom Environment

   IV. Effective Instruction

   V. Promotion of High Standards and Expectations for Student Achievement

   VI. Promotion of Equity and Appreciation of Diversity

   VII. Fulfillment of Professional Responsibilities

Narrative

Francine is in her second year at Sample School, moving to the 4th grade this year after one year in the Learning Center. Francine agreed to teach 4th grade when there was uncertainty about the availability of the Learning Center position. Although the Learning Center position eventually became available, Francine honored her commitment to 4th grade. She did so with magnificent spirit and an incredible amount of work and preparation, and she has met with enormous success. Her classroom is one of the nicest places in our school. Children are consistently productive, engaged and thoughtful with one another. All of Francine's colleagues find her a true team player. It is refreshing to ask Francine to do something; her response is always thoughtful and framed in terms of how the most productive thing for children can happen. Not surprisingly, I have received numerous comments from parents such as, "Caroline adores Ms. Fourth—this is her best year in school" and "We just had our parent conference, and I was extremely impressed with how well Francine knows Max as a person and as a student. She is a wonderful teacher."

I. Currency of Curriculum

Francine takes a great deal of initiative around learning curriculum (**claim and judgment**). Last summer, she took a week long class at Northeastern in order to prepare for the Math Investigations curriculum (which she was teaching for the first time this year). Francine calls on her experience teaching 4th grade at Lincoln School two years ago, and in fact met with her teaching partner there in preparation for this assignment. Francine also works very constructively with the other 4th grade teacher at Sample and has accessed the resources and expertise of the 4th grade teacher she is replacing this year. Francine also makes extremely effective use of the Curriculum Coordinators. For example, she worked closely with the Science Coordinator in planning for the botany unit she taught at the start of this year. She met with the Language Arts Coordinator to plan both writing and spelling programs. She is likewise meeting with the Social Studies Coordinator (**evidence of the claim above**). As a result Francine is very knowledgeable about current curriculum expectations (**interpretation**).

Francine has been extremely thoughtful about the MCAS (Massachusetts Comprehensive Assessment System) tests as well, seeking to integrate strategies that are called for throughout the year. (See observation write-ups of 11/5/00, 11/24/00 and 12/21/00.)

II. Effective Planning and Assessment of Curriculum and Instruction

Francine has a magnificent ability to plan for a wide range of students within the confines of each lesson. She develops lessons at many levels simultaneously (**claim and judgment**). For example, during the human body unit, some students were expected to learn all of the parts of the cell (normally taught in grade 7), as well as the function of various types of cells. Other students were required to read material with a partner and draw and label a cell. If there are twenty math problems, some students are expected to do all of them; others a limited number. There are spelling programs for children learning ten words a week, children learning fifteen words and children who are working on challenge words (**evidence**).

Within each unit, each lesson meshes well with the next in a seamless manner (**claim/judgment**). Because of the level of advance organization that Francine does an excellent job of building into each lesson, children are able to function quite independently (**claim/judgment/interpretation**). All of these characteristics were observed during a math lesson on November 5th, excerpts of which follow:

[The following contains the evidence for the claim and interpretation above and evidence of additional claims, interpretations and judgments contained within this section. Please also note that the evaluator has used the time-saving technique of cutting and pasting evidence from previously written observation write-ups. The italicized sections were pasted from the observation write-up. See the section in this book titled "Where Do I Find Time for All These Write-ups? Try These Tips! (page 81) for additional time–saving ideas." —William Ribas]

This is a lesson on constructing graphs. The goal of the project is to teach children how to analyze the data they have collected from their plant unit to make a bar graph. Francine starts the lesson with an overhead of a bar graph about the life cycle of plants. She starts by going over the parts of the graph, the title, etc. She discusses with the class how the vertical axis of the graph is constructed. She asks the children why the graph starts at 5 days and increases in increments of 5. She has a nice way of guiding the discussion and of calling on a broad range of children. She also has a very good way of restating what the children say. For example, when one child says the graph would be too big if every day were labeled, Francine expanded this to talk about how the graph is used to summarize information. She presses on this issue to extend thinking—i.e., you decide what the intervals on the graph should be, based on the actual data you have. "You have to think about what numbers you have." She asks how many more days it takes one plant to develop vs. another. She has a good tolerance for wait time. When Tobias answers, she asks the class to raise hands if they agree. On another question, she asks why the answer (between 60 and 65) could be 63 or 64 but not 61. When Francine is certain that the class has understood how to read this graph, she moves to the next part of the lesson.

For this section of the lesson, a written exercise in reading a graph, children move to their old seats so they can work with their science partners. Francine has excellent management techniques, and the children move effortlessly from one situation to the next. She reminds children to take pencils, and she tells them who will pass out graphs and how they will be distributed. When this is finished, Francine says, "You and your partner should have your question sheet and your graph." Before the children start, Francine read them a narrative about the sample graph. The questions that the children have to answer about this graph are parallel to the questions she has gone over on the overhead. The topic is different—the written exercise involves a growth chart and the overhead was about plants. The class quickly settled into the working partnerships and worked very productively. When voices were a little loud, Francine reminded them to "use one-inch voices," and this did the trick.

For the next few minutes, Francine went over the exercise with the class. She read the first question and got responses from the class. Francine again pressed the answer—she reminded the kids to pay close attention to the question being asked— i.e., the question was not to double but to find the answer as "more than twice as tall." On the second question, one student said the answer was yes—most of the kids agreed. However, Francine checked to see if anyone thought the answer was no.

During the last part of the lesson, Francine told the class what was going to happen the next time. She told them they would be getting graph paper (she showed them a sample). She told them how they would create their own graphs. She had them get their science folders and science notebooks. Ariel distributed the graph papers. Francine referred the children to rough draft graphs they had made. She reminded them that they had these, the sample on the overhead and the graph for the practice exercise—all of these references could be used to help them. She told them that for the last few minutes of the class, they could talk with their science partners about how they would plan their graphs.

This was an excellent class. It was carefully planned, and it met the children exactly at their learning step. One of the most impressive things about Francine's teaching is the way she presses around questioning—she routinely asks extension questions, and she checks to make sure that everyone understands. She also invites and respects minority opinions—the goal is to find out the how and why—not just to recite the right answer. The tone of the class is excellent. Francine has a very nice way of interacting with the children—she makes lots of positive remarks such as "good point, excellent." Her directions are very clear—children are able to move smoothly from one part of the lesson to the next. A lot of the class involves group work and the children stay on task and talk with each other in a respectful way. I would like to add that the classroom itself is attractive and well organized (Francine opened this room this year). Materials are well organized and easy to access. Student work is nicely displayed. Overall, Francine is an impressive teacher.

Although the class just described masterfully utilized mixed-ability groups, Francine also utilizes performance-level groups as appropriate.

III. Effective Management of Classroom Environment

Francine is a masterful manager in the classroom. So much of what happens looks like it is happening "by magic," but every moment is the result of careful planning (**claim and judgment**). The class is structured in "teams" that rotate monthly. Teams have a variety of ways that they earn points for working cooperatively and productively together. Francine uses a range of mechanisms, including homework charts on which students mark off their assignments with small stickers. There are rewards such as lunch with the teacher given for a certain number of days of handing in homework on time. One of the funniest encounters I had with a child this year was with a girl from Francine's class who had left her backpack on the bus. She was unconcerned about her lunch, money and other personal possessions, but she was driven to tracking the backpack down because her homework was in it and this child was determined to maintain her perfect record (**interpretation and evidence**) . . . Of course, all of this works because Francine's expectations are both challenging and doable at the same time (**claim and judgment**); because Francine checks with students to make sure that they understand what to do in numerous ways (**claim and judgment**); because all of the routines are predictable; because Francine speaks to her class with the utmost respect (**claim and judgment**) . . .

An observation of a science class on December 21st demonstrated Francine's ability to manage a class most effectively. A summary of that class follows:

This is an observation of a science lesson. The class is going to be meeting in their "tree groups." The lesson starts with the overhead. Francine reviews by telling the class that all six research groups have presented. The goal of today's lesson is to have each group make a study sheet for the class. Francine explained that each student would get six study sheets which they would be able to use for a quiz; that the group that was the expert on, for example, palm trees, would make the study sheet for their group. Francine had prepared a worksheet for each group. She went over the worksheet with the class. Mickey asked about how they would get information from a student who was not here. Francine told him that they could refer to the posters of students not here.

Francine went through the worksheet in a question-and-answer format. The worksheet, which was very clearly laid out, asked for the names of trees included in the group, description of the trees in the group, how the tree was used and interesting facts. For each question, Francine had a student explain what was called for. Francine has a nice way of predicting and, therefore, preventing problems. For example, the worksheet called for four or five interesting facts. Francine acknowledged that kids had more than this, but that they needed to pick the most important and interesting ones. Francine reviewed the process for filling out the sheet—how to take turns and how the people who were not writing could be preparing the next question. Francine next told the kids where they were going to be working. She emphasized that if there were six groups talking, they would need to keep their voices down. The task needed to be finished before lunch (they would have about twenty-five minutes). All of this advance organizing—i.e., previewing the sheet, answering questions and predicting problems, was very useful. Francine pays attention to nice details—such as how to take a poster down without ripping it.

The transition to the small groups was very smooth and efficient, although it involved a lot of steps—taking down posters, getting information cards, etc. Francine made sure each group got started. The groups set to work with amazing efficiency. Due to absences, the groups ranged in size from five students to two students. Francine moved among the six groups, helping kids decide among the array of information sources available to them. She reminded kids that the information could be recorded "in note-taking form" rather than in complete sentences. Without exception, the groups stayed with the task at hand, conversations among the children in each group stayed on topic and they were all able to fill out the worksheet. The fact that these worksheets were going to be used as study sheets by their classmates gave them a clear purpose.

About five minutes before lunch, Francine stopped the groups. She said that some people were finding they needed more information to make the sheet complete. She said that they should see what information they needed to complete the sheet, who was going to get it and that they needed to bring it in tomorrow to finish the task. Francine made a final round among the groups to see what information needed to be completed. Francine had the children put everything away in a completely organized manner. She had the children organize their homework folders for the close of the day.

Once again, this was a well organized, thoughtful class. Francine built on previous assignments—i.e., information gathering and making posters—and was moving the children to the next level of application—how you would teach this information to somebody else. The posters and cards (from previous classes) were well prepared, so the kids all pretty much had the tools at hand to complete today's assignment. Each step of the research project built beautifully on the steps that preceded it. Francine is a master at advance organizing and because of this, things that could become problems in less skilled hands (i.e., who is going to be the recorder in a group, what to do about missing information, what to do about absent students) were avoided here. The class was all content— virtually no effort was spent on management problems. As always, the tone of this class was very productive; children talked in their groups in an animated way, but they remained on task. An excellent class.

IV.   Effective Instruction

Francine sets clear goals, and uses these as a basis to assess instruction on a daily, weekly and monthly basis. For example, Francine gives a weekly math assessment to review concepts taught that week. She corrects the assessment over the weekend and then on Monday divides the class into two groups; students who need to review concepts work with the Learning Center teacher, while Francine does a supplementary lesson with the rest of the class. Francine uses the idea of pre- and post-assessments in other areas of the curriculum as well. Students are asked to draw or write on what they think about a topic (i.e., the parts of a plant or bee, what a Native American looks like) before a unit begins. As illustrated above in the description of the science class, Francine concludes units by frequently having children teach what they have learned to someone else. Francine is also skilled at using a range of instructional strategies. For example, Francine uses whole-class books, book groups, independent reading and reading aloud in her reading program. She incorporates teacher-directed lessons, hands-on activities and practice and application, as appropriate. This range of instructional approaches was evident in a math class I observed on November 24th. Excerpts from that observation follow:

This is a math class—children are learning about silhouettes of solid geometric shapes. The first part of the lesson is a review of something they have done before. They are predicting what geometric shapes would look like on an overhead projection. They predict that a cone held upside down would be a circle—in fact, when Francine does this on the overhead, this is what they see. The children continue to give reasons why this is so. The next shape is a triangle prism—each time students say what shape they think it will be, they give a reason. When stood on end, the top is blurry—on its side, it is clear. On its side, the shape looks like a rectangle—again, Francine has children give reasons why this is so.

Francine next has the class open their math books to page 9 of their workbook. The task is for each team to build the landscape that is pictured. Francine explains that she will be giving each group a bag of geometric solids and a sheet of paper on which to build the landscape. She answers questions about the order of the shapes, etc. Francine does a lot of advance organizing—i.e., the place where the structure is to be built, putting it all on a book so the structures won't tip, given the uneven desk surfaces. The directions are very clear, which results in the children being able to start the task in a purposeful way. As Francine walks around the class, she reminds children to look at the picture—says that there may be extra pieces in the bag. In a couple of minutes, all the groups complete this part of the task. Francine comments that in some teams there is a difference of opinion about some of the shapes. She places the diagram on the overhead and goes over it.

Francine said they were now going to talk about looking at things from different points of view. Ultimately, they would draw how things looked from different points in the room. Francine focused on the point between the two rectangles on the overhead—asked what you would see if you faced various ways. Francine said, "Pretend that you are a little person at each of these letters—what would you see from each point?" She went on to ask how the desks in the classroom would look to a little baby and to Michael Jordan. From there, they went on to do the three exercises on the worksheets with partners.

Francine told them that now they would be drawing what they saw in the classroom from their perspectives. She wanted them to draw what they saw from where they were sitting. There was a good discussion about why Charlie, for example, could see the flag and the window, whereas Alyssa would see the desk next to her. Francine said the goal was to draw your spot so clearly that if it were given to another person, they would be able to figure out who did it. There were a lot of questions about what to draw—should it be just what was in front of you, or to the left, right, etc.? Francine said they would start this today—spend five minutes on it and finish it tomorrow. The children seemed to have a fairly good idea of how to go about doing this. Francine told them not to put their names on the drawings, but to put them in their math folders, and that they would finish them tomorrow.

This lesson presented extremely challenging and often ambiguous concepts . . . Francine gave good clues as the children were drawing—i.e., think about the size of things—the size of your desk in comparison to the chalkboard . . . As always, Francine's tone with the group is very positive. Children work on the task at hand in a productive manner, even when they are confused. All of the organizational details and the preparation of the materials are well accounted for, and this keeps things flowing nicely from one activity to the next.

V. Promotion of High Standards and Expectations for Students' Achievement

Francine has an extraordinary range of students in her classroom (even by Brookline's standards), due in part to the fact that it was not possible to accommodate a developmentally delayed child in her class at another school; Francine has thus worked with staff at our school to develop an interim program for her. At the other end of the spectrum, Francine has two children in her class who are the most intellectually gifted children in 4th grade and among the highest-ability children in the school. To accommodate this range, Francine works with teachers in two learning centers, the remedial reading teacher and the E.S.L. teacher. These specialists work both on a pull-out basis and in Francine's classroom. In addition, Francine has set up a special reading group with the librarian for the highest-level children and participated in a special math pilot with the town-wide gifted and talented coordinator. Within the classroom, Francine has developed groups for spelling, reading and math to accommodate the range in her class. Francine is a master of the concept of "personal best." She simply insists that a child put forth his or her best work, and children are required to redo work that was rushed through or incomplete. Francine works in tandem with parents around this concept, so that standards for homework and schoolwork are consistent. Francine also insists on standard writing conventions such as complete sentences, paragraphing and punctuation.

VI. Promotion of Equity and Appreciation of Diversity

Francine has a genuine respect and appreciation for each child in her class (**claim and judgment**). She honors each student for his or her strengths (**claim and judgment**). Francine takes a genuine interest in the lives of her students outside of the classroom—be it sports, music, scouting, drama or family events (**claim and judgment**). As she wrote, "I try to publicly recognize each student, giving them positive attention and praise when they succeed in a specific area (**claim and judgment**). For example, J., a new student and struggling reader, is a wonderful artist. I., a low-functioning child, is a wonderful football player with a great sense of humor. Ji, another child who struggles academically, has a great personality and a wonderful way of cheering up her peers.

Francine uses the curriculum as a basis for teaching about diversity (**claim and judgment**). For example, in teaching about Native Americans, Francine used this study as a sequel to previous teaching about stereotypes (**evidence**). Francine frequently uses class discussions and meetings to address issues of diversity and equity (**claim and judgment**).

VII. Fulfillment of Professional Responsibilities

Francine works most effectively with everyone on our staff—the librarian, SPED staff, ESL–Bilingual staff and regular education teachers all find Francine a delight to work with (**claim and judgment**). She is flexible and adaptable, and will do virtually anything that will make her classroom a stronger place (**claim and judgment**). Interestingly, two of the specialists I am evaluating this year asked me to do their observations in Francine's classrooms. This shows it is a comfortable and positive place for other professionals as well as for children (**evidence and interpretation**). Francine is a master at collaboration and team teaching (**claim and judgment**).

Francine's skills in working with parents was addressed at the start of this report. She makes herself available to parents on a daily basis, yet her contacts with parents are always appropriate and professional. Like her colleagues on the faculty, parents also find Francine easy to talk to and helpful (**claim and judgment**).

[You will note that many there are many positive claims, judgments and interpretations that are not backed up by evidence. In districts where a full time evaluator's load is limited to ten people, the evaluator is able to provide evidence for most or all of the subjective statements. However, in districts in which evaluators have over twenty evaluations (as is the case for this evaluator), valuable time documenting evidence must be focused toward the lower performers. I speak more about this later in the chapter which discusses time-saving techniques for evaluators with large loads).—William Ribas]

Francine's enthusiasm, positive attitude, ability to forge strong and positive relationships with children, colleagues and parents, her strong work ethic and the intelligence and common sense she brings to her work, make her a wonderful teacher to have on the Sample faculty. We are lucky to have her.

_____ This evaluation indicates performance with no areas of concern.

__X__ This evaluation indicates performance with need for improvement in one or two areas (see recommendations).

_____ This evaluation indicates performance with need for improvement in several areas (see recommendations).

_____ This evaluation indicates performance which is below the standard expected of staff in the Sample Public Schools (see recommendations).

X

Overall Evaluation: Satisfactory   Unsatisfactory

_____   _____
Signature of evaluator   date

_____   _____
Signature of teacher   date

Signature signifies receipt of, not concurrence with, this evaluation. Teachers are encouraged to submit comments. Please make comments on the back of this form or on an attached sheet.

PEER SUPPORT WITH WRITING OBSERVATION WRITE-UPS AND END-OF-YEAR EVALUATION REPORTS

It will feel very cumbersome to evaluators when they first start writing evaluations that

- consistently label teaching moves with the district's common language
- translate literal notes into evidence
- make interpretations that point to the impact on students and/or the school culture and use language consistent with the district's performance standards
- make value judgments that are consistent from teacher to teacher and use the district's evaluation language

The evaluators' comfort level will grow as they gain experience. The speed at which they write will also increase as they gain experience using this style.

For both beginning and seasoned evaluators, it is helpful to have them work with colleagues from whom they can get feedback about drafts of observation write-ups or final evaluation reports. Below is a peer conferencing guide that administrators can use to help each other write their evaluation documents more clearly, concisely and quickly. This is a good activity for an administrators' meeting. Much is written about the value of peer coaching for teachers, but peer coaching is equally effective for administrators. It provides them with both technical and emotional support.

Read the Write-Up You Have Been Assigned and Answer the Following Questions

1. Does the evidence (objective information) in the write-up directly support the claim, judgment and/or interpretation (subjective statements)? Do you have suggestions on how the writer can better support his/her statements with observed and/or verified information?

2. Is there a way for the writer to describe the evidence that is more concrete, observable or verifiable? Do you have suggestions for the writer for improving his/her descriptions?

3. Does the writer make it clear how the teacher's behaviors affect the students' learning or well being, negatively or positively?

4. Does the writer use the language of the district's performance standards in the write-up?

5. Does the writer make value judgments about the teaching moves observed?

6. What other comments/questions do you have about the example?

CONFERENCING TO CREATE CHANGE: WHAT YOU ASK A TEACHER AND HEAR FROM A TEACHER IS OFTEN MORE IMPORTANT THAN WHAT YOU TELL A TEACHER

At the beginning of the chapter, I spoke about the importance of writing in clear, concise and honest language. We also spoke about the importance of the above being accompanied by speaking in conferences and discussions with teachers about their performance. This is particularly true when the discussion is about areas for improvement. The next section provides a framework for effectively having these types of supervision and evaluation conferences with teachers.

Pre-conferences, post-conferences and impromptu conversations with teachers are excellent opportunities to create positive change in a teacher's practice. Effective questioning and listening during conversations with a teacher give the evaluator much of the information (evidence) he/she needs to make judgments and interpretations about the teacher's performance. Questions that force the teacher to reassess his/her practice and reconsider less effective practices can be far more effective in causing behavioral change than recommendations merely stated by the evaluator. Below are six steps evaluators can use to get teachers to think about, talk about and reassess their practices. These stages are an adaptation of the steps found on pages 54 and 55 of Thomas Gordon's book, *Leadership Effectiveness Training* (1977).

Six Stages of Listening and Questioning to Promote Behavioral Change
Stage I: Door Openers

- Choose the best location/setting for the conversation. The best setting can be determined by the situation. For example, some teachers may prefer complete privacy when you are addressing areas they need to change in their performance. In these cases, in your office behind a closed door is probably the best place. However, I have known other teachers who prefer to have conversations of this sort in their classrooms. They feel more comfortable in familiar surroundings and are more at ease discussing your assessment of their teaching.

- Door Openers indicate you want to have a two-way conversation about the teacher's practice and don't just want to give the teacher feedback. This is best achieved with questions that push the teacher to think about his/her practice in a different way. At this point the questions should be open-ended to get the teacher talking and thinking. Some post-conference door openers can include the following:

    How do you think the lesson went?

    How did you feel during the lesson?

    What did you observe about the students during the lesson?

Stage II: Passive Listening

Passive Listening is a technique you can use to create an environment where the teacher feels he/she can talk freely.

- The most important thing to do is "bite your lip and listen." Resist the urge to give the teacher the answer or advice too soon. It may be quicker (and more gratifying to you) to give the teacher your feedback than to wait for him/ her to discover a "better way" during the discussion. However, changes in practice that are discovered by the teacher are far more likely to be implemented than those you give as advice that is not requested. Harry Truman said it best: "There is no limit to what you can achieve when you don't care who gets the credit."

- Use body language that indicates your openness to hearing what the teacher has to say. Your physical deportment can signal to the teacher that what he/she says is important to you.

Stage III: Acknowledgment Responses

Eye contact, nodding, comments such as "I hear you" and "I understand" and paraphrasing the teacher's statements all send the message that you are listening. Remember that acknowledging is not agreeing! There will be ample opportunity to discuss areas of disagreement at the appropriate time.

Stage IV: Active Listening

Active listening gives the speaker tangible evidence of the listener's understanding. For example, a listener labels a teacher's feelings about the situation (e.g., as anger, excitement, pride, frustration, confusion). The listener uses clarification questions and follow-up questions to gather additional information. For example, effective assessment is an area teachers typically struggle with because of the recent changes in practice resulting from an increased emphasis on standards. At the end of this section, you will find a set of questions that are based on one school district's performance standards on assessment. An evaluator may use these questions to learn more about how a teacher assesses students and to push the teacher to examine his/her assessment practices.

Stage V: Closing the Gap Between the Evaluator's and the Teacher's Perception of Performance

- Identify differences between your perception and the teacher's perception of the situation, and generate options that sound reasonable to both of you. Ask questions that help the teacher discover inconsistencies between his/her perception of a practice's impact on students and the real impact. You want the changes teachers make to "stick." The more teachers buy into the changes in their practices, the more likely they are to permanently implement them. Of course if a teacher's practice is detrimental to the students, you will not have the option of allowing the teacher time for self-discovery. In those situations you may need to be more direct about the inappropriateness of the behavior that you wish to change.

- Be open to the idea that you may not be completely correct in your perceptions. Listen to and consider the teacher's rationale before making a final judgment. Remember that there is a difference between a rationale and an excuse. A **rationale** is a true and convincing explanation of why the teacher's practice is better for students then your suggested change. An **excuse** is a reason why it is better for the teacher to use his/her practice, rather than to use the better practice for students.

- Do an internal check of your frustration/defensiveness meter. If your frustration and/or defensiveness is growing faster than the progress you are making in closing the gap between your perception and that of the teacher, it might be best to end the discussion and schedule a time to get together again in the near future. This will keep you from making non-productive statements and give you time to reflect and decide on whether there are other ways to word your concern that will better enable the teacher to hear and "own" those concerns.

Stage VI: Concluding the Discussion
- Generate options for next steps.
- Be aware of the consequences (alternatives to coming to agreement or ATAs) of not reaching consensus on the next steps. The extent to which you require next steps with which the teacher does not agree or continue to generate options until there is agreement often corresponds to the degree to which the teacher functions successfully or not.
- Summarize the conclusions reached in the conference.
- Set a date, time, location and tentative agenda for a follow-up discussion.

The framework as outlined in the *Conferencing to Create Change* section, pages 73–75, must always be considered within the context of the individual with whom the evaluator is meeting. Some teachers prefer that the evaluator "cut to the chase" if they believe the evaluator is working up to an area for improvement. Most, however, prefer the evaluator work through the stages and appreciate the give-and-take that this type of conference provides. Below are some sample questions that can be used with various performance standards.

Questions an Evaluator May Ask a Teacher About the Following Performance Standards on Assessment

Standard 1: The teacher effectively plans assessment of students' learning.

Standard II: The teacher monitors students' understanding of the curriculum effectively and adjusts instruction, materials or assessments when appropriate.

The following list is adapted from Colby's article (1999).

- How do you make decisions about the appropriate assessments to use?
- What types of assessments do you use in your classroom?
- How and when do you gather assessment information?
- What type of grading system do you use and how effective is it?
- What must students do to demonstrate proficiency on each curriculum standard?
- What supports do students who are not progressing receive?
- How is progress communicated to students and parents?

Questions an Evaluator Asks a Teacher About Professional Development Portfolios

Standard VII C: The teacher is a reflective and continuous learner.

The following list is based on Painter's article (2001).

- What ten to twelve artifacts can you put into your portfolio that represent your professional growth on all seven standards?
- What performance standard(s) does each artifact represent?
- Why is each artifact better than other artifacts that you could choose to represent this standard(s)?
- Can you explain the rationale for each artifact to someone who is viewing it out of the context of knowing a great deal about your classroom?
- How do the artifacts you chose represent to you and others your growth as a teacher?

With some teachers, no matter how well the evaluator tries to address social–emotional dynamics by presenting the information in a way that can be "heard," the response will still be angry and defensive. These teachers often believe you (the evaluator) can't relate to the specifics of the difficulties in their classrooms, because you don't walk in their shoes. For those teachers, the following section on teaching sample lessons can be a very effective tool for addressing that emotional defense mechanism. Don't panic! Just read on. You will see that by using the structure outlined in the next section, teaching sample lessons is less scary and time-consuming than you have always thought.

EVALUATORS TEACHING SAMPLE LESSONS: A POWERFUL TOOL FOR CREATING A CULTURE OF OPENNESS TO CHANGE AND RECEIVING FEEDBACK ABOUT AREAS FOR IMPROVEMENT

Teaching sample lessons is a powerful tool for supervisors and evaluators. However, few supervisors and evaluators ever teach model lessons despite the fact that most agree they are very valuable. Most of the evaluators I speak with about teaching sample lessons give two reasons why they don't teach them, despite acknowledging their value. The first is the time it takes to prepare a lesson for a group of students and for a curriculum they do not teach on a regular basis. The other reason is one they tend to admit with more reluctance. It is the fear they feel about not being able to teach the lesson with the level of excellence they attained when they taught full time. They are afraid to open themselves up to the staff's ridicule. These emotions cause many evaluators to consciously or subconsciously avoid teaching model lessons.

> You are teaching to create a context for discussion about teaching and learning, not to demonstrate a model of perfection. Be clear about this with the teacher when you agree/volunteer to model a lesson.

The tips below are designed to assist evaluators with these concerns. They will help evaluators find the time and courage to maximize the use of sample lessons.

1. Don't panic. You are supposed to make mistakes, but not on purpose. Many supervisors and evaluators believe that a sample lesson must be perfect to be of benefit to the observers. Since no lesson can be perfect, supervisors who believe they can be are reluctant to do sample lessons. A sample lesson need not be perfect or even excellent to be valuable. It should demonstrate your best teaching, given the unusual circumstances such as the limited amount of teaching you do and your lack of familiarity with the content, physical location and students, especially as compared to that of the regular teacher. Mistakes will occur during the lesson and can be as valuable supervision tools as your successes.

2. As stated above, you are teaching to create a context for discussion about teaching and learning, not to demonstrate a model of perfection. Be clear about this with the teacher when you agree/volunteer to model a lesson.

3. Save time! Invite several teachers for whom you think modeling would be valuable to observe the same lesson. You don't need to model a separate lesson for each teacher to gain most of the value derived from a model lesson. There is significant value in having several teachers give their views of the lesson in a group post-conference.

4. You are presenting a model for openness to hearing corrective feedback. In the pre-observation conference, be sure the teacher(s) knows he/she must give you specific feedback about areas for improvement. Require that the recommendations for improvement be based on the district's performance standards. By doing so you will force the teacher(s) to more thoroughly internalize the performance standards. Again, reinforce with the teacher(s) that you will do your best to make it a very good lesson. There will be areas for improvement, however, and the teachers should focus on those areas and their impact as well as on the moves that work. Hearing this feedback will be difficult the first time. However, it will get easier each time you do this. Modeling lessons may eventually be a lot of fun for you and the teachers!

5. Teachers may not say it to you, but most will respect and admire your "guts" in your willingness to walk in their shoes. They will respect your willingness to teach with an audience of adults and to accept feedback from them on areas for improvement. Your model lessons will increase the teachers' comfort level with being observed by supervisors and peers and increase their openness to hearing feedback about areas for improvement.

6. Ask a high-performing teacher to give you feedback on your plan before teaching. It will be helpful to you, and that teacher will feel his/her excellence is recognized and appreciated by you.

7. Keep the lesson brief. You need only teach long enough for the lesson to have a beginning, middle and end. Fifteen minute lessons take less planning and preparation and can have as much value to the observer(s) as forty-five minute lessons. There will be much to see and discuss in a fifteen minute lesson.

8. The post-conference is key to maximizing teachers' learning from the model lesson. Here are some tips.

    a. The observing teachers will be reluctant to criticize you. If the post-conference starts off as a pep rally for your teaching, thank the observing teachers for their encouragement, but sensitively push the teachers for specific areas of weakness and suggestions for improvement.

    b. Teachers tend to give the feedback in general terms without specific evidence, because they have never received training in the effective analysis of teaching. Push them to remember specific behaviors you used that were less effective than alternative behaviors.

    c. Get the teachers to focus on the impact of these behaviors on student performance.

    d. When they do compliment you, push the teachers to explain how the behavior they described positively changed the performance of the students in the lesson and how it will be a benefit to students in the future.

9. Be realistic about how often you can do sample lessons. Start with just a few lessons and add more gradually. If you don't presently do any, commit to teaching two lessons in the upcoming year. Try to work yourself up to at least three or four per year. You will find that the more model lessons you do, the less time each one will take to plan. You will be better able to maximize the benefit for the teachers you observe.

COMMON LANGUAGE AND STANDARDS

A district's supervision and evaluation is improved when the district has a common language teachers and administrators use to describe effective teaching in terms of the district's standards. Earlier in this chapter we looked at samples of evaluation write-ups that use and/or refer to a district's common language and standards for curriculum and instruction. Chapter 7 includes the performance standards used in two districts as a common language all administrators and teachers use to describe teaching in those districts. A number of districts in Massachusetts, Vermont, New Jersey, New Hampshire, Maryland, Virginia, Maine and other states have further defined the language of their teaching performance standards by training their administrators to use the language described in books such as *The Skillful Teacher* by Jonathon Saphier and Robert Gower (1997), *Instruction for all Students* by Paula Rutherford (1998), and *Understanding by Design* by Jay McTighe and Grant Wiggins (1999). Chapter 7 contains a district's document developed along with one of the authors of *The Skillful Teacher*, Jonathon Saphier, to help administrators use language from that book to expand their repertoire of terms for describing teaching. The document was later expanded by the district to include connections to *Understanding by Design*.

You will note in the document under discussion that the first performance standard, *Principle of Effective Teaching I*, refers to the learning expectations, which are the district's curriculum standards. The last performance standard, *Principle of Effective Teaching VII*, refers to the responsibilities of teachers that reach beyond the realm of classroom teaching. This standard is helpful for generating a discussion with teachers about their role in public relations. Both standards reflect the value that a good teacher is someone who does more than teach effectively in the classroom.

The document is designed to provide teachers and evaluators with three levels of specificity related to the language of teaching. Moving from left to right through the columns, the teachers and evaluators are given more specific examples of the standard indicated in the left-most column.

Expanding the language base used to describe performance and curriculum standards has been particularly useful to administrators who are working with under-performing teachers. (Chapter 5 covers more about working with under-performing teachers.) In one district, in addition to their staff development in the curriculum standards and the performance standards, a teacher in need of additional coaching attends a six day course that provides in-depth instruction in effective instructional strategies. The instructors of this course use the same textbook used in the course that teaches classroom observation and analysis skills to administrators. The result is that the teacher and evaluator have a significant body of common practice information, standards and language with which to analyze and discuss the teacher's performance as measured against the performance and curriculum standards.[3] This common basis allows more effective formative and summative evaluation relationships between the evaluators and the teachers.

Most supervision and evaluation training programs have a textbook that clearly describes behaviors leading to effective instructional performance. It is important that those districts who use an outside (as opposed to a program developed in the district) program for training administrators in clinical supervision and evaluation develop documents and/or training that connects the district's own curriculum and performance standards to the language used in the training. Larger districts who develop their own clinical training programs should make sure that there is a seamless connection in that training between curriculum standards, performance standards and the language that administrators and teachers use to describe those standards.

One district I work with is presently struggling with the issue of supervisors and evaluators using *three sets of terms* to describe some of the same teaching practices. One set of terms is written on their contracted evaluation forms that have existed for many years. The second set of terms was developed several years ago in response to the state Department of Education's issuing regulations that require districts to develop new performance standards meeting a minimum specified level. The standards in the evaluation documents did not meet this level, so new standards were developed without changing the evaluation forms. The third set of terms is language given to teachers and administrators in a program teaching instructional practices and promoting standards-based education. All three of these documents/programs are excellent in isolation. However, one can easily see the potential for confusion as the district works to increase inter-rater reliability between and among over sixty evaluators without a structure for connecting the three sets of language in use.

---

[3] The courses used by this district are the teacher course, Understanding Teaching, and the administrator course, Observing and Analyzing Teaching. Both courses are taught by trainers from Research for Better Teaching in Acton, MA.

WHERE DO I FIND THE TIME FOR ALL THESE WRITE-UPS?

Try These Tips!

Administrators with large evaluation loads often feel frustrated by the time it takes to provide a quality evaluation for every member of their staffs. It is important that every teacher receive evaluations that incorporate the principles from Characteristics of Excellent Evaluators, discussed earlier in this chapter. However, if the structure of an administrator's department or building leaves the administrator with a large number of evaluations, there are time-saving strategies that have a minimal negative impact or no impact on the supervision and evaluation of the staff.

Administrators also vary greatly in the time it takes them to complete the various tasks related to supervision and evaluation. Administrators are always aware that it takes a great deal of time to supervise and evaluate well, however, they are often not sure which activities take up most of that time. The amount of time spent on each activity can vary by administrator. It can be helpful to have administrators complete the survey on the next page prior to teaching them time-saving techniques. This preparation enables each administrator to choose those techniques that will lead to the greatest benefit. It is important to remember that the techniques below are a menu, not a recipe. Administrators must pick and choose those that will save time without undermining the quality of their work. It is also important to note that the assumption is made that the evaluators have had sufficient training in the skills needed to capture, analyze and communicate orally and in writing about the complex interactions involved in teaching prior to implementing these timesaving techniques.

1. **"Imitation is the highest form of flattery,"** even if you're imitating yourself. Don't be afraid to repeat a good sentence or paragraph on several evaluations. If more than one of your teachers is experiencing success or needing a recommendation in a particular area, it is fine to use the same acknowledgment or recommendation for two or more people, as long as it fits their situations. The purpose of your evaluations is to reinforce excellent practices and cause positive changes in ineffective performances. They are not exercises in original prose.

2. The strategy above also applies to using effective text from evaluations by other evaluators. Borrowing phrases from others can be particularly helpful with areas for improvement, which are the most difficult and time-consuming to write. I have seen this work particularly well when small groups of evaluators meet and exchange evaluations (with the names

concealed) of low-performing teachers. The evaluators then borrow clear, concise but sensitive recommendations for use in their evaluations. Regarding recommendations for improvement, evaluators often spend more time deciding how to phrase them than deciding what needs to be said.

TIME STUDY SURVEY

Evaluator's name: _____

Evaluator's position: _____

Date: _____

Number of evaluations you must do this year:

Tenure _____ Non-Tenure _____ Total _____

1.   How much time in the course of the year (in hours and minutes) does it take you to schedule all of your observations and pre-/post-conferences? Below, briefly describe how you do this scheduling.

_____

_____

_____

_____

_____

Tenure high	Tenure average	Tenure low	Non-tenure		
____	____	____	____	2.	In what percentage of the observations do you pre-conference? *100%*
____	____	____	____	3.	How many minutes does it take you to prepare for one pre-observation conference? *15*
____	____	____	____	4.	How many minutes does it take you to complete one pre-observation conference? *30* *45*
____	____	____	____	5.	How many minutes does it take you to prepare for one observation? *5* *50*
____	____	____	____	6.	How many minutes does it take you to complete one observation? *75* *125*
____	____	____	____	7.	How many minutes does it take you to prepare for one post-observation conference? *5* *130*
____	____	____	____	8.	How many minutes does it take you to complete one post-observation conference? *45* *175*

Tenure high	Tenure average	Tenure low	Non-tenure	
___	___	___	___	9. How many minutes does it take you to complete one observation write-up report?
___	___	___	___	10. How many minutes does it take you to write one summative evaluation document?
___	___	___	___	11. How many minutes does it take you to prepare for a meeting with one teacher about the summative evaluation document?
___	___	___	___	12. How many minutes does it take you to meet with one teacher about the summative evaluation document?

(handwritten notes: 180, 225 =, C5 hrs)

List the other activities related to evaluation that you must undertake in the course of the year and how many minutes each activity takes to complete.

Other (please describe)

_____

_____

_____

Other (please describe)

_____

_____

_____

3. In final year-end evaluation documents, don't try to write again from scratch what you observed and wrote about during the year. Cut and paste claims/judgments or evidence from your observation reports. It also saves time to refer to the report with citations such as, "In one class I observed (see observation report 3/2/97) Ed's tone was sharp and curt in reaction to the students' behavior and lack of cooperation . . . "

You can then attach the observation report or cut and paste from the report, rather than rewriting all the information related to this incident. On page 62, I included a sample final evaluation report that uses both cut and paste and citing of the observation report as ways to save time.

4. A dictaphone can save time once you get used to using it. Using a dictaphone is a skill that needs to be learned both by the administrator and the secretary typing the dictation. Begin by practicing with short pieces of one or two paragraphs. This strategy will also enable your secretary to practice on small pieces. Once you have mastered the dictaphone, an observation write-up can be dictated in fifteen minutes and then revised after it is typed in draft form.

5. Laptop computers are another time-saving device that takes practice. The evaluator should only try using one if he/she is a fair-to-good typist. It is also important for an evaluator using this technique for the first time to let the teacher know ahead of time. It has been disconcerting to some teachers when the administrator who has formerly arrived in his/her room with only a pad and pen shows up with an unexpected laptop computer. However, it very soon becomes the norm with the computer causing no more anxiety than a pad and pen.

6. **"Give a person a fish, and he/she eats for a day. Teach a person to fish, and he/she eats for a lifetime."** This proverb applies to evaluators as well. Principals, superintendents and assistant superintendents who evaluate teacher evaluators often hesitate to delegate a sufficient number of evaluations to others. There are good reasons for this in districts where there is insufficient training and coaching of all evaluators. A poorly done evaluation can be more work for the administrator supervising the evaluator than doing the evaluation himself/herself. However, in the long run a principal, superintendent or assistant superintendent would be better off spending a year carefully coaching and closely overseeing the subordinate evaluator as he/she does the evaluations. Evaluators, like teachers, can really surprise you when they have had sufficient training, coaching, assessment and reteaching. Teach your evaluators to "fish" and it will save you time in the long run.

    WARNING! I wish to include a clear disclaimer about the next two suggestions. I feel they should be employed only with the approval of the superintendent or assistant superintendent responsible for overseeing evaluation in the district. He/she needs to be the person who determines which evaluators' loads, in which years, warrant implementing the following time-saving techniques.

7. Your most extensive reports (particularly in regard to the writing of evidence) need to be those for teachers who are not performing well. These are the reports most likely to be contested by teachers and even litigated and, therefore, need to be the most thoroughly and carefully written. This is not to say that excellent teachers don't need and deserve affirmation and recommendations. However, the amount of evidence you include in the reports of high-performing teachers can be much more limited because you don't need to legally prove your claim/judgment. In all my years evaluating teachers I have never been asked by a teacher or a teacher's union representative to provide sufficient evidence to justify a compliment! There are also many ways to acknowledge and celebrate your highest-performing teachers. Some ideas for commending their performances can be found in the sections of this book on sample lessons and peer coaching. Other ideas include sending brief handwritten notes or emails acknowledging high performance or assigning high performers to mentor new teachers.

> The amount of evidence you include in the reports of high-performing teachers can be much more limited because you don't need to legally prove your claim/judgment. In all my years evaluating teachers I have never been asked by a teacher or a teacher's union representative to provide sufficient evidence to justify a compliment!

The following two activities are designed to help the evaluator prioritize his/her time based on a general assessment of all staff members scheduled to be evaluated. The first activity should be done just prior to the start of the school year and should include all teachers scheduled to be evaluated in that year. The second activity should be done in March or April and include all the teachers scheduled for summative evaluation in the following year. Since these designations are an estimate and not fully supported by evidence, the evaluator should keep these exercises confidential. Their purpose is only to help the evaluator prioritize his/her supervision and evaluation time. The suggested exercises make use of an overly simplified way of thinking about teaching. However, they are essential activities if you want to budget your time in a way that creates the greatest impact for students.

DIVIDING INTO THIRDS

List the *tenured* teachers (*professional teacher status* in some states) by the three categories below, based on where you think they rank in your department or school. *Be certain to have an equal number of teachers in each category.*

- Circle the name of the teacher who is your lowest performer.
- On the back, list the ways you can recognize your top third teachers other than with lengthy evaluation write-ups.
- On the back, list the performance issues, by performance standard, of the teacher circled.

Highest-performing third:

_____

_____

_____

Middle-performing third:

_____

_____

_____

Lowest-performing third:

_____

_____

_____

Ways I can facilitate the growth of my top third teachers and acknowledge their successes, other than by lengthy observation write-ups and final evaluation documents:

_____

_____

_____

_____

The issues related to my lowest-performing tenured (professional teacher status) teacher, connected to the appropriate performance standard, and including a list of the supports I need to effectively work with this teacher:

_____

_____

_____

_____

DIVIDING INTO THIRDS, . . . PREPARING FOR NEXT YEAR

This activity is designed to help evaluators prioritize their time by determining which of the teachers in their evaluation load in the *upcoming* year will need a disproportionate amount of time and other resources. *This information is confidential and should only be used by the evaluator.*

1. Think about the tenured (professional teacher status) teachers in your school or department whom you will evaluate next year. List them below in the appropriate category.

2. Circle the name of the teacher in the bottom list who is the lowest performer in the group.

Highest-performing third:

_____

_____

_____

Middle-performing third:

_____

_____

_____

Lowest-performing third:

_____

_____

_____

The issues related to my lowest-performing tenured (professional teacher status) teacher, connected to the appropriate performance standard, and including a list of the supports I need to effectively work with this teacher.

Issues: _____

_____

_____

Performance standard: _____

_____

_____

Supports I will need to address the issues: _____

_____

_____

Where I will go for those supports: _____

_____

_____

8. Documents such as the Brookline performance standard document in chapter 7 enable evaluators to easily reference a small group of comprehensive resources on effective teaching. You will note that the Brookline document gives specific phrases and sentences in the second column. The third column connects each performance standard to two widely used books on the subject of classroom teaching. An evaluator can effectively write seventy-five percent or more of his/her evaluations using that document and the two reference books. For most busy evaluators, it is better to have a small group of excellent references that you use consistently, than a large library of references that become frustrating when trying to find specific information.

> For most busy evaluators, it is better to have a small group of excellent references that you use consistently, than a large library of references that become frustrating when trying to find specific information.

9. I spoke earlier about the value of evaluators teaching sample lessons. Remember, a great deal of time can be saved by keeping the lesson to fifteen minutes and inviting several teachers to observe and conference

about the same lesson. See the section on sample lessons on page 77 for specifics.

Evaluators can also gain the significant value of model lessons without spending a great deal of time by running one or more staff meetings as sample lessons. A good staff meeting uses many of the teaching moves in a good classroom lesson. The meeting can be conducted using effective classroom teaching techniques, and then leaving ten to fifteen minutes at the end for teachers to give feedback on the presentation, based on the district's performance standards. In many of the districts in which I conduct training, the teachers often complain that administrators always ask them to use interesting and engaging teaching techniques, but run dull meetings themselves. A faculty meeting designed to use effective teaching techniques would be an opportunity to run an effective meeting, discuss effective teaching techniques with the entire staff and model a school culture in which the professionals are open to experimentation and feedback on areas for improvement. Below is a sample from a handout or overhead the administrator may use at the end of the meeting to achieve this goal.

a.   Read the seven teacher performance standards.

b.   In your group, evaluate my running of today's meeting over the last fifty minutes in terms of my presentation related to the performance standards.

c.   Agree on one area for improvement that falls within the standard assigned to your group.

d.   Select one person in the group to post-conference with me about the area identified for improvement.

10.   Practice may not make perfect, but it sure can make for quicker: Time yourself the next time you do a final report or an observation write-up of a teacher whose performance ranks in the top third of your school's faculty. If it takes more than ninety minutes to write these documents, try the following.

a.   Get an oven timer and set it for one hour. Write as you normally would for the hour. Use cut and paste (computer or the actual scissors and paper kind) wherever possible.

b.   When the oven timer dings, set it again for thirty minutes. Use that thirty minutes as a deadline for completing the report.

c.   When the report is "finished", if you feel compelled to proofread and revise, set the timer again for thirty minutes. Work to finish the report before the thirty minutes is up.

d.   Give it to the teacher as is. You will be very uncomfortable the first couple of times. However, after a while you will work more efficiently and learn that the world will continue to spin even if that high-performing teacher doesn't get a perfect report. There are other ways to recognize his/her hard work that are less time-consuming.

Remember: This short cut is for high-performing teachers only.

11. Peer review for your highest-performing teachers. High-performing teachers often feel (and rightfully so) that a disproportionate amount of the evaluator's time is devoted to low-performing teachers. Creating a structure that allows the evaluator to choose a pair of his/her highest-performing teachers to work together in a formal peer supervision process reduces his/her load by two evaluations for that year. It also creates a stimulating professional growth opportunity for those teachers.

Peer review/coaching should not completely replace the teacher–evaluator interaction. It is important that the evaluator complete a comprehensive summative evaluation at least every four years. Even high-performing teachers need (and most want) a comprehensive evaluation from their administrators at least every four years.[4]

In some districts, peer supervision is done formally as a contracted alternative to the administrator evaluation. In other districts where there is no formal peer supervision or coaching role within the contracted evaluation process, the evaluator prepares a "minimum contract compliance evaluation." The administrator's evaluation meets the minimal requirements of the contract or the law. The teachers involved and the evaluator are aware that the productive feedback the teachers receive for that year will come in the work they do as partners and that the evaluator will spend very little time working with them directly. (See example 1 in the following peer review section.) Below is a sample of an observation write-up in a district in which

> High-performing teachers often feel (and rightfully so) that a disproportionate amount of the evaluator's time is devoted to low-performing teachers. Creating a structure that allows the evaluator to choose a pair of his/her highest-performing teachers to work together in a formal peer supervision process reduces his/her load by two evaluations for that year. It also creates a stimulating professional growth opportunity for those teachers.

---

[4] In a district in which I consult, the administration requires as few as one comprehensive evaluation every five years for a teacher with ten years of successful experience in the system. However, the district requires intensive peer coaching and supervision in at least two of the intervening years. The district procedures also permit the evaluator to comprehensively evaluate any teacher in any year if the evaluator wishes to do so.

the evaluators had high evaluation loads. In this district, the evaluators completed the Dividing Into Thirds activity above and used minimum contract compliance evaluations with their highest-performing teachers. Teachers in the top third of the faculty received observation write-ups and final evaluations similar to the following. They were then provided with peer coaching opportunities through the staff development program as noted in the preceding discussion.

SAMPLE MINIMUM CONTRACT COMPLIANCE OBSERVATION WRITE-UP FOR A HIGH-PERFORMING TEACHER BY A PRINCIPAL WITH A LARGE EVALUATION LOAD

Wednesday, September 26, 2001   Sample School
Observer: Mr. Principal
Mr. Hamilton's Fifth Grade   9:00 to 9:35

Mr. Hamilton's review lesson on factors of whole numbers was fast-paced and clear. Mr. Hamilton checked for understanding with a series of probing questions that forced his students to use advanced thinking skills: "What is a factor?", 3 x 2 "What would be the first factor of 100?", etc. A forest of hands greeted each question, indicating that students felt familiar with the material and comfortable with sharing their thinking: "Are there others?", "What's 5's partner?" . . . As he asked questions, Mr. Hamilton used the white board to record answers, in the form of a "rainbow model." This graphic organizer/metaphor was intended to help students see the range of factors. The combination of his steady stream of questions and effective use of the board kept students focused.

He rarely used an attention move, other than one pause to wait for everyone to focus, and to remind a student to wait before sharpening his pencil: "Ben, I'm going to ask you to wait; you don't even know what we're doing yet." The management of the class seemed "invisible." You couldn't see the strings, but it was evident that in just two weeks, Mr. Hamilton had established an expectation of attention and a pattern of routines which kept students involved.

Mr. Hamilton kept momentum of the lesson going through a variety of moves. Just before he gave new instructions, he asked students to put their hands on their heads, so they would stop working, writing, etc., and pay attention to the next set of instructions. Then he continued, "I want you to work with the people at your table; I'm going to set the timer for 5 minutes." Again as he was moving toward passing out calculators, which he had on hand for each group, he anticipated that there might be some confusion with their use. "What don't I want?" Stella replied, "No fractions." "Right, whole numbers, not decimals." Mr. Hamilton gently shaped Stella's answer to remind students that while calculators will provide answers in decimals, he was looking for factors that were whole numbers. This anticipated possible confusion and kept the class on task.

The review lesson quickly moved into a practice and application session. Mr. Hamilton moved the students into groups of three, which he had drawn up ahead of time. He set them to work on a series of factoring problems to apply what they had done in their review of factors of 100. By inference, one could tell that his objective, aside from learning the concept of factoring, was for students to be able to broaden their range by working on other numbers. His lesson showed evidence of careful planning and the classroom was provisioned to keep the smooth flow going. As a result, students were able to review and practice the factoring of multiples of 100 in a focused twenty-five minute session. Engagement was near 100% and Mr. Hamilton circulated throughout the practice time, checking in at each table to ascertain if the students had questions or were stuck. Mr. Hamilton had a lesson in which the tasks and objective were clear.

Signature of teacher	date

Signature of observer	date

Signature signifies receipt of, not concurrence with, this evaluation. Teachers are encouraged to submit comments.

The next section of this chapter talks about peer review and its various forms. The evaluation of high-performing teachers, described above, is just one of many effective educational purposes for which peer review is effective.

12. **Effective mentoring and induction programs for teachers new to the district.** In the last five years there has been a significant increase in the hiring of teachers. In some states, districts are reporting a 100% or even 200% increase in the number of teachers hired each year compared with hiring patterns from just five years ago. As a result, evaluators are starting the year with significantly more new teachers, some of whom are less experienced than was the case five years ago. They are spending more time evaluating teachers, since many states require that teachers new to the district receive a comprehensive evaluation every year rather than every second, third or fourth year as required for tenured teachers. This is requiring an inordinate amount of the evaluators' time in working with new teachers, time which was previously available for the supervision of veteran teachers. Much of this time is spent on basic orientation, induction and, in some cases, in developing fundamental planning and

classroom management skills. Providing each new teacher with an experienced and well-trained mentor, coupled with new teacher induction seminars, enables the evaluators to focus their time on the summative assessment of new teachers. This takes far less of the evaluators' time than training each new teacher to the district in Our District 101, Classroom Management 101 and Classroom Planning 101. As much as evaluators may hate to admit it, mentor teachers usually do a much better job!!

PEER REVIEW/EVALUATION/SUPERVISION/COACHING (ALL OF THE ABOVE)?

Much has been written lately about peer involvement in the supervision and evaluation process. When people hear the terms "peer review," "peer coaching" or "assistance" they apply many meanings to the them. They often use these terms interchangeably and/or make incorrect assumptions about their definitions. Districts talking about the role of peers in changing teachers' performance need to be clear in their own minds whether they are interested in peers taking on formative or summative roles. Districts should be clear about whether they are interested in the peer interaction as a professional development function or an evaluative function.

Most districts do not yet have a formal peer program. However, those programs that do exist take forms as varied as the meanings that come to people's minds. The American Federation of Teachers and the National Education Association in their guide, *Peer Assistance & Peer Review: An AFT/NEA Handbook* (1998), defines peer review and peer assistance as very different systems.

> **Peer assistance** aims to help new and veteran teachers improve their knowledge and skills. Such a program links new teachers or struggling teachers with consulting teachers who provide ongoing support through observing, modeling, sharing ideas and skills and recommending materials for further study.

> **Peer review** adds one significant element to peer assistance—consulting teachers conduct formal evaluations and make recommendations regarding the continued employment of participating teachers.

An entire book can be written about the range of options for peer involvement in the process of supervision and evaluation and or that of staff development. Recent research supports the contention that peer interaction is an effective means for building teacher competency. The 1999 Milken Family Foundation Report, *A Matter of Quality*, quotes the work of The National Center for Education Information, *Profiles of Teachers in the U.S. Survey* (1996), in which educators identified the four most valuable factors in developing competency to teach as follows:

- Own teaching experience   92%
- *Other teachers*   *72%*
- Studying on one's own   43%
- Education methods courses   37%

The concepts of peer coaching, peer assistance and/or peer review is one school boards, administrators, teachers and teachers' associations/unions support. However, the specific way such a program will operate is a question that can raise significant labor relations (*legal*) differences between school boards and teachers' associations/unions. Districts considering a peer component in their supervision and evaluation programs, therefore, must clearly define the role of the peer and the objective of the peer program.

The programs presently in use range along a continuum from peer formative assistance and feedback to peer review for the purpose of making employment decisions. In some programs, peer involvement is optional and completely formative and is identified by the district as staff development rather than as a part of the supervision and evaluation program. Example 1 below is a sample of this type of program from one of the communities in which I have worked. In this community, everyone agreed that teachers play an important role in helping other teachers improve and grow. However, the state teachers' association was adamantly opposed to teachers' involvement in the summative review of their colleagues. The state association disagreed with the national union's position paper mentioned in the preceding paragraph. The school board and teachers' association could not agree on a program within the evaluation process that would meet the objectives of both groups, therefore, we developed the program below within the professional development program as a compromise that met most of the needs of both groups. The program met the objectives of the school committee, teachers' association and many of the district's teachers to empower a group of teachers each year with the opportunity to learn and grow from one another rather than participate in a comprehensive evaluation with an administrator.

The program met the following school board objectives to

- provide an effective staff development option for high-performing teachers
- allow the evaluators to choose which teachers would participate (with final review by the superintendent), thereby recognizing the teachers' history of high performance
- reduce the administrators' evaluation time with high-performing teachers during that year to a contract minimum. This enabled administrators with large evaluation loads to focus on those teachers

who needed a higher level of the evaluator's feedback and support (see the section on time-saving techniques for evaluators to see how this was done without causing the high-performing teachers to feel neglected)

The program met the following teachers' association objectives to

- ensure that teachers played no role in making summative decisions about their colleagues
- see that the program did not require large amounts of additional time from teachers
- require that the administration did not arbitrarily choose teachers for varying forms of the contract-mandated evaluation processes

This district's program falls far to the left on the continuum shown in Figure 6.

Those activities falling to the far left of the continuum are solely formative assistance programs. The programs to the far right require summative judgments and even employment decisions by the peer evaluator.

In another district in which I am working, the state teachers' association fully embraces the concepts identified in the national union's position paper. This district has developed a program similar to the Cincinnati model in which teachers play a significant role in making summative employment decisions about their colleagues. Teachers observe low-performing teachers and write reports, presented to a panel of fifteen people, that recommend continued employment or dismissal for these teachers. The panel reviews the

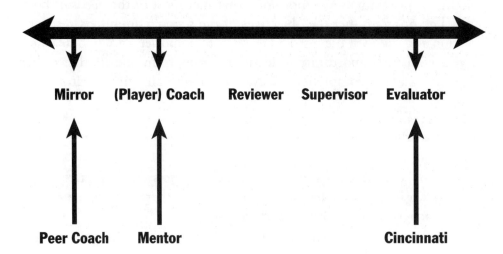

The Role of Peers in Supervision, Evaluation and Staff Development

Mirror   (Player) Coach   Reviewer   Supervisor   Evaluator

Peer Coach   Mentor   Cincinnati

Figure 6

recommendations and makes a final report to the superintendent. This district's program places it at the far right of the continuum below.

EXAMPLE 1

In this district, the peer review process is solely a supplemental process for teachers who have demonstrated high performance for a specified period of years. These teachers are given the option to forgo one year of extensive evaluation by their administrator to work intensively with a peer. The evaluating administrator's role is reduced to one that meets the absolute minimum required by the contract and state regulations. It is understood by the administrator and the teachers that the benefit the teachers derive from this experience will come from their self- and peer-assessment. The program provides three benefits: 1) High-performing teachers often grow more from peer- and self-assessment experiences then they do from traditional administrative evaluations; 2) The program also frees the supervisors and evaluators to focus their evaluation time on those teachers who would benefit the most from an administrative evaluation; 3) Teachers chosen for the program are the ones who would benefit most from a peer experience. The teachers chosen feel very good about being recognized for their status as excellent practitioners.

Sample School Peer-/Self-Feedback Plan for Excellence by Empowering Teachers

This year we seek to maximize the value of reflection on one's own practice and/or the extent to which we all are able to learn a great deal from our colleagues. Research indicates that reflecting on one's own teaching and honest feedback from peers are two of the most effective means of improving teachers' performance.

By September 30 of this school year, the teacher will have completed a self-assessment based on the district's performance standards. The teacher will have met with the peer colleague to develop a pre-test self-assessment plan and an observation/ meeting plan for the year. The plan should include a schedule of at least ninety minutes of observations.

By October 15 of this school year the teacher will attend the district-sponsored workshop on peer coaching.

By March 15 of this school year the teacher will complete a peer- and self-reflection paper or a portfolio[5] that demonstrates his/her growth during the school year, based on the district's performance standards. The teacher will have observed a colleague for a total of at least ninety minutes. The

---

5 For information on developing portfolios, see the questions found in chapter 2 and the article note in the sources on which these questions are based.

teacher will pre-conference with the colleague before each observation and post-conference after each observation.

In those classrooms without an intern, a substitute will be provided for one day of coverage, so each peer dyad can complete observation and conferencing.

By April 1 of this school year, each teacher will have produced a reflection paper or portfolio demonstrating the learning that has emerged from this year. The report or portfolio should list areas of current growth and recommendations for future growth, based on the district's performance standards. The teacher will give the principal a two-page summary of the year's activities and the growth that has resulted from the peer- and self-reflection experience.

Principal's Role: The principal will recommend to the superintendent up to 25% of the tenured teachers scheduled for summative evaluation to participate in this program during the school year

[**Note:** A typical summative evaluation load in this district is between 15 and 28 teachers for a non-teaching administrator.—William Ribas]

The teachers chosen must be deemed by the principal as excellent teachers, based on the district's performance standards.

The evaluator will complete the minimum contract requirements for an evaluation of a tenured teacher. The goals will have been set out in the plan completed by the teacher by September 30. The evaluator will complete one announced formal observation that is thirty minutes in length. The observation will be followed by a one-page progress report. In addition, the evaluator will submit the Annual Report of Teacher Effectiveness by the date indicated in the contract.

The following teachers are recommended for the program above for the 200_ School Year.

_____   _____

_____   _____

Principal's signature: _____

Date: _____

EXAMPLE 2

In another school district, teacher peer review teams have a significant role in reviewing and evaluating the professional development plans of all teachers during the years in which they are not involved in an administrative evaluation. Teachers with administrative evaluation ratings at or above the district standard work with the Peer Review Committee during the three years following their administrative evaluation years. Below is a description of the Peer Review Committee's responsibilities, as they are defined in the teacher's contract for that district. The role of teachers in this supervision and evaluation process falls to the right of example 1 above on the figure 5 continuum and to the left of the Cincinnati model.

Peer Review Committees

Peer Review Committees (PRCs) play an important role in the Evaluation and Professional Growth Cycle for teachers with tenure. Peer Review Committees are to be established in each elementary school and in each high school house. All professional status teachers are expected to serve a term on a Peer Review Committee. These committees are non-evaluative in nature and are composed of three teachers who will each serve a two-year rotating term. Members of the Peer Review Committee shall be provided reasonable release time to perform these duties.

Each Peer Review Committee reviews individual and collaborative professional growth activity plans submitted by teachers to (a) make sure the plans meet the criteria established for the particular phase of the evaluation cycle and (b) provide feedback regarding the plan should the teacher request it, or if the plan does not meet the criteria.

At the end of the school year, teachers in Phases II–IV of the evaluation cycle submit a record of their professional growth activities and a one- to two-page summary statement of what they learned from the experience to the Peer Review Committee for review. The Peer Review Committee reviews all records submitted by teachers. The Peer Review Committee will not be expected to comment to the administrator on the perceived quality of any teacher's professional growth activity, but will be expected to sign and submit the Certification Form in each phase of the evaluation.

All teachers are required to serve a term on the Peer Review Committee on a rotating basis.

EXAMPLE 3

A third type of program is one in which teachers work in pairs for a year of collaborative work. An example of this type of program (Year 2 Collaborative Year) can be found in chapter 7 of this book, in the Lexington Public Schools evaluation document. The peer work is primarily formative, but it is a requirement for all teachers in the four year supervision and evaluation cycle. In this example, the peers have an equal role to one another as is the case in example 1. However, differing from example 1, all teachers are required to participate, as they are in example 2.

EXAMPLE 4

The public schools in Cincinnati, Ohio, Montgomery County, Maryland, Minneapolis, Minnesota, New York City and a number of other school districts across the country have developed comprehensive peer *assistance* and *assessment* programs. As in examples 1, 2 and 3, these programs provide teachers with peer formative assistance to improve their performances. In addition, the programs in these districts have effectively given teachers an important part of the summative assessment component for veteran teachers who were identified by their evaluators as performing below standard and probationary teachers. To quote the Cincinnati program,

> . . . through the Intervention Component, the program seeks to assist experienced teachers who exhibit serious instructional deficiencies. When assigned, consulting teachers work with those teachers to improve their instructional skills and to bring the teachers to a satisfactory level of performance. In cases where improvement of serious instructional deficiencies does not occur, peer assistance and evaluation may result in the removal of such teachers from the classroom and/or the non-renewal/termination of teaching contracts. (American Federation of Teachers and the National Education Association, 1998)

The actual description of these programs is contained in the supervision and evaluation guides for each district. However, an excellent twenty-page explanation of the NEA and AFT's recommendations for programs of this type can be found in joint publications by the two national teachers' unions/associations. I would recommend that those who are interested in learning more about these programs begin by obtaining a copy of *Peer Assistance & Peer Review: An AFT/NEA Handbook,* (American Federation of Teachers and the National Education Association [AFT/NEA], 1998). The handbook was distributed at the AFT/NEA Conference on Teacher Quality held September 25–27, 1998, in Washington, D.C. The following explanation is based on the information in this guide and also on my experience in consulting to one of the districts implementing such a program.

In these peer assistance and assessment programs, the district selects and trains a group of teachers known as consulting teachers. Consulting teachers work with all probationary teachers new to the district and those probationary teachers whose contracts were renewed for a second year and are deemed by their evaluators as needing additional assistance and review. Consulting teachers are assigned to tenured teachers who are evaluated by their administrators as below standard. (AFT/NEA, 1998)

The handbook lists the following qualifications for consulting teachers:
- have taught successfully for a specified number of years
- be recognized as outstanding classroom teachers
- demonstrate deep knowledge of the disciplines they teach
- possess a repertoire of effective classroom management strategies and instructional techniques
- have strong verbal skills, both orally and in writing
- have the ability to work cooperatively and effectively with others

(AFT/NEA, 1998)

The consulting teachers are typically selected by the joint governance committee known in some districts as the Peer Assessment and Review (PAR) Panel. Consulting teachers make recommendations to the PAR panel about the teachers with whom they work. For probationary teachers, these recommendations lead the PAR panel to tenure the teacher, renew the teacher's contract without tenure or to deny renewal of the teacher's contract. For tenured teachers, the PAR recommendations lead to placement back in the professional development cycle (as opposed to continued intensive support and assessment), a second year of intensive support and assessment by the consulting teacher or dismissal.

The role of the PAR governance panel is described as follows:
- select, oversee, train and evaluate consulting teachers
- determine the process for selecting participating teachers
- review the reports and recommendations for consulting teachers
- accept or reject consulting teacher recommendations
- consider and act on appeals of participating teachers regarding the consulting process
- make recommendations concerning teacher competence (and in some districts, continued employment) to the superintendent
- ensure fair treatment for all participating teachers

(AFT/NEA, 1998)

CONCLUSIONS

Nationally, the role of teachers working with their peers to enhance professional performance is on the rise. It is important, however, that districts involved in peer programs be very clear about the purpose and structure of those programs. Teachers, teachers' unions/associations, school boards and administrators must decide whether

- the program is purely a formative professional development experience for teachers
- the program is purely a summative assessment program
- or, in cases in which it is both formative and summative, the degree and limits of the peer reviewers in making summative decisions

SOURCES

American Arbitration Association. (1995). Decision regarding the Lexington, Massachusetts, Public Schools.

American Arbitration Association. (1994). Decision regarding the Little Rock, Arkansas, School District.

American Federation of Teachers and the National Education Association. (1998). *Peer assistance & peer review: an AFT/NEA handbook.* Washington, D. C.

Archer, J. (1999, May). Sanders 101. *Education Week,* 26.

Colby, S. (1999, March). Grading in a standards-based system. *Educational Leadership,* 52–55.

Curriculum frameworks. (1995). Malden, MA: Massachusetts Department of Education.

Gordon, T. (1979). *Leadership effectiveness training.* New York: Bantam Books.

Holloway, J. (2000, February). A value-added view of pupil performance. *Phi Delta Kappan,* 84–85.

Koppich, J. (2001). New York, New York. *Investing in teaching,* The National Alliance of Business, The Business Roundtable, National Association of Manufacturers and the U.S. Chamber of Commerce. p. 29

McTighe, J. & Wiggins, G. (1999). *Understanding by design.* Alexandria, VA: Association of Supervision and Curriculum Development.

Milliken Family Foundation. (1999). *A matter of quality: a strategy for assuring the high caliber of America's teachers.* Lowell Milliken.

Painter, B. (2001, February). Using teaching portfolios. *Educational Leadership.*

Principles of effective teaching. (1995). Malden, MA: Massachusetts Department of Education.

Ribas, W. (2000, April). Ascending the ELPS to excellence in your district's teacher evaluation. *Phi Delta Kappan,* 585–589.

Rutherford, P. (1998). *Instruction for all students.* Alexandria, VA: Just ASK Publications.

Saphier, J. (1993). *How to make supervision and evaluation really work.* Carlisle, MA: Research for Better Teaching.

Saphier, J. & Gower, R. (1997). *The skillful teacher.* Carlisle, MA: Research for Better Teaching.

What teachers should be able to do. (1994). Washington D.C.: National Board for Professional Teaching Standards.

Chapter 4

THE PUBLIC RELATIONS (POLITICAL) SKILLS AND KNOWLEDGE NEEDED TO BE AN EFFECTIVE SUPERVISOR AND EVALUATOR

SAVVY TEACHERS' ASSOCIATIONS/UNIONS WANT TO BE YOUR PARTNER IN ENSURING EFFECTIVE SUPERVISION AND EVALUATION

In 1982 I served as vice-president of a local NEA affiliate in New Hampshire. In that position, I chaired the contract negotiations committee and the grievance committee. Over the last two decades, I have moved from labor to management. I worked as a vice-principal, principal, director of pupil-personnel services and, for the past seven years, as an assistant superintendent for personnel. I have also been a consultant to various school districts' teachers and administrators on the topic of supervision and evaluation of teachers and peer coaching, assistance and/or review. My role changed in these years, however, I saw very few changes in the basic structure and political forces that impacted school labor–management relations between 1982 and 1995.

Since 1995 the context of school labor–management relations has been changing at an accelerating pace. Public schools have been placed in a competitive environment unparalleled in other areas of public employment. Voucher programs, for-profit schools and charter schools have provided alternative education avenues to many families for whom alternatives were previously unavailable. Unlike the students who have historically attended independent schools, students who access these alternatives often take tax money that was earmarked for the local public school district with them to their new school setting. During the 1999–2000 school year, *Education Week* (Schnailberg & Walsh, 1999) ran a series of front page articles about the growth of for-profit education and for-profit schools. Since the publication of those issues, *Education Week* has included articles on the status of voucher programs and charter schools in various states and in the courts in almost every issue.

We have also seen a shift in political support for voucher programs and other alternatives to public schools. During the 2000 presidential election the Democratic candidate for vice president came from a group of senators who had a record of favoring voucher programs! He seriously tempered that view once he was on the ticket. However, for most Americans, a Democratic candidate with this type of record would have been inconceivable just two years earlier.

A dozen for-profit companies now operate public schools. Beginning in the late 1990s, articles started to appear in the *Wall Street Journal* and *Business Week* describing the investment opportunities available in for-profit education. A front-page article written by Michael T. Moe, a research director for Merrill Lynch and Company, in the August 13, 1999 (Friday the 13th, mind you) *Wall Street Journal* gave the following analysis of the for-profit market.

> There are fewer than two dozen companies managing public schools now, and many operate only one or two schools. Education-management companies will grow over the next ten to fifteen years to account for 10% of U.S. elementary and secondary spending—about $36 billion dollars a year.

Venture capitalists and other investors continue to invest large sums of money into these education companies, despite the fact that they have yet the turn a profit. An article in *Education Week* (Walsh, 2001, p. 5) indicated that venture capitalists invested 1.942 **BILLION** dollars in education companies during the year 2000 alone. The good news about the bad news is that during first half of 2001 that amount has only (if only is the right word when you are discussing this much money) been 558 million dollars (Walsh, p. 5). Investors are predicting that the lobbying efforts they support to increase the number of voucher programs and charter schools will result in a significant increase in the shift of public education dollars toward for-profit education providers. From 1994 to 1999, the number of charter schools has soared from 100 to 1700. In 1999, then U.S. secretary of education, Richard Riley, predicted the number of charter schools will reach 3,000 by 2002 (Symonds, 2000, p. 64).

United Mind Workers, a book about public school labor–management relations has been praised by the Rochester, NY, Federation of Teachers and American Federation of Teachers' leader Adam Urbanski as making "a timely and significant contribution to the future of labor management– relations." As this book states, The assault on "tenure now forming in state capitals is partly the result of the failure of school systems to create substantive evaluation systems and the failure of unions to develop peer review or other robust professional means of ensuring quality." (Kerchner, Koppich & Weeres, 1997, review on jacket)

Many school labor leaders recognize that public school boards and teachers' associations/unions need to prove to parents, taxpayers and legislators that school boards, administrators and teachers' associations/unions are working together to ensure that every child in the public schools receives a public education that is equal or better in quality then the other alternatives that are now becoming available to parents.

As the for-profit education movement increases its lobbying efforts in Washington, D.C., and in state capitals, we see an increase in the flow of public money to public school alternatives. Savvy teachers' associations/unions, school boards and administrators see the enlightened self-interest served by developing effective systems of supervision and evaluation. They understand that an effective method of instructional quality control is one of the most powerful ways to counteract messages such as the following from a *Wall Street Journal* article:

> . . . because American public education in the 20th century has been organized much as a Soviet enterprise was . . . like one of those Soviet factories, it could just keep pumping out defective products . . . A nation made up of charter schools would entrench accountability, because every four years a district would reevaluate whether to renew the charter or hand the school to someone else . . . (*Wall Street Journal*, November 16, 1999).

The concern about voucher programs and for-profit schools has shifted the playing field for local, state and federal leaders of teachers' associations/unions. Prior to 1995, *A Nation at Risk* and other reports placed some public-relations (political) pressure on teachers' associations to look at their roles in ensuring high levels of performance. However, efforts of people such as Adam

Urbanski, the late Albert Shanker and Bob Chase to respond proactively to these pressures were often met with internal opposition from the membership. The opposition to the "New Unionism" was difficult for leaders to counteract because the threat to the traditional union bread and butter issues (wages, benefits, working conditions and job security) posed by these reports was more distant and abstract. These forces, coupled with the fear of lawsuits from members not given maximum protection (see the explanation in chapter 5 of a union's failure to meet the duty of fair representation) often forced all but the most visionary teachers' associations/union leaders to continue a course that protected low-performing teachers, even when management provided reasonable formative supports and adequate due process.

Today, the rapid growth of voucher programs and for-profit schools has made the threat to wages, benefits, working conditions and job security from loss of public funds more immediate for younger teachers. If these education alternatives capture ten percent of the students presently in public schools, as some predict could occur by 2010, there will be a significant decline in the number of public school teaching positions. This decline could lead to the layoff of younger staff. These teachers would be forced to take lower-paying jobs in charter, independent, religious and for-profit schools. A decline in public school jobs will also mean a decline in membership revenue for the teachers' associations/unions. This will decrease the financial ability of teachers' associations/unions to lobby and to maintain public information programs that promote public education. In my opinion, this is the *most difficult* time to be a teachers' association leader *in more than thirty years of teacher unionization.* The associations are squeezed between the financial and political pressures to reform and from long-time members opposed to reforms that may negatively impact their present working conditions.

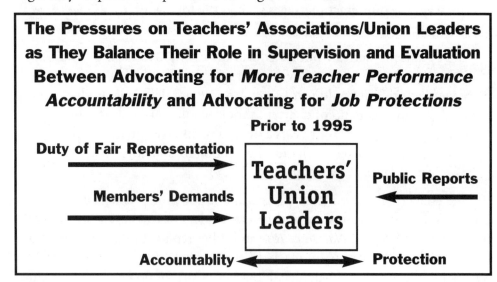

Figure 7

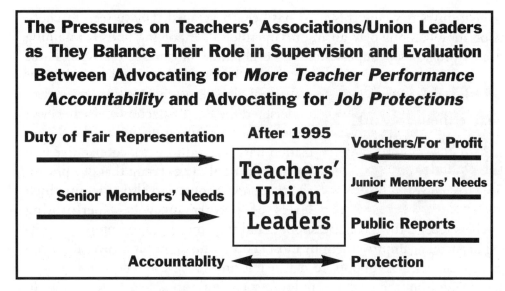

The Pressures on Teachers' Associations/Union Leaders as They Balance Their Role in Supervision and Evaluation Between Advocating for *More Teacher Performance Accountability* and Advocating for *Job Protections*

Duty of Fair Representation   After 1995   Vouchers/For Profit

Senior Members' Needs   **Teachers' Union Leaders**   Junior Members' Needs

Public Reports

Accountablity ⟷ Protection

Figure 8

It takes a skilled and visionary local president to balance these forces. All local presidents are elected by today's membership. In a time when most of the membership is within five to ten years of retirement age, it is difficult for association/union leaders to build support for programs that may increase accountability at some cost to protection. The members who will benefit from a policy geared toward maintaining the long-term viability of public education (by moving the association's support toward accountability for high performance) are likely to be in the minority of younger teachers or future teachers, whereas high-seniority teachers face the prospect of decreased protection without a quid pro quo benefit during their remaining years in the teaching work force. We should have tremendous respect for the many local presidents who maintain support for a policy that strives to achieve a balance between protecting rights and being accountable for high performance.

SUPERVISION AND EVALUATION: QUALITY CONTROL FOR PUBLIC EDUCATION

The trust needed between management and labor to enable them to work together on quality control through supervision and evaluation takes time and work to develop. Teachers' associations/unions need to see that teachers identified as performing below standard will be given reasonable supports and a reasonable time period to improve. Evaluating administrators need to see that teachers' associations/unions will ensure reasonable supports and time to improve for their members, but they will not impede administrators from requiring all teachers to maintain a level of performance that ensures public education is competitive in quality and cost with charter, independent, religious and for-profit schools.

In districts where this trust has been developed, I have seen teachers' associations/unions play an important role in supporting and maintaining quality programs of supervision and evaluation for tenured teachers. These

> The trust needed between management and labor to enable them to work together on quality control through supervision and evaluation takes time and work to develop.

are districts in which administrators and teachers' association representatives are trained to understand the E.L.P.S. factors in teacher evaluation. The administration and teachers' association have learned to work cooperatively to balance the need to be certain that due process rights are not ignored and also to require high levels of performance. Low-performing teachers receive the feedback, support and time they need to improve, resulting in adequate improvement by most. Those who do not improve, after adequate feedback and support, recognize it is time to leave and do so (often with counseling from the teachers' union/association), are asked to leave and do so or are dismissed using the appropriate legal standards for due process.

THE PUBLIC RELATIONS (POLITICAL) SOLUTION

I believe the following quote from the joint AFT/NEA manual on *Peer Assistance and Review* (1998) best sums up the public relations battle that faces teachers' associations/unions, school boards and administrators if they are to reverse the momentum in the United States toward increasing the number of voucher and charter school programs to the detriment of the public schools.

> The public, for its part, is concerned about the quality of schools and about the quality of the teachers in them. While a large majority of the public (85%) trusts teachers to make sound educational decisions (National Center for Education Information, 1996), citizens believe that a small percentage of teachers are not qualified and should not be teaching. Moreover, the public is frustrated by what it perceives as an inability to remove inadequate teachers from the classroom. The public attributes the difficulty in firing bad teachers to rules and regulations developed by teacher unions.

The 33rd Annual *Phi Delta Kappan*/Gallup Poll of the Public's Attitudes Toward the Public Schools

The following statistics from polls in 1993, 1998 and 2001, jointly sponsored by *Phi Delta Kappan* and Gallup, (Gallup & Rose, 2001) seem to indicate the slide in confidence in public pchools has begun to reverse direction. We must continue to build public confidence with demonstrated high quality supervision and evaluation.

1. Do you favor or oppose allowing students and parents to choose a private school to attend at public expense?

National Totals	2001	1998	1993
Favor	34%	44%	24%
Oppose	62	50	74
Don't know	4	6	2

2. A proposal has been made that would allow parents to send their school-age children to any public, private or church-related school they choose. For those parents choosing nonpublic schools, the government would **pay all or part of** the tuition. Would you favor or oppose this proposal in your state?

	National Totals			Public School Parents		
	2001	1998	1994	2001	1998	1994
Favor	44%	51%	45%	52%	56%	48%
Oppose	54	45	54	47	40	51
Don't know	2	4	1	1	4	1

3. (Last asked in 1998) In the voucher system, a parent is given a voucher which can be used to pay all the tuition for attendance at a private or church-related school. Parents can then choose any private school, church-related school, or public school for their child. If a parent chooses a public school, the voucher would not apply. Would you favor or oppose the adoption of the voucher system in your state?

	National Totals	Public School Parents
Favor	48%	55%
Oppose	46	42
Don't know	6	3

4. (Last asked in 1998) In the voucher system, a parent is given a voucher which can be used **to pay part of the tuition** for attendance at a private or church-related school. Parents can then choose any private school, church-related school, or public school for their child. If a parent chooses a public school, the voucher would not apply. Would you favor or oppose the adoption of the voucher system in your state?

	National Totals	Public School Parents
Favor	52%	58%
Oppose	41	37
Don't know	7	5

The issue of low-performing teachers not being required to improve or leave is a real one in many districts. However, it is not present in all districts. We must ask ourselves why it is that two districts in the same state, with the same statewide union leadership, the same labor laws and the same resources can exist side-by-side with one effectively dealing with low-performing teachers while the other district is virtually ineffective in dealing with this issue? To place the blame solely on the union in that state or district is unfair and inaccurate.

Chapter 5 examines the roadblocks that inhibit districts' ability to adequately address their low-performing teachers' performance issues. The chapter describes how some districts effectively address the issue. You will see that there is sufficient blame to go around. Yes, there are some state union uniserve workers and some local association presidents who still respond to the issue of addressing low-performing teachers as if the political dynamics were the same as they were in 1990. You will also see, however, that most districts have neither trained their evaluators adequately, nor created adequate support structures for evaluators so they can perform the difficult task of addressing unsatisfactory teaching. The result is that the number of districts and evaluators in those districts that can adequately address low-performing teaching is relatively low, regardless of the teachers' associations'/unions' influence.

The key to reversing the public relations and political disaster we create for ourselves by not adequately supervising and evaluating all teachers is for the following to take place.

1. Evaluators and school boards must stop pointing fingers at the associations/unions with accusations that they are protecting bad teachers and must accept the responsibility for effectively training and supporting evaluators so they can effectively evaluate all teachers, particularly low-performing teachers. (See chapter 1 for more information about effective training.)

2. Union leaders must teach, coach, and assess the way their state uniserve consultants, local presidents and grievance people respond to evaluators when a teacher is being intensively supervised and evaluated for low performance. These leaders must be taught the difference between actions that ensure a member's rights and those that protect bad teachers.

EACH PARTY MUST OWN ITS PART OF THE PROBLEM! A CASE OF INSTITUTIONAL FINGER POINTING

The first time I worked with a district to improve system-wide supervision and evaluation, I met with various groups in the district to ask why supervision and evaluation didn't work in that district. The first group I spoke with was the principals. The perspective from principals was that the "union's grievance philosophy is to protect the worst-performing teachers to the fullest, regardless of how well the evaluation is completed." A number of the principals related stories ranging from one about the state uniserve person yelling at them in final evaluation meetings to another in which the uniserve representative threatened the principal physically. A high school department head, whose administrators' union was represented by the same local as the teachers' union, told of his attempt to evaluate a low-performing teacher. A local teachers' union grievance person walked into his office, closed the door and said, "We're all in this together. It's us (unionized employees) against them (the senior administration and school committee). Why are you taking their side against one of your own?"

In a subsequent conversation with the superintendent, he confirmed that the incidents related in these stories had indeed taken place. After the physical threat, the superintendent called the local president to ask his assistance in moderating the actions of the uniserve representative. The president responded that he fully supported the uniserve person's behavior. The superintendent sent a letter to the uniserve person expressing his dismay, but felt powerless to do more. The principals felt besieged and threatened by the union and powerless to appropriately evaluate low-performing tenured teachers. Their response to parents' complaints about these tenured low performers was to tell parents that they could do very little because of the union's aggressive protection of bad teachers. This caused the concerned parents to voice their concerns to the superintendent and school committee. The superintendent, being new to the district and powerless to deal with tenured low-performing teachers because of an ineffective evaluation process, was forced to transfer low performers to other schools and/or reassign them to lower-level jobs at their teacher's salary.

When I began my work with this district, I had just finished seven years as a principal in another district. My experience had been with a local president and vice president who required any principal evaluating a low-performing teacher to be clear about expectations and provide adequate supports, frequent feedback and time to improve. If the evaluator took these steps however, the association/union ensured the teachers' rights were not violated, but also participated as a positive force for improvement in all meetings related to the evaluation. The district provided its administrators with constant training in topics such as difficult conferences and observing and documenting teachers' performance. The district also provided evaluators of low-performing teachers with legal coaching by a labor attorney well versed in teacher evaluations. Four times in those seven years I had undertaken the supervision and evaluation of teachers performing below standard. In two cases the teachers improved their performance and continued to teach for many years thereafter. In two other instances I had to find the teachers unsatisfactory and move toward further action. In the first of these two, I informed the teacher that she needed to improve in a fixed period of time or she would be dismissed. She was eventually dismissed. In the second, the teacher was started on a year-long improvement plan with intensive support and summative evaluation when I left the district. At no time did I ever feel the teachers' association/ union was threatening or in any way unreasonable in their requests.

The next group I spoke with about the district's performance on evaluation was the local president and the chairs of the grievance committee. I asked why they thought low-performing tenured teachers were not required to improve or leave. The group's response was that the evaluators weren't doing their jobs. They reported that the evaluators were not following the contracted process, nor were they meeting the due process standard and, in many cases, they were not even doing their evaluations. They further reported that there were no consistent standards among the evaluators (no inter-rater reliability). Some evaluators gave everyone glowing evaluations. Others evaluated the same performance in a very different way. After the meeting, I spent a considerable amount of time reading the evaluations that had been completed during the previous year. I found that all the claims of the association/union members were correct. Only 30% of the required evaluations had been completed in the previous year. Of those 30%, only a third had used the correct forms and procedures. Evaluators had not had any district-sponsored training in supervision and evaluation for over five years. After reading a number of evaluations, I called one principal who had been doing a good job to compliment her on her work. She stopped me midway through a sentence, saying, "I can't believe you read my evaluations! I've been a principal here for fifteen years and I don't think anyone ever read any of the evaluations before. This is wonderful."

Five years later, this district has gone from having one of the most dysfunctional supervision and evaluation systems I've worked with to having one of the most effective supervision and evaluation programs in the state. The district has gone from effectively addressing none of its low-performing tenured teachers to addressing all of its low-performing tenured teachers (2% to 3% of the teaching staff as is indicated in the literature) using the program outlined in the next chapter. Comprehensive training, coaching and assessment is provided for all evaluators. The teachers' association/union grievance people meet to discuss cases and most have responded in a far less aggressive manner as the evaluators have improved their inter-rater reliability and overall performance. It is still my hope that the quality of training for evaluators will increase and that those grievance people who are most effective in this area will train and further influence their colleagues.

> Without a commitment from superintendents and school boards to train and support evaluators so they can effectively evaluate all teachers, a district cannot have a successful system of supervision and evaluation. Without a commitment from state and local teachers' associations/unions to train uniserve people, local presidents and grievance people to ensure rights without protecting bad teachers and to avoid intimidation tactics, teachers' associations/unions are doomed to be targeted by the public as roadblocks to effective public education.

The crucial factor in the example above from a public relations (political) point of view, is that the district's evaluators and parents no longer have reason to say that supervision and evaluation of low-performing tenured teachers is impossible within the present set of state laws. Without a commitment from superintendents and school boards to train and support evaluators so they can effectively evaluate all teachers, a district cannot have a successful system of supervision and evaluation. Without a commitment from state and local teachers' associations/unions to train uniserve people, local presidents and grievance people to ensure rights without protecting bad teachers and to avoid intimidation tactics, teachers' associations/unions are doomed to be targeted by the public as roadblocks to effective public education. Unless management and labor each do their part in providing adequate training and support, public schools are destined for extinction or to be solely for those children in our society whose parents lack the knowledge, assertiveness and/or skill to access the so-called "better options" for their children.

SOURCES

American Federation of Teachers and the National Education Association. (1998). *Peer assistance & peer review: an AFT/NEA handbook.* Washington, D. C.

Curriculum frameworks. (1995). Malden, MA: Massachusetts Department of Education.

Gallup, A. & Rose, L. (2001, September). The 33rd annual *Phi Delta Kappan*/Gallup Poll of the public's attitudes toward the public schools. *Phi Delta Kappan,* 41–58.

Johnson, J. & Immerwahrl, J. (1994). *First things first: what Americans expect from public schools.* New York: The Public Agenda Foundation.

Kerchner, Koppich & Weeres. (1997). *United mind workers.* San Francisco: Jossey & Bass.

McTighe, J. & Wiggins, G. (1999). *Understanding by design.* Alexandria, VA: Association of Supervision and Curriculum Development.

Moe, M. T. (1999, August 13). Tesseract and others march briskly ahead in school privatization. *Wall Street Journal.*

Profiles of teachers in the U.S. survey. (1996). Washington, D.C.: National Center for Education Information.

Ribas, W. (2000, April). Ascending the ELPS to excellence in your district's teacher evaluation. *Phi Delta Kappan,* 585–589.

Schnailberg, L. & Walsh, M. (1999, November/December). The new business of schooling. *Education Week,* Volume XIX, Nos. 13, 14, 15, and 16.

Symonds, W. (2000, February). For-profit schools. *Business Week,* 64.

Turning schools right side up. (1999, November 16). *Wall Street Journal* [Editorial].

Walsh, M. (2001, August 8) Seed money drying up for education-related businesses, *Education Week,* 5.

What teachers should be able to do. (1994). Washington D.C.: National Board for Professional Teaching Standards.

Chapter 5

THE LEGAL PROCESSES AND STANDARDS AS THEY RELATE TO SUPERVISING AND EVALUATING LOW-PERFORMING TEACHERS

Successfully supervising and evaluating a low-performing teacher[1] is one of the most difficult, time-consuming, emotionally charged and important tasks that administrators undertake. The difficulty of the task is due in part to the natural conflict that occurs between the techniques the evaluator must employ to meet the legal requirements while balancing the social–emotional impact of the evaluation on the teacher and the department/school as a whole. The legal procedures require sensitive yet clear and frank discussion about inadequate performance and a significant amount of written documentation. These requirements in turn raise the teacher's anxiety level and, at times, that

---

[1] The formative suggestions in this chapter have application to provisional teachers as well as to teachers with tenure. However, the summative standards related to the law concerning dismissal are typically only applicable to tenured teachers. In most states, provisional teachers who have not achieved tenure do not have due process protections unless they are dismissed in the middle of the year. Typically, the contract of a low-performing teacher without tenure is just not renewed for the subsequent year. Due process in these situations only becomes an issue if there is the possibility of a discrimination claim based on race, religion, age, sex or handicap.

of his/her colleagues. The meetings, observations and written documents these evaluations require may make a single difficult evaluation as time-consuming as five to ten of the administrator's other evaluations.

It is important for evaluators to understand the legal basis for the evaluation procedures used by their districts. In most districts, evaluators typically become aware of the "L" in the E.L.P.S. only when one of their evaluations of a low-performing teacher is challenged. At that point it is usually too late to effectively use the legal information. An example is that of an administrator who worked collaboratively with a representative of the teachers' association on a low-performing teacher's evaluation. The administrator wrote an improvement plan and reviewed the district's performance standards with the teacher at the start of each of two years. She observed the teacher's classes frequently, providing the teacher with clear written and oral feedback, several staff development opportunities and a colleague mentor. (See the seven tests for just cause, on pages 121–122.)

> Successfully supervising and evaluating a low-performing teacher is one of the most difficult, time-consuming, emotionally charged and important tasks that administrators undertake.

As is important, *the evaluator maintained the hope and belief that the teacher could improve* and complete her career satisfactorily.[2] Unfortunately, even with this support, the teacher still could not be successful. The administrator decided that she needed to find the teacher to be unsatisfactory and recommend dismissal. The school district's labor attorney reviewed the documents from the administrator's two years of work with this teacher and determined that the case would likely be upheld in arbitration. The assistant superintendent, who had monitored the evaluation throughout the two years, knew how much time the evaluator had devoted to the evaluation and asked the administrator how her other evaluations were progressing. The administrator became quiet and reported that since she had been so busy with this evaluation she did not think she would be able to complete the other evaluations on time. The evaluator thought this wouldn't be a problem, since the other teachers were performing well. Fortunately, it was early enough in the school year to correct the error and have the administrator complete the other evaluations on time. Had she not done so, the administrator's evaluation of the low-performing teacher might have been open to claims that she had not applied the system's standards evenhandedly. (See the seven tests of just cause,

---

2 I call this the Pollyanna Principle. At the outset of an intensive evaluation, the administrator must force him/herself to believe the teacher can improve to a satisfactory level. This is often one of the most difficult ideas to teach to an administrator. Some teachers will disappoint you and eventually need to leave the profession, however, most will surprise you by the progress they make when you have followed the procedures in this chapter.

on pages 121–122.) The administrator may have jeopardized the comprehensive evaluation she had prepared for the low-performing teacher.

Teachers' associations are legally bound to provide a *reasonable level* of representation to their members. An association that does not provide this level of representation leaves itself open to being sued by teachers for failure to meet its duty of fair representation. (See the explanation of the duty of fair representation legal standard, on pages 122–124.) In the example above, the teachers' association representative had been involved as an observer and appropriate advocate and support resource for the teacher throughout the two years of the formal supervision and evaluation process. The representative knew that the administrator and the district made genuine efforts to provide support and an opportunity for the teacher to succeed and that the teacher had not sufficiently improved. Had the procedural problem mentioned above not been caught in time, however, the teachers' association may have found itself in a situation where it believed it needed to represent the teacher through arbitration in order to avoid being charged with failure to meet its duty of fair representation.

> Accepting the need to change *is one of the most significant differences* between teachers who do improve and continue in the profession and those who do not. A skilled representative is often better able to help the teacher understand and accept the need to change than the evaluator would be.

The key words related to the test of fair representation are *reasonable level* of representation. Most association representatives ensure a reasonable level to protect themselves and their members, but they will not protect a poorly-performing teacher who has received reasonable notice, support and time to improve, but still has failed to be consistently successful on the district's performance standards. At times, an association representative may unreasonably protect a teacher because he/she does not know the standard for fair representation or does not wish to offend the teacher. This is more likely to occur in districts where there has been inadequate dialogue between the association and the administration about the public relations component of the E.L.P.S. Fortunately, many association representatives are aware of the legislative and public relations implications on public education of their role in supervision and evaluation. They are committed to reasonable representation, but not to protection for low-performing teachers who have failed to improve.

Having a skilled association representative at all meetings with low-performing teachers may be helpful. Negative information about one's performance is often difficult for someone to understand and accept. The association representative may serve as a safe person with whom the teacher may discuss the information in private. Accepting the need to change *is one of the most significant differences* between teachers who do improve and continue in the profession and those who do not. A skilled representative is often better able to help the teacher understand and accept the need to change than the evaluator would be.

Involving the association representative early gives the association an opportunity to help the teacher explore all alternatives for improvement and to access emotional support such as counseling. It allows the association to put its energy and resources into assisting rather than protecting teachers. Should the evaluation not lead to improvement after a reasonable period of time and support, the association representative has access to career and retirement counseling resources for the teacher. Even in those cases in which a teacher must leave the profession, administrators and the teachers' association both want to help the teacher leave with dignity. If the representative has been involved throughout, the association has clearly met its duty of fair representation.

> Involving the association representative early gives the association an opportunity to help the teacher explore all alternatives for improvement and to access emotional support such as counseling. It allows the association to put its energy and resources into assisting rather than protecting teachers.

This section contains documents and procedures that will assist administrators in meeting the legal and educational requirements while balancing the public relations and social–emotional components of working with low-performing teachers. The work with low-performing teachers in districts using this program has resulted in some low-performing teachers leaving the profession. However, most of the teachers supervised and evaluated in accordance with the procedures outlined in this chapter have improved to a satisfactory level of teaching and consequently feel more fulfilled in their jobs.

WHAT DO DUE PROCESS AND JUST CAUSE MEAN?

A public employee's right to due process prior to discipline or dismissal is embedded in three levels of law: contract, state and constitutional.

The procedural requirement that governs the evaluation of most pubic employees is *just cause.* Typical contract language concerning just cause reads as follows:

No teacher (administrator) who has acquired tenure (professional teacher status in some states) shall be discharged or otherwise disciplined without just cause.

A typical example of state law is the following language from the Massachusetts General Laws, chapter 71, section 42:

A teacher with professional teacher status (tenure), shall not be dismissed except for inefficiency, incompetency, incapacity, conduct unbecoming a teacher, insubordination, failure on the part of the teacher to satisfy the teacher performance standards developed . . . or other *just cause*. (Finnegan, 2000, pp. 71–74) (emphasis added)

The United States Supreme Court has determined that a person's job is a property right and is therefore protected under the Fourteenth Amendment to the United States Constitution:

No state shall make or enforce any law which shall abridge the privileges or immunities of citizens of the United States; nor shall any state deprive any person of life, liberty *or property* without *due process*. (emphasis added)

The following description is adapted from a training document that was written by Robert Fraser (1996), a partner in Stoneman, Chandler & Miller, a law firm that represents numerous school districts in labor relations and teacher evaluation matters. Dr. Fraser is a practicing attorney and has a Ph.D. in Education. He has worked as a uniserve representative for the Massachusetts Teachers Association and as an assistant superintendent of schools prior to practicing law and representing school boards in cases of labor law.

Among the earliest cases (defining just cause in teacher dismissal) was a 1984 decision in which Arbitrator Archibald Cox (of Watergate fame) stated that just cause is absent *unless* three requirements are satisfied:

1. The employee committed the offense or was guilty of the shortcoming ascribed to him;
2. The misconduct or shortcoming justified the disciplinary measure; and
3. The procedure was consistent with fundamental fairness.

(Needham Education Association and Needham School Committee, 1984)

The Cox definition, which although better than none at all, falls far short of giving school officials the guidance they need in order to determine whether or not just cause exists to discipline a teacher whose performance has been unsatisfactory. Just cause cannot include reasons that are arbitrary, unfair or generated out of some petty vendetta. (Briggs v. Board of Directors of Hinton Community School District, 1979)

Traditionally, in determining whether or not an employer had just cause to dismiss an employee, arbitrators will pose the following questions.

[The paragraphs in italics have been added by the author to connect the seven standards to the daily tasks of teacher evaluation. —William Ribas]

1. Was the employee informed of management's rules and expectations?

   Districts should make all teachers aware of the district's performance standards. Some districts give the performance standards to every teacher at the beginning of each school year. At the very least, the performance standards should be given to teachers and discussed with them at the beginning of years in which those teachers will receive a summative evaluation.

2. Were management's rules and expectations reasonable?

   In states where the performance standards are collectively bargained, the standards themselves are considered by all parties to be reasonable. It is the implementation by individual administrators that may be questioned.

3. Was the employee's alleged infraction investigated?

   Administrators must gather adequate evidence. Later in this chapter is a detailed explanation of the rules of evidence as they relate to teacher evaluation.

4. Were the procedures followed by the employer fair?

   In many states, the due process procedures are collectively bargained and therefore certified as fair by management and the union. In these states, it is often the implementation of the standards by individual administrators that may be questioned.

5. Has management applied its rules or standards evenhandedly?

   The degree to which administrators consistently implement the standards and procedures (inter-rater reliability) *is important.*

6. Was the employee given an opportunity to improve?

   The use of improvement plans that include monitoring systems and supports is discussed in depth later in this chapter.

7. Did the penalty fit the "crime"?

   The concept of progressive discipline and its connection to supervision and evaluation is discussed in chapter 6.

A negative response to any one of the foregoing questions may indicate a lack of just cause for the employer's action. (Fraser, 1993, as cited in Fraser, 1996).

THE DUTY OF FAIR REPRESENTATION

Along with the right of the union to be the exclusive representative of all employees in the bargaining unit goes the duty of the union to represent everyone fairly. The legal term for this is the duty of fair representation (a.k.a. DFR).

The Massachusetts collective bargaining law, Massachusetts General Law Chapter 150E, does not specifically refer to this duty. (All states have a similar law defining the rules related to collective bargaining/contract negotiations for teachers.) However, section 5 of the law has been interpreted by judges to require the duty of fair representation. The applicable court cases have defined that duty to mean that a union

1. has a duty to fairly represent all the employees in the bargaining unit, both in collective bargaining and in the enforcement of the contract through the grievance and arbitration procedures

2. must serve the interests of all members of the unit without hostility or discrimination toward any

3. must exercise its decision-making power with good faith and honesty and must avoid arbitrary conduct; therefore, decisions, must be made in a reasonable and rational manner

Grievances: The decision of the union whether or not to process a grievance must be based on the merits of that particular grievance and on a thorough investigation of the facts of the particular situation. The decision whether or not to process a grievance may not be based on personal hostility, political opposition, illegal discrimination or any other irrational or unreasonable basis.

Under Massachusetts law, an individual may pursue a grievance on her/his own, without assistance from the union. However, the union must be given the opportunity to be present at any meetings between the grievant and supervisors/management representatives to ensure that any adjustments made are consistent with the terms of the contract.

Arbitration: As with grievances, the decision whether or not to take a grievance to arbitration must be based on the merits of the grievance. The basis of the decision must be reasonable and rational. The decision to arbitrate a grievance belongs to the union. However, in the case of dismissals, a teacher may appeal her/his dismissal to arbitration without assistance or approval from the union, as provided by the Education Reform Act of 1993, which modified Massachusetts General Law, chapter 71, section 42, which is related to the dismissal of teachers. (Dorine Levasseur, Massachusetts Teachers Association Field Consultant, 1999).

Legal Standards for Determining if the Union/Association Has Violated Its Duty of Fair Representation for a Member

The American Federation of Teachers and the National Education Association provide its state and local affiliates with information designed to inform its representatives about the duty of fair representation. The following guidelines for unions/associations appear in a jointly published document entitled *Peer Assistance & Review: An AFT/NEA Handbook* (American Federation of Teachers and National Education Association, 1998).

1. If the decision not to pursue a grievance was not arbitrary, capricious, based on discrimination or hostility toward the grievant or was rational, a court will not second-guess the wisdom of that decision (by the union/association).

2. Honest mistakes or misjudgments by the union do not constitute violations of the duty of fair representation.

3. Before finding a DFR violation, courts will look for evidence of improper motive or bad faith by the union.

WEINGARTEN RIGHT

This explanation of the Weingarten right is based on an article that first appeared in the *BEA Educator* in November, 1999. It is adapted here with the permission of the *BEA Educator* and the author, Dorine Levasseur, Massachusetts Teachers Association Field Representative.

The name comes from a 1975 United States Supreme Court case that held that it is unlawful for an employer to deny an employee's request that a union representative be present at an investigative interview which an employee reasonably believes might result in disciplinary action. The following rules tell teachers how to access those rights.

Rule 1: The teacher must make a clear request for union representation before or during an interview or meeting (*unlike the "Miranda" right that requires police officers to explain a person's rights before the meeting begins*). If the teacher believes an interview might lead to discipline somewhere down the road, or that's the way the meeting begins to unfold, the teacher may immediately tell the supervisor conducting the meeting that he/she wants to suspend the meeting until a union representative is present.

Rule 2: The supervisor must grant the request and wait until a union representative can be present, deny the request and continue the interview or give the employee the choice between having the interview without representation or ending the interview. Teachers are typically advised by their unions that in such situations the teacher should not continue without representation.

Rule 3: If the supervisor denies the request for representation and continues the interview, the teacher has the right to refuse to answer questions. However, the teacher must sit there until the supervisor terminates the interview. Teachers are typically advised by their unions/associations that if the supervisor continues the meeting, the teacher should take notes. In my experience, it may often be advantageous to the supervisor to delay the meeting for a reasonable period of time to permit representation. Most of these discussions are to obtain information and a delay of several hours or a day does not negatively impact the situation. In fact, the presence of a representative may make the conversation run more smoothly and be less confrontational. However, the administrator should not delay the meeting if there is a possibility the teacher will commit an inappropriate act if he/she is not given a clearly stated expectation by the supervisor immediately.

AN EVALUATOR'S GUIDE TO GATHERING AND VERIFYING EVIDENCE

Gathering and documenting evidence is important in all evaluations. Stating evidence in conferences and write-ups is an effective way to recognize and acknowledge hard work and excellent performance. It is also a way to mirror for teachers their performance so they can self-evaluate. For these purposes, evidence is a formative, educational and social–emotional tool. The evaluator need not be concerned with the legal aspects of gathering and documenting evidence. The situation changes, however, when the evaluator is working with a less than satisfactory teacher. Since in these cases there is always the possibility of a dismissal or disciplinary hearing, it is essential that the evaluator understand the legal requirements for gathering and verifying evidence. This section is written to help evaluators better understand the legal concept of *evidence* as it relates to the supervision and evaluation of low-performing teachers.

> Gathering and documenting evidence is important in all evaluations. Stating evidence in conferences and write-ups is an effective way to recognize and acknowledge hard work and excellent performance. It is also a way to mirror for teachers their performance so they can self-evaluate.

Evidence is " . . . any species of proof, or facts, legally presented at the trial or arbitration hearing of an issue" (Liacos, 1999). Administrators or supervisors involved in evaluations that may be challenged should remember that most evidence will be introduced through the evaluator's testimony, making the fact-gathering process very important. **Testimony** is "evidence given by a witness under oath either orally or in the form of affidavits or depositions" (Liacos, 1999).

Direct evidence is, " . . . evidence in the form of testimony from a witness who actually saw, heard or touched the subject of interrogation" (Garner, 1999, pp. 576–580). Direct evidence, if believed, will prove a fact without any *inference*. The most common type of *direct evidence* used in an evaluation is evaluator observation. These include observing the teacher in the classroom, outside of the classroom and reviewing artifacts such as assignments, assessments, classroom design, etc.

A second type of *direct evidence* is written or oral complaints or reports given to the evaluator by another party who witnessed the behavior. In schools, this information usually comes from another staff member, a student or a parent who has been directly impacted by or has directly observed the teacher's action. Initially, this is considered to be indirect or hearsay evidence. (See the explanation below.) However, if an evaluation goes to arbitration or another type of hearing, this evidence can be made direct if the person giving the testimony is willing to testify at the arbitration or submit an affidavit under oath.

Most frequently, this second type of evidence in an evaluation comes from parents and so, for purposes of illustration, I will use actual parent examples. In most situations when evaluators receive parents' complaints, the best course of action is to refer the parents to the teacher to discuss the issue. It often empowers the reticent parent to speak to the teacher if the evaluator also offers the person the opportunity to come back if the parent does not have a satisfactory discussion with the teacher. In cases in which the parent has already spoken to the teacher without success or the parent is afraid to speak to the teacher alone, the next course of action is usually a meeting with the teacher, the parent and the evaluator. This type of meeting serves two purposes. First, it allows the evaluator to mediate, moving the pair toward a win–win solution. Second, it enables the evaluator to thoroughly investigate the situation and determine whether or not the problem is the result of problematic teacher behavior. I have, in a select few instances, delayed this joint meeting and met with the teacher alone with permission to use the parent's name. I have done this when I felt that either party's level of emotion might preclude a productive meeting. In those cases, separate meetings allowed me to help each party work through his/her emotions, until he/she was able to resolve the issue by dealing with the facts.

> The major difficulty for evaluators with statements from other witnesses is verification of testimony by parents who refuse to have their names used.

The major difficulty for evaluators with statements from other witnesses is verification of testimony by parents who refuse to have their names used. Often a parent may call with information about an issue of which the evaluator was not aware, but the parent refuses to allow the evaluator to use his/her name. Typically, this reluctance is due to a fear that the teacher will take retribution on the student.[3] If the evaluator cannot persuade the parent to allow

---

3 During my nine years as a vice principal and principal, I supervised and evaluated over eighty teachers. I had dozens of calls from parents who were initially afraid to have their names attached to a complaint about a teacher for fear that there would be retribution on their child. In every case, I encouraged the parent to speak with the teacher about the complaint. In the one instance when I suspected a teacher may punish a child for a parent's complaint, I met with the teacher early in our supervisory relationship and shared that this was a concern of the parents. I told her that I wasn't assuming it to be true, however, I wanted her to know I would consider behavior of that sort a very serious breach of professional ethics and conduct unbecoming a teacher. In nine years, I did not have one instance of a teacher taking retribution on a child. This is not to say it would never happen, but I believe the occurrence of such behavior is extremely rare.

use of his/her name, yet judges the complaint as worthy of further investigation, the evaluator may then make observations in an attempt to establish the veracity of the complaint. (See the Indirect Evidence Decision Tree on page 133.) In most cases, however, a complaint from a person who wishes to remain anonymous is difficult to verify and, therefore, of little or even no use as credible evidence in an evaluation.

Circumstantial evidence is "testimony not based on actual personal knowledge or observation of the facts in controversy, but of other facts from which deductions are drawn, showing indirectly the facts sought to be proved" (Garner, 1999, pp. 576–580). An example of this type of evidence would be a consistently lower enrollment rate for a particular high school teacher as compared to that of other colleagues teaching the same class. A lower enrollment during only one year is probably not evidence of a performance issue. However, an *accumulation* of occurrences of this situation would lead a reasonable person to *infer* that there is a problem that requires further investigation and possible intervention. One school district faced with this situation took the following steps to deal effectively with the alleged problem without violating the teacher's rights.

1. The evaluator, in this case the department head, increased the level of unannounced observation in the teacher's classroom. This activity was deemed warranted to gather additional information with which to verify or negate the claims made by parents and students.

2. The principal directed the assistant principal in charge of scheduling students to fully enroll that teacher's classes for the start of the next school year.

3. The principal directed the guidance counselors (who typically removed students from the class during the summer at parents' requests) to refer disgruntled parents to the teacher and, if necessary, meet with the parents and the teacher to resolve the issues and keep the students in the class. If these interventions failed, counselors were directed to refer the parents to the department head/evaluator.

4. The evaluator then worked with the situation in the way described earlier in the description of *direct evidence* by a witness other than the evaluator. If, after a reasonable period of time and effort, the student was not successful, the evaluator would recommend to the principal that the student be removed from the class. The evaluator kept notes of all discussions and actions taken throughout this process. When a student was removed, the evaluator documented all of these steps in a memo to the teacher.

Hearsay evidence is "evidence not proceeding from the personal knowledge of the witness, but from the mere repetition of what he has heard others say" (Garner, 1999, pp. 576–580). Hearsay evidence is often not admissible in court, but it is generally admissible in administrative hearings such as arbitrations. The arbitrators will determine the appropriate weight given to the hearsay evidence. Arbitrators place greater credibility on hearsay evidence when it is cumulative. An example of this is the parent input letters elementary principals often receive in the spring when they are making classes for the upcoming year. These letters often express the same or similar concerns about a teacher's ability to effectively teach the parents' children. In some cases, these letters are first-hand accounts from parents who previously had other children in the teacher's classes. In most cases they are hearsay accounts based on information the parents received from other parents. The accumulation of these hearsay accounts may cause a reasonable person to deduce that a problem exists, thereby making this evidence circumstantial.

CASE STUDY: USING THE VARIOUS TYPES OF EVIDENCE

One example of using various types of evidence in an evaluation was a first year principal who, upon arrival in the district, heard a number of accounts from parents and staff about a fourth grade teacher who had a reputation for intimidating students. A review of the teacher's file showed no documentation of the problem by the previous principal. In fact, the previous evaluations of the teacher had been quite positive. When the new principal asked about the teacher, however, the retiring principal shrugged his shoulders and said that the problem had been going on for years. The way the retiring principal had dealt with parents' concerns about class assignments for the upcoming year was to put only sixteen students in the class while the other fourth grade classes each had twenty-one or twenty-two students.

During the course of the next year, the new principal had two complaints from parents of students in the class about their children being afraid of this fourth grade teacher. He referred each parent to the teacher, as suggested earlier. In the case of one child, after the parents had two meetings with the teacher, the principal met with the teacher and parents to try to resolve the issue. Two other meetings of this type were required when the child refused to come to school, and the parents had to physically carry the child into the classroom. The child was eventually switched to another class. During that year, the principal had only two other complaints of children being afraid of their teachers from the parents of the other 539 students in the building. No other child needed to be removed from any class.

The principal observed the teacher six times. Three were scheduled observations and three were unannounced observations. He wrote comprehensive observation write-ups for each. The teachers' association president attended all the post-observation conference meetings between the teacher and the principal.

As was typical, in early May the principal sent a letter to parents inviting their written input to the staff about the development of class assignments for the upcoming year. There were twenty classroom teachers in grades 1 through 5. The parents of the 450 students going into grades 1 through 5 sent ninety-three input letters. (This was a K–5 school, but the input mechanism for incoming kindergarten parents was separate.) Twenty-three of the letters indicated teachers that the parents' believed could not meet the needs of their children. Twelve of those letters were about the one fourth grade teacher being investigated. The remaining eleven were scattered among the nineteen remaining teachers. No other teacher was brought up more than twice.

The upcoming school year was scheduled to be the fourth grade teacher's evaluation year. The principal met with the teacher in late May and shared the parents' concerns from the letters. The teacher said she had some minor problems with parents in previous years, however, the parents' reactions were due to inaccurate gossip rather than fact. The principal explained that he was not accepting the letters as fact at this time, though he did want the two of them to develop a plan to deal with the parents' perceptions. He also told the teacher he would be observing more often than typical in the upcoming year, so he could respond to the parents with first-hand knowledge of the teacher's performance.

The principal worked intensely with the teacher throughout the year. The principal's observations and discussions with the teacher that year indicated an inordinate use of criticism (as opposed to encouragement and positive reinforcement) by the teacher and a lack of activities that engaged her students in learning. The teacher argued that these were just philosophical differences and parents' complaints during the year, about events when the principal was not in the room, were the children's fabrications. The principal continued to work formatively with the teacher, but summatively documented the observations and parents' concerns. That year the principal and teacher had to work with two more parents who reported their children were afraid of the teacher. One child was removed from the class after a number of interventions that included several visits to a child psychiatrist to deal with the school phobia. At classroom placement time, parents' letters again showed that the teacher received more than ten times the average number of complaints. The principal wrote an unsatisfactory evaluation citing the following evidence:

1. *Direct evidence* from classroom observations and conference discussions with the teacher which indicated excessive use of criticism, a lack

of smiling and positive affect and a lack of interesting and stimulating instructional activities. The direct evidence also included non-classroom observations of the teacher on the playground and at special assemblies that showed a lack of interaction and participation with the children in a way that would build the relationship between teacher and students. (See the example of a reprimand for Jane Doe in chapter 6.)

2.   A large amount of *evidence* in this example was derived from the testimony of investigated complaints from the parents of students in the class that year. These complaints indicated that the teacher had frequently responded abruptly to students when the principal was not in the room. The parents' testimony of students' complaints as reported by the administrator in a hearing is often known as **double hearsay** because it was communicated from the student to the parent and then to the administrator. Some of the parents were willing to provide more direct *hearsay evidence* by testifying directly or submitting an affidavit from themselves or their children for a hearing. In this example, the age of the children led the parents and administrators to conclude that it was not in the children's best interest to testify at the hearing (*direct evidence*).

3.   The following *cumulative hearsay evidence* was well documented, leading to a *reasonable person's* conclusion that there is a factual basis for the claims.

     a.   Logged parents' and students' complaints and parents' letters of complaint indicating the information in 2 above (The evaluator was prepared to present this information at a hearing)

     b.   Two consecutive years of an inordinate number of written and oral requests from parents not to place their children in the class

     c.   The fact that of the three cases of school phobia in the building, two were in this fourth grade teacher's classroom, even though a special effort had been made during the class assignments not to place students who might be susceptible to school phobia in the class

The principal alerted the association president that he was going to find the teacher unsatisfactory. The unsatisfactory evaluation was given to the teacher and reviewed in a meeting with the association president. The teacher was informed that failure to significantly improve in the upcoming year could lead to dismissal. Two subsequent meetings were held with the association president to develop an improvement plan.

The teacher resigned at the end of the school year. Subsequent information got back to the evaluator that indicated the teachers' association was instrumental in providing the teacher with the personal and career counseling that led the teacher toward a new career. The teacher eventually went back to school, received an MBA and went on to a career in the travel industry. (Dopazo & Ribas)

HARASSMENT?

I'm often asked by readers why the evaluator in the example above was not charged with harassment, because he began immediately to work with the teacher at a higher level than he had with other staff members. For example, six observations were conducted in the first year despite the fact that this was not a formal evaluation year for the teacher.

As described above, the administrator had heard an inordinate number of accounts from parents the summer before his first school year as principal indicating issues with the teacher. The principal decided he would visit the classroom early in the year so he could determine for himself if the claims were founded or not. It soon became obvious to the principal that the teacher needed to change her practice. He began working more intensely with the teacher, providing coaching and feedback. The intent of the administrator in this first year was to improve the teacher's practice, not to remove the teacher. Assisting the teacher with this change required a high level of interaction between the principal and the teacher.

In this case, the principal had the following reasons for interacting differently with this teacher than with the other tenured staff members.

1. The evidence of teachers' and parents' complaints led the principal to reasonably *infer* that the teacher may need assistance and/or closer monitoring.

2. The principal's direct observations supported these claims.

3. The principal's intent in increasing his interactions with the teacher was to *improve* not *remove* the teacher.

As a result, the principal was honestly and openly meeting his responsibilities as a supervisor and his responsibility to ensure the best interests of the students. Therefore, he was *not* harassing the teacher.

DECISION TREE FOR ADMINISTRATORS RESPONDING TO INDIRECT CLAIMS

The principal in the preceding example utilized a decision tree chart (figure 9 on facing page) to address parents' complaints. You will note that the principal treats all parents' complaints similarly unless he has a reason to do otherwise. Following a procedure of this type insulates the principal from charges from teachers (and parents) that he/she acts in an arbitrary or capricious manner when dealing with claims from indirect sources.

It is important to note that a procedure such as that below is a guide to administrative action. Since every incident has its own unique characteristics, it is impossible to develop a chart such as this that accounts for all the varied circumstances that may arise. Therefore, it is important that administrators effectively exercise professional judgment throughout the decision tree. The evaluating administrator must have access to a person in the senior administration (or a consultant) from whom he/she may receive coaching when confronted with a difficult judgment in responding to complaints about a teacher. The following section of this chapter describes a framework used by some districts to provide peer coaching for administrators confronted with difficult evaluation or disciplinary situations. In the chart below, those times in which the principal needed to exercise his professional judgment are shown with a dotted line around the box.

Investigation Hint: You will note that the investigation of this type of complaint may include interviews with other students to obtain information when there are no adult witnesses or only insufficient ones. When conducting such interviews of students, it is important to record the questions you asked and ask each child the same questions to the extent possible. When a union files a grievance concerning the administrator's actions in situations of this type, administrators are often accused of asking leading questions when interviewing students in an investigation. Writing down the questions and sticking to the script (to the extent possible) is one way an administrator may show he/she did not ask leading questions designed to push the students toward responses that would incriminate the staff member being investigated.

Indirect Evidence Decision Tree

Strategies for Addressing an Indirect Claim

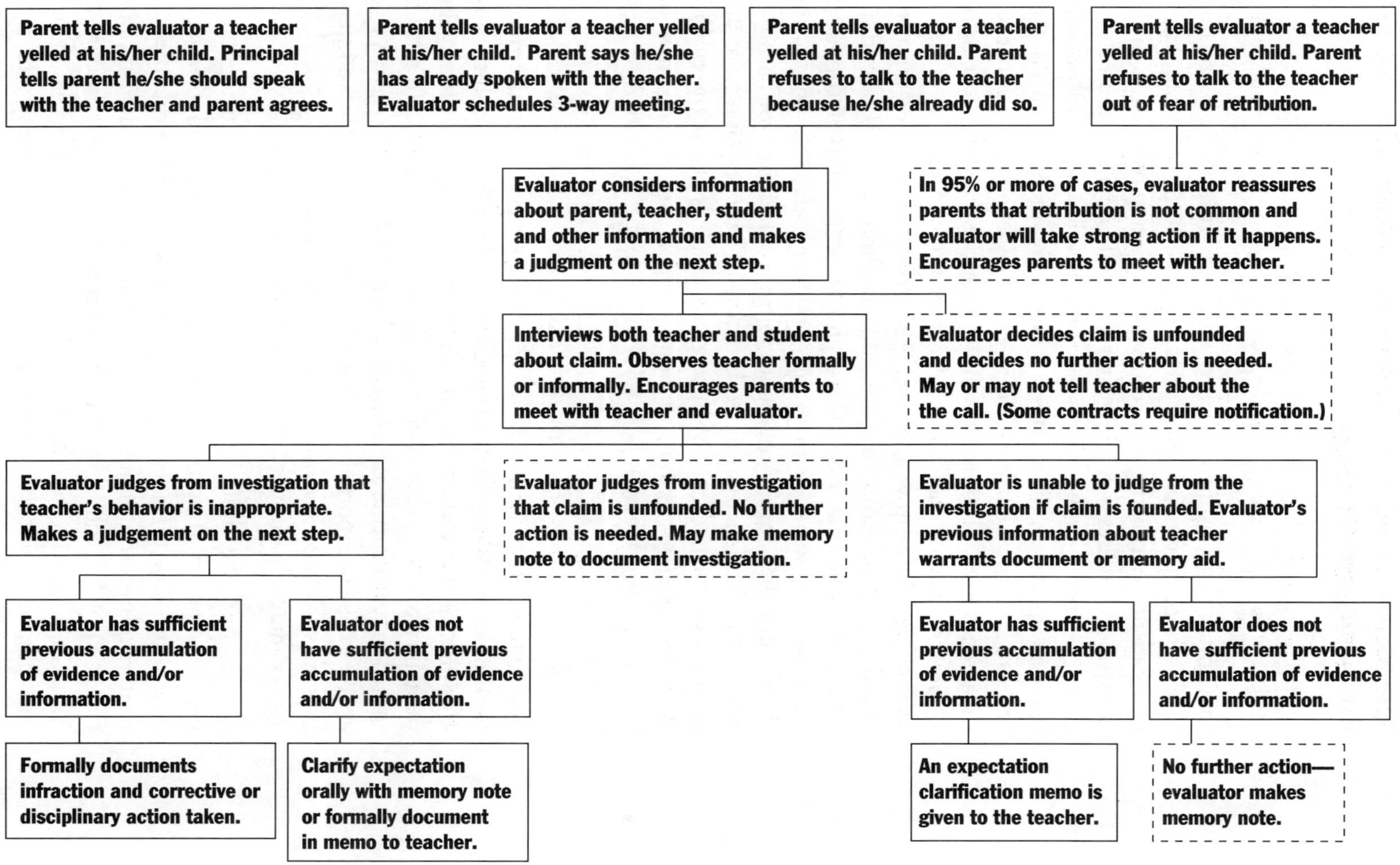

Parent tells evaluator a teacher yelled at his/her child. Principal tells parent he/she should speak with the teacher and parent agrees.

Parent tells evaluator a teacher yelled at his/her child. Parent says he/she has already spoken with the teacher. Evaluator schedules 3-way meeting.

Parent tells evaluator a teacher yelled at his/her child. Parent refuses to talk to the teacher because he/she already did so.

Parent tells evaluator a teacher yelled at his/her child. Parent refuses to talk to the teacher out of fear of retribution.

In 95% or more of cases, evaluator reassures parents that retribution is not common and evaluator will take strong action if it happens. Encourages parents to meet with teacher.

Evaluator considers information about parent, teacher, student and other information and makes a judgment on the next step.

Interviews both teacher and student about claim. Observes teacher formally or informally. Encourages parents to meet with teacher and evaluator.

Evaluator decides claim is unfounded and decides no further action is needed. May or may not tell teacher about the the call. (Some contracts require notification.)

Evaluator judges from investigation that claim is unfounded. No further action is needed. May make memory note to document investigation.

Evaluator is unable to judge from the investigation if claim is founded. Evaluator's previous information about teacher warrants document or memory aid.

Evaluator has sufficient previous accumulation of evidence and/or information.

Evaluator does not have sufficient previous accumulation of evidence and/or information.

No further action—evaluator makes memory note.

An expectation clarification memo is given to the teacher.

Evaluator judges from investigation that teacher's behavior is inappropriate. Makes a judgement on the next step.

Evaluator has sufficient previous accumulation of evidence and/or information.

Evaluator does not have sufficient previous accumulation of evidence and/or information.

Formally documents infraction and corrective or disciplinary action taken.

Clarify expectation orally with memory note or formally document in memo to teacher.

Figure 9

The Team Approach to Supporting and Coaching
Evaluators Involved in Difficult Evaluations
or
Reducing the "Ghost Town" and "Goldilocks" Effects

Chapter 1 of this book briefly spoke about the social–emotional factors that impact the evaluators when working with a low-performing teacher. Most schools and departments are designed so the evaluator (e.g., principal, department head) is the sole evaluator of a group of teachers in the school or department. In these situations, it is a typical human reaction for the teacher's colleagues to be emotionally supportive. Even when staff members privately encourage the administrator to work more intensely with the teacher, very few ever indicate that position to the teacher or other teachers. Soon after the intensive work begins, the administrator realizes that little or none of that earlier prodding for action translates into public support of the administrator's efforts to improve the teacher's performance. The administrator steps into the "middle of the street" to confront this difficult issue and turns around to find the streets and sidewalks a "ghost town," empty of supporters. In some instances, the low-performing teacher publicly berates the administrator to other staff members. Some colleagues join the administrator bashing, but most respond with silence or active listening. These responses are taken by the teacher as concurrence with his/her complaints about the evaluator. It creates a lonely and stressful situation in which the evaluator may be prone to second-guessing whether he/she is being too direct or not direct enough with the teacher.

Those of us responsible for supervision and evaluation throughout the district can help limit the ghost town effect for evaluators in three ways. First, we should maintain a reasonable level of inter-rater reliability in the district. Common practice and expectations in the district limit the evaluators' vulnerability to claims that their work is personally motivated rather than connected to system-wide expectations. Using the assessment techniques noted in chapter 2 is an important first step. The best way to achieve inter-rater reliability is with good teaching, coaching and assessment of the skills of supervision and evaluation.

Second, we should provide periodic meetings during the year when groups of administrators involved in difficult evaluations or staff discipline situations come together to discuss their work with a qualified coach. This enables administrators to learn from one another and to receive coaching from a knowledgeable expert from the senior administration or a consultant. More importantly though, the social support of this type of meeting reassures administrators that they are not alone and that the system supports them during this difficult yet very important work.

The first meeting of this type in your district should be used to analyze a sample case study together. (See the sample cases later in this section.) This activity will model for the evaluators the steps involved in productively analyzing a difficult evaluation. In subsequent meetings, the evaluators bring their own difficult cases for discussion and coaching. In preparation for the meeting, evaluators should consider the following background facts and impressions (without including the staff members' names) prior to the session. This preparation will enable evaluators to give the group and the coach the information needed to productively participate in the discussion. It should be understood by all participants that all information related to these meetings is strictly confidential and should not be discussed beyond the meeting.

Below is a questionnaire that should be given to evaluators at least a couple of days before the seminar, so they can arrive ready to talk about their cases in a way that will maximize the quality of the feedback they receive.

DIFFICULT EVALUATION/PROGRESSIVE DISCIPLINE SUPPORT AND COACHING SEMINARS

The evaluator-coaching seminar we are having next week is designed to provide administrators with ideas, strategies and supports when working with difficult supervision, evaluation and/or progressive discipline situations. Often these situations involve confidential information. Because of this we ask that you not use the staff member's name when posing your questions. We also must insist that the issues discussed not be shared with anyone other than the appropriate administrator outside of the meeting.

Consider the pertinent background information requested in the questions below. What questions do you have about your case that will help you to better work with this teacher?

1. How many years has he/she been teaching? How many years in this district? (Give an estimate if you're not sure.)
2. What is the teacher's age?
3. What is the teacher's overall health (physical and mental)?
4. What is the teacher's personal support system in and out of school?
5. How does the teacher respond to recommendations for change?
6. How would parents describe the teacher?
7. How would students describe the teacher?
8. How would colleagues describe the teacher?
9. How would the teacher describe his/her performance to you?

10. How would the teacher describe his/her performance to a trusted friend?

11. How would you describe the teacher's performance? What are the issues?

12. How do the above descriptions compare to one another?

13. What supervision techniques have worked with the teacher? Why?

14. What has not worked with the teacher? Why?

15. Are there any other legal issues that might be raised (e.g., discrimination based on age, sex, race, religion or handicapping condition)?

Third, we should match these evaluators as partners or groups of three to provide each of them with constant support between the regularly scheduled meetings. Typically, there are two kinds of partner relationships. In one type of partner relationship, the second administrator has no direct contact with the teacher being evaluated. In these situations, the partner is a "critical friend" who assists the evaluator with analyzing the teacher's issues and deciding on appropriate interventions, but does not observe or meet with the teacher. The other partner relationship is the second evaluator/supervisor model. In these cases the second administrator conducts observations and participates in meetings with the teacher. I strongly advise against having the second evaluator/supervisor be a person with a full evaluation load, for this will only dilute his/her effectiveness on those evaluations. In either case, addressing the evaluation as a case study with the partner, using the information from the preceding questions, may be very helpful. It is understood by both parties that all information related to the teacher and his/her evaluation is strictly confidential.

The partners may also use one another to help with observations that are difficult to write, final evaluations and/or memos to the teacher. In chapter 3, I noted how helpful administrators find peer coaching about observation write-ups and end-of-year reports. In cases of low-performing teachers, this activity is not only helpful, it is essential! Below is a format for peer-editing evaluation documents of low-performing teachers.

PEER CONFERENCING TO HELP YOUR PEERS WITH WRITE-UPS OF LOW-PERFORMING TEACHERS (EVALUATIONS, MEMOS, OBSERVATIONS, ETC.)

1. Start with an area in the write-up that is done well. Be sure to be specific about what is done well and give evidence that supports why you believe that part is done well.

   - Don't say, "This is really good."
   - Do say (see C.E.I.J. examples in chapter 3), "You did a good job of supporting the claim that is underlined by indicating the time the students came in, the fact that the teacher arrived after the students and the time the teacher addressed the class."

2. Do the labeled teaching moves (claim) identify the teacher behavior in terms of one of the district performance standards?

3. Does the evidence (objective information) in the write-up directly support the claim, judgment and/or interpretation (subjective statements)? Do you have a suggestion as to how the writer may better do this?

4. Are the interpretations worded in language consistent with the performance standards?

5. Have clear judgments been made about the claims that indicate whether the teacher is satisfactory in each standard described in the document? Have the judgments been made in language that is consistent with the statements of judgments used in the district's final end-of-year evaluation document?

6. Is there sufficient evidence to support any judgments about performance standards on which the teacher has been judged unsatisfactory?

7. Is there a way for the writer to describe the evidence in a more concrete, observable or verifiable manner? Do you have a suggestion for the writer as to how he/she may better do this?

8. Do you, as the reader, understand the impact (negative or positive) on the students' learning (or well being) of the behaviors described in the write-up of the class or activity?

9. Does the document objectively state the case and avoid "digs" that may result from the evaluator's frustration with this teacher?

After the information is provided, the partners may then discuss together the Questions to Ask Yourself When You Are Supervising and/or Evaluating a Teacher (Administrator) You Suspect Is Unsatisfactory (or Barely Satisfactory), on page 145–146 and A Checklist of Tests for Unfair Evaluation found on pages 147–148 of this section. These documents will help map out a plan of action that addresses the whole E.L.P.S. As the evaluations progress, there are additional questions for the partners to discuss. These questions can be found at the end of the sample case study that follows.

CASE STUDY OF A DIFFICULT SEVENTH AND EIGHTH GRADE SCIENCE TEACHER EVALUATION (SAMPLE OF A FOUR-YEAR CYCLE)

Read the case study and follow the directions that appear at the end.

This example takes place in a district with a four-year evaluation process for tenured (professional teacher status) teachers. The first year is a summative evaluation. Years two, three and four are formative, with significant professional development components. In those years, the principal does not complete a summative evaluation of the teacher. For an example of this type of evaluation process, see chapter 7.

Jane Doe is a seventh and eighth grade science teacher. She is forty-two years old and has taught in the system for fifteen years. Jane taught for two years in another district before coming to Sample District. She works with a staff of seventh and eighth grade teachers who, for the most part, are quite strong. However, there is one other teacher on the team, John Moe, who performs below average, but still satisfactorily. John is one of Jane's closest confidants. They typically sit together at faculty meetings and often have lunch together.

Jane is liked by other members of the staff, but by no means loved. She attends all the staff's social events and is generally cordial with colleagues. However, she can at times be moody and short with colleagues. Jane and John Moe are part of a group of six to eight teachers from the school who get together quarterly for coffee. Jane stays connected to the teachers' association by attending social events and some of the informational meetings, but she is not an active participant in the operation of the union.

Jane's first seven years were excellent. She actively took courses, eventually getting her master's degree. She served on system-wide committees, showed up at some of the seventh and eight grade sporting events and plays, and participated in the eighth grade overnight trip. During this period, she built strong relationships with parents. Parents whose children had Jane during that time still speak highly of her in the community, though they no longer have children in the school. Jane's performance warranted excellent evaluations and tenure (professional teacher status) at the end of her third year. Years four through six were supervisory years (phases two through four) and her performance in evaluation year seven (phase one) continued to be excellent.

Years eight to ten were a plateau for Jane. One of her own two children started to have difficulties in school and at home due to some emotional issues.

Jane periodically discussed her concerns about the child with the principal, but the child's problems were a continual source of concern. As a result, Jane cut back on her committee work, professional development and attendance at events. Her teaching remained good (but not excellent) partly on the strength of the knowledge and skills she had developed in her first seven years. The principal began to notice the plateau effect in evaluation year nine (phase three of the four-year evaluation cycle). She gave the issues some thought, but decided to give an evaluation with no areas of concern because Jane's performance was still quite good in the classroom. She believed the plateau would end and Jane would again begin to grow as a teacher, if she gave Jane positive and supportive comments during Jane's phase one administrative evaluation in year ten.

Years eleven to thirteen saw a slow but steady decline. Jane stopped keeping up with changes in instructional strategies and curriculum. As her teaching declined further from her first seven years of excellence, parents' complaints increased slowly and steadily. Parents were reporting the slow return of work. Their children expressed boredom with the primarily lecture format and reported that Jane was, at times, overly critical of students. In administrative evaluation year fourteen (phase 1 of the four-year cycle), the principal realized the supportive approach of the last two years was not moving Jane forward. In fact, Jane's performance was declining due to a lack of willingness (or ability) to change at the pace needed to stay current with curriculum and instruction. She could no longer be sustained by the excellence of her first seven years.

In evaluation year fourteen (phase one) the principal made three recommendations and marked Jane as being below standard on one of the seven performance standards. The principal believed Jane should have been marked below standard on two and possibly three of the standards, but didn't do this because she was sure Jane would react very strongly to such an evaluation. There were also some fleeting hopes that Jane would still be able to turn things around. Upon receiving the evaluation, Jane made an appointment with the principal. She expressed her strong concern about receiving the below standard rating. After talking with the principal, she still disagreed but decided not to pursue the issue any further. After school closed for the year, the principal received two letters and several other comments from parents of graduating eighth graders about their disappointment with science during these last two years.

During year fifteen, when Jane was in phase two of the evaluation cycle, Jane's performance flattened out at the level of the previous year. Although the principal believed a number of improvements were needed to bring Jane up to the Sample District standard, Jane did not see the issues.

After the first principals' meeting in October, the principal takes you aside, shares this situation and asks for your advice. What will you tell her? Why?

Case Study of a Difficult Third Grade Evaluation (Sample of a Two-Year Cycle)

Read the case study and follow the directions that appear at the end.

This example takes place in a district with a two-year evaluation process for tenured (professional teacher status) teachers. The first year is a summative evaluation. The second year is a supervisory year in which no summative evaluation is completed, unless the teacher is placed in an out-of-cycle summative evaluation. For an example of this type of evaluation process, see chapter 7.

Jane Doe is a third grade classroom teacher. She is forty-two years old and has taught in the system for fifteen years. Jane taught two years in another district before coming to Sample. She works with two third grade colleagues and a grades three to six resource room teacher who are very good teachers. Next door to Jane is a fourth grade teacher, John Moe, who is below average, but still satisfactory. John is one of Jane's closest confidants.

Jane is liked by other members of the staff, but by no means loved. She attends all the staff's social events and is generally cordial with colleagues. However, she can at times be moody and short with colleagues. Jane stays connected to the teachers' association by attending social events and some of the informational meetings, but she is not an active participant in the operation of the teachers' association.

Jane's first seven years were excellent. She actively took courses, eventually getting her master's degree. She served on system-wide committees and attended some of the grade four and five after-school and evening events to support her previous students. Jane's performance warranted excellent evaluations and tenure (professional teacher status) at the end of her third year. Years four and six were supervisory years and her performance in evaluation years five and seven continued to be excellent.

Years eight to ten were a plateau for Jane. One of her two children started to have difficulties in school and at home due to some emotional issues. Jane periodically discussed her concerns about the child with the principal, but the child's problems were a continual source of concern. As a result, Jane cut back on her committee work, professional development and attendance at events. Her teaching remained good (but not excellent) partly on the strength of the knowledge and skills she had developed in her first seven years. The principal began to notice a lack of positive change in her teaching in evaluation year nine. All of Jane's teaching seemed to be a "rerun" of previous years. She gave the issues some thought, but decided to give an evaluation with no unsatisfactory areas. Jane's performance was still satisfactory in the classroom overall, even though her currency in curriculum and in some instructional areas was below the standard. The principal believed the plateau would end, and

Jane would again begin to grow as a teacher if she were given positive and supportive comments during supervisory year ten.

Years eleven to fourteen saw a slow but steady decline. Jane stopped keeping up with changes in instructional strategies and curriculum. As her teaching declined further from her first seven years of excellence, parents' complaints increased slowly and steadily. Parents were reporting the slow return of work. Their children expressed boredom with the number of worksheets and teacher-directed activities and reported that Jane was at times negative with students. In evaluation year eleven, the principal realized the supportive approach of the last two years was not moving Jane forward. In fact, Jane's performance was declining due to a lack of willingness (or ability) to change at the pace needed to stay current with curriculum and instruction. She could no longer be sustained by the excellence of her first seven years.

In evaluation year eleven, the principal made two or three recommendations and marked Jane as below standard in one area. The principal marked Jane as "satisfactory" overall. The principal believed Jane should have been marked with two or three areas below standard, but didn't because she was sure Jane would react very strongly to such an evaluation. There were also some fleeting hopes that Jane would still be able to turn things around. Upon receiving the evaluation, Jane made an appointment with the principal. Jane expressed her strong concern about not receiving all satisfactory ratings. After talking with the principal, she still disagreed but decided not to pursue the issue any further. After school closed for the year, the principal received several comments from parents of her third graders about their disappointment with their childrens' year. The principal also received six letters from second grade parents asking that their children not be placed in Jane's class for third grade. During supervisory year twelve, Jane's performance flattened out at an overall unsatisfactory to barely satisfactory level. A number of areas for improvement persisted, however, Jane did not see most of them as issues.

After the first principals' meeting in November the principal takes you aside, shares this situation and asks for your advice. What will you tell her? Why?

CASE STUDY OF A DIFFICULT HIGH SCHOOL EVALUATION (SAMPLE OF A THREE-YEAR CYCLE)

Read the case study and follow the directions that appear at the end.

Jeff Doe is teaching French to seniors. He is forty-two years old and has taught in the district for thirteen years. Jeff taught for two years in another district before coming to this district. He works with a staff which is quite strong for the most part. However, there is one other teacher on the team, John Moe, who is below average, but still satisfactory. John is one of Jeff's closest confidants. Jeff is liked by other members of the staff, but by no means loved.

Jeff attends all the staff's social events and is generally cordial with colleagues. However, he can at times be moody and short with them. Jeff stays connected to the teachers' association by attending social events and some of the informational meetings, but he is not an active participant in the operation of the union.

Jeff's first seven years were excellent. He actively took courses, eventually getting his master's degree. He served on system-wide committees, showed up at some of the high school sporting events and plays and participated in the "Can We Talk?" diversity awareness program. Jeff's performance warranted excellent evaluations and tenure (professional teacher status) at the end of his third year. Years four and five were alternative evaluation pathway years and his performance in evaluation year six (observation cycle) continued to be excellent.

Years eight through ten were a plateau for Jeff. One of his two children started to have difficulties in school and at home, due to some emotional issues. Jeff periodically discussed his concerns about the child with the curriculum coordinator, but the child's problems were a continual source of concern. As a result, Jeff cut back on his committee work, professional development and attendance at events. His teaching remained good (but not excellent) partly on the strength of the knowledge and skills he had developed in his first seven years. The foreign language coordinator (department head) began to notice a plateau in observation cycle year nine. She gave the issues some thought, but decided not to confront the areas of concern because Jeff's performance was still quite good in the classroom. The coordinator (department head) believed the plateau would end, and Jeff would again begin to grow as a teacher if she gave Jeff positive and supportive comments in his observation cycle evaluation during year nine

Years ten and eleven saw a slow but steady decline. Jeff stopped keeping up with changes in instructional strategies and curriculum. As his performance declined further from his first seven years of excellence, parents' complaints increased slowly but steadily. Parents were reporting the slow return of work. Their children expressed boredom with the primarily lecture format and reported that Jeff was, at times, overly critical of his students. In the observation cycle evaluation in year twelve, the Foreign Language Coordinator realized the supportive approach of the last several years was not moving Jeff forward. In fact, Jeff's performance was declining due to a lack of willingness (or ability) to change at the pace needed to stay current with curriculum and instruction. He could no longer be sustained by the excellence of his first seven years.

In evaluation year twelve, the coordinator made three recommendations and marked Jeff as barely satisfactory[4] on two of the performance standards. The coordinator believed Jeff should have been marked unsatisfactory on at

---

4 The categories for summative ratings in this district were exemplary, satisfactory, barely satisfactory and unsatisfactory.

least one of those performance standards, but she didn't do it. She was sure Jeff would react very strongly, since this was the first time he was ever marked below satisfactory. There were also some fleeting hopes that Jeff would still be able to turn things around. Upon receiving the evaluation, Jeff made an appointment with the coordinator. Jeff expressed his strong concern about receiving barely satisfactory ratings. After talking with his coordinator, Jeff still disagreed, but he decided not to pursue the issue any further. After school closed for the year, the coordinator received two letters and several other comments from parents of graduating seniors about their disappointment with French class during these last two years.

At the start of year thirteen, Jeff was in the out-of-cycle stage of the evaluation cycle. Jeff's performance was no better than it had been during the previous year. Although a number of improvements were needed to bring Jeff to a satisfactory rating on all of the district's performance standards, Jeff did not see these areas of his teaching as areas for growth or unsatisfactory.

After the administrative council meeting on October 3rd, the coordinator (department head) takes you aside, shares this situation and asks for your advice. What will you tell her? Why?

CASE STUDY ACTIVITY

You have ten minutes to discuss this case with a partner. You will then have another ten minutes to discuss it as a group. If there is other information you need about this case to answer the following questions, please ask. At the end of the twenty minutes, give a report from your group on how you will advise your colleague. Some things you may want to consider in your advice are

1. Should the principal (or the curriculum coordinator in the third case) involve the central administration? If so, how? If not, why not?

2. What is the principal's next step?

3. How may the principal monitor the impact on other staff members of his work with the low-performing teacher? Will the principal's work with this teacher impact the building staff as a whole? If so, how? If not, why not?

4. What is the role of the building peer review committee or teacher support team (if one exists in your district)?

5. Does the principal need any more information about the low-performing teacher? If so, what?

6. What educational, legal, political or social–emotional information and support does the principal need? To whom should the principal go for this information and support?

7. Will the principal's work with this teacher impact the school system as a whole? If so, how? If not, why not?

8. Should the teachers' union be involved in any way? If so, how? If not, why not?

    ** *Your answers to the questions above are focused on helping your colleague with the evaluation from this point forward. Now, review the situation with the benefit of hindsight.*

9. Is there anything this principal should have done differently during the prior years? If so, what?

A SECOND EVALUATOR–SUPERVISOR MODEL

As discussed in chapter 2, when a teacher has more than one supervisor–evaluator it is important that the administrators communicate well. In cases of low-performing teachers, in which the partner is more actively involved as a second evaluator–supervisor, this partner attends meetings and observations with the teacher. For these situations, the following guidelines are essential.

1. Come to agreement on the priorities and goals of the evaluation. The administrators should review the teacher's performance related to the district's performance standards and work out any differences they may have prior to the start of the evaluation. I have seen many evaluations of low-performing teachers seriously compromised right from the beginning because of the failure of the supervising and/or evaluating administrators to provide a consistent message to the teacher. Failure to do this

    In districts where there are multiple evaluators you always deal with the "Goldilocks effect." Prior to a district's participating in significant training, this effect may be caused by the tendency of evaluators to function like the chairs of the three bears in the Goldilocks story. Some may have a predisposition to be *too hard,* others to be *too soft* and still others to be *just right* in their approach to a low-performing teacher.

    also makes it more difficult for the association to play a positive role in moving the teacher toward change.

2. Plan with your partner before each meeting, so you send the same message to the teacher. The message that a person needs to change is *emotionally* very difficult for people to hear. The more clearly and concisely the message is given and reinforced, the more likely it will be accepted by the teacher. A consistent message also helps the association representative to reinforce the suggested changes in private conversations with the teacher.

3. Use your partner's areas of strength.

4. Be ready for the period of *regression*. This process is always "two steps forward and one step back." Remind your partner of this when he/she is frustrated and ready to give up.

5. Support each other through the periods of *aggression*. There will be times when the teacher will lash out at one of you more than the other. Be willing to share the heat that results from telling the teacher about areas in which he/she needs to make a change.

6. Share the work. These evaluations require a tremendous amount of time. Try to keep the work as evenly distributed as possible.

I've developed the following questions to help evaluators align their evaluations with the seven tests of just cause described on pages 121–122. Evaluators may use these questions alone. However, it may be extremely helpful for an evaluator to review these questions with his/her partner or supervisor for a "reality check." In districts where there are multiple evaluators you always deal with the "Goldilocks effect." Prior to a district's participating in significant training, this effect may be caused by the tendency of evaluators to function like the chairs of the three bears in the Goldilocks story. Some may have a predisposition to be *too hard*, others to be *too soft* and still others to be *just right* in their approach to a low-performing teacher.

QUESTIONS TO ASK YOURSELF WHEN YOU ARE SUPERVISING AND/OR EVALUATING A TEACHER YOU SUSPECT IS UNSATISFACTORY (OR BARELY SATISFACTORY)

1. Had I reviewed the district's performance standards with the teacher with reasonable thoroughness prior to identifying problems? *Note:* Many districts now require evaluators to review the district's performance standards with their entire staff at the start of each year to ensure that all teachers are "informed of management's rules and expectations." (See the seven tests of just cause on pages 121–122.)

2. What has changed since the last satisfactory evaluation to warrant a change in my judgement of this person's performance from satisfactory to unsatisfactory (or barely satisfactory)? Remember, this change may be in the teacher's performance or in the evaluator's and/or the district's ability to deal with the type of low performance that this teacher has previously exhibited. In cases where there has been a change in evaluator, what is the reason for the difference between my interpretation in the most recent evaluation and that of the previous evaluator?

3. On which of the district's performance standards do I believe the teacher is performing unsatisfactorily?

4. What evidence do I have that supports this belief?

5. Have I clearly and specifically communicated my concerns in language consistent with the district's performance standards? (See the questions related to editing observation and final evaluation write-ups found on page 137.)

6. Have I factored in extenuating circumstances to a reasonable extent? For example, a teacher's health issue may require a *reasonable accommodation* to enable the teacher to perform satisfactorily on the performance standards.[5] However, it does not excuse a teacher from satisfactorily meeting the performance standards.

7. Have I given reasonable support and allowed sufficient time to enable improvement?

8. What additional knowledge do I need to be reasonably qualified to make judgments about what constitutes satisfactory teaching in this person's assignment? If I need more knowledge, where or to whom do I go for this information?

9. Is there another administrator who can give me a second opinion on the teacher's performance or act as a sounding board as I make critical decisions throughout this process?

10. To what extent does the teacher agree/disagree with my assessment of his/her performance? How do I close the gap between our differing assessments? (See the section on Conferencing to Create Change on page 73 of chapter 3.)

11. How does the teachers' association respond when an administrator addresses the deficiencies of a low-performing teacher with tenure? How will I work with the teachers' association when addressing my concerns about this teacher?

12. Is my supervisor fully apprised of my concerns, the evidence and my plan for next steps?

[5] Edwin M. Bridges, in his book, *The Incompetent Teacher* (1992), found that in nearly half the cases of incompetent teaching that administrators described during his research, the teachers suffered from some type emotional distress, burn-out, health problems, marital difficulties and/or financial problems.

REASONS CONTRIBUTING TO TEACHERS AND TEACHERS' ASSOCIATIONS NOT BELIEVING JUST CAUSE HAS BEEN DEMONSTRATED IN AN EVALUATION

The document below comes from the files of a teachers' association in Massachusetts. The author is unknown. This document is a fairly comprehensive list of the claims that teachers have made over the years to refute unsatisfactory evaluations. It is an older document that comes from a time prior to the political focus on voucher programs and charter schools, when the focus of many local teachers' associations/unions was more on protection at all costs then on representation. For an in-depth explanation of this change in the manner of representation by teachers' associations, see the discussion in chapter 4 on current public relations (political) circumstances affecting how teachers' associations/unions represent their members. Despite recent political changes, the following document has value as a helpful set of questions for evaluators to ask themselves when involved in difficult evaluations.

A CHECKLIST OF TESTS FOR UNFAIR EVALUATION

This checklist of tests for unfair evaluation is drawn from court decisions and arbitration awards and should prove to be a classic.

The following checklist should be read by the individual in the event of a poor evaluation by the evaluator. Any one or more of the following statements that apply to your situation might be sufficient grounds to challenge the evaluation in the form of a grievance.

1. Cited facts are inaccurate.

2. The evaluation failed to consider constraints of pupil background, overcrowding, school conditions, etc.

3. The evaluator is not competent to evaluate in my field and/or lacks understanding of current acceptable pedagogical practice or board policy or law.

4. My evaluator relied on hearsay.

5. My evaluator failed to observe me for a sufficient amount of time to make a valid judgment.

6. My evaluator failed to give me adequate forewarning of this down rating, in that he did not give me sufficient time or assistance to improve, specify the incompetent performance or unprofessional conduct with such particularity as to furnish me with an adequate opportunity to make sufficient improvement or offer specific suggestions and recommendations for improvement.

7. This evaluation is excessive for the wrongs cited.

8. This evaluation fails to consider the extenuating and mitigating circumstances as cited on my initial conference form.

9. This evaluation is irrelevant to my fitness to teach, in that the wrongs cited do not adversely affect students or coworkers to any material extent.

10. I am being down rated for an assignment outside my field.

11. The objectives, goals, standards or rules cited are so broad as to be void for reasons of vagueness.

12. The objectives, goals, standards or rules are unreasonable, arbitrary, capricious and/or impossible of observance or attainment.

13. This evaluation is inequitable or discriminatory in that the cited standards or rules have not been consistently enforced at my school inasmuch as coworkers in the same situation have done the same thing without reprimand or down rating.

14. The wrongs cited exceed the jurisdiction of the board which jurisdiction is limited to the orderly, safe and efficient operation of the school district.

15. The citations on my evaluation form violate constitutional guarantees to my free speech, association, political advocacy or to the standards of academic freedom accepted in the profession.

16. I was given no opportunity to confront my accusers.

17. The adverse citations occurred a long time ago before the evaluation and did not recur.

18. This evaluation ignores my past record of achievement and unjustly punished me for a single recent wrong which is not likely to recur.

19. My performance has been adversely affected by extreme stress and duress due to unreasonable administrative harassment.

FORMAT FOR AN IMPROVEMENT PLAN

At a minimum, an improvement plan should be a written document that includes areas for improvement, recommendations for improving those areas, supports available to the evaluatee and the monitoring system. These plans may take many forms. Evaluators interested in other improvement plan formats are encouraged to read a book by Platt, Tripp, Ogden & Fraser (2000) called *The Skillful Leader: Confronting Mediocre Teaching.*

An improvement plan is used in years when the typical level of supervision or evaluation is insufficient to address the areas needing improvement.

It should always be used when someone has been placed in an out-of-cycle evaluation (removed from the scheduled supervisory year and placed in summative evaluation) for performance reasons. Improvement plans may also be used in a regular evaluation year or in a supervision year when it has been determined that a more intensive relationship is needed.

1. The **areas for improvement** section spells out to the teacher exactly which areas of performance are in need of improvement. Statements should relate directly to the district's performance standards (a.k.a. principles of effective teaching in some states). It is helpful to describe these areas in such a way that the teacher or administrator understands *what is not happening* and *what should be happening*. The area of concern must also be one that has been observed by or verified by the evaluator. At times, an evaluator may have circumstantial evidence pointing to a possible issue. In these cases, it should be noted as an expected area for improvement until evidence verifies or disproves what is suspected. To avoid confusion about expectations, it is important to note in the plan that the evaluation will focus on areas for improvement but will also include an assessment of all the performance standards.

2. The **recommendations for improving these areas** section explains what the employee is expected to do to overcome the concerns identified in the areas for improvement section of the plan. It is best to actively involve the evaluatee in generating these activities. This may be difficult, however, when the evaluatee does not believe there are issues. Specific, realistic and achievable activities to be pursued by the evaluatee are delineated. Some evaluators place the recommendations in a separate section. Other evaluators include the recommendations in the areas for improvement section, with connected recommendations following the description of each area identified for improvement.

3. **Supports available to the evaluatee** includes the resources (people, materials, workshops, etc.) that are available to assist the evaluatee in his/her efforts to improve. Some evaluators list the supports in a separate section. Other evaluators connect them to specific recommendations. For example, an evaluator may recommend that a teacher improve his/her knowledge of the subject matter by attending a specific course at a college or university.

4. **The monitoring system** describes how progress on the plan will be measured. It should include the pattern and approximate time lines for observations, conferences and interim and final reports. This section should also include the anticipated next steps based on whether the evaluatee is fully successful, partially successful or unsuccessful in his/her efforts to improve.

SAMPLE IMPROVEMENT PLANS

The following pages contain samples of improvement plans that have been used successfully with teachers. In the first two examples, the teacher and administrator reached agreement on the contents of the plan. Both then signed the plan without further comment. In the third example, the teacher and administrator could not reach agreement after several discussions. The administrator wrote the plan and included some of the teacher's ideas that he considered to be appropriate. The teacher was then permitted to make comments related to any areas of disagreement.

In each case, these plans were written after the end-of-year evaluation. Therefore, the evidence that lead to the judgment that improvements were needed in these areas was well established in that evaluation. In the final example, the plan for Karen Sullivan, I included the final evaluation report on which the improvement plan was based. In some cases the improvement plan is included in the final yearly evaluation.

IMPROVEMENT PLAN FOR MARK MCWIRE SAMPLE SCHOOL GRADE 5

1. Areas of Focus

III. Effective Classroom Management

To ensure that the classroom environment is one in which students feel safe and comfortable

To ensure the transition of students back to class from learning center and other activities is smooth and supportive

V. Promotion of High Standards

To ensure the judicious use of high quality, curriculum-related support materials (e.g., movies)

To ensure the communication of high standards in a tone and manner that is perceived by students as positive and supportive

VI. Promotion of Equity and Diversity

To ensure the classroom environment, instructional techniques and management techniques are sensitive to gender differences

VII. Fulfillment of Professional Responsibilities

To constructively initiate interactions with parents and solicit their contributions while being receptive to them

To work with administrators to ensure that the level of parent satisfaction is equivalent to the level that is typical for Sample School teachers

2. Recommendations for Improvement

a. Send a summer letter to students and parents asking parents to write information about their children.

b. Have beginning-of-the year meetings with each child's parents to learn about their child.

c. Have a breakfast or celebration activity focused on the children and invite the parents to attend.

d. Increase the level of constructive communication with parents.

e. Use parents as helpers in art and/or other classroom projects.

f. Look for opportunities early in the year to tell parents about positive things their children are doing.

g. Think about why the majority of concerns are related to girls and if there are changes that must be made in your interactions with girls.

h. Coordinate with Integrated Services (special education teachers, speech therapists, etc.) staff to ensure smooth transitions that are positive for the children.

3. Support Available

a. Principal Bob Martin will meet with you on a weekly or biweekly basis to provide supervision between now and the November meeting. We will determine the frequency of meetings beyond that point at that meeting.

b. Bob will assist Mark in planning regular meetings with service providers.

c. Please let Bob know if there are other supports that would be helpful.

4. Monitoring System

a. Bob will complete at least five formal observations between September and April 30. At least two of these observations will be announced.

b. Bob will make frequent informal visits and observations in and out of the classroom.

c. Jennifer (association representative), Mark and Bob will meet in October, January and April to check the status of the evaluation to that point.

d. Bob will write an evaluation based on all of the performance standards with a focus on the areas noted above.

_____   _____
Principal's signature   date

_____   _____
Teacher's signature   date

Signature signifies receipt of, not concurrence with, this improvement plan.

IMPROVEMENT PLAN FOR SAM MAMOSA

The Sample School

Office of the Principal

MEMORANDUM

DATE: October 7, 1999
TO: Sam Mamosa
FROM: Any Principal
RE: Improvement Plan

1.   Areas for Improvement:

I.   Effective Planning and Assessment of Curriculum and Instruction:

A. The teacher plans instruction effectively.

• Sam needs to make sure that there is one focused learning goal for the class period and that he tailors the instruction to the wide variety of students and abilities present in his class.

• Sam must leave appropriate, complete and clear lesson plans when he will be out of school. He must not rely on phone conversations with the sub or faxed plans.

B. The teacher plans assessment of student learning effectively. Assessment:

• Sam needs to make his expectations clear to the class and outline how the students are to meet those expectations. He must also discern, throughout the class, whether student learning is occurring. At the end of class, Sam must summarize the lesson and assess if the students have met his expectations.

C. The teacher monitors students' understanding of the curriculum and effectively adjusts instruction, materials or assessments when appropriate.

• Sam needs to make sure that all students are engaged in the activity for the day and that this is focused work, not copious idle conversation.

II.   Effective Management of Classroom Environment:

• Sam needs to check regularly that all students are working on the lesson for the day—not just discussing social issues.

• Sam needs to have an introduction, lesson and concluding activity for all classes.

• For behavioral problems, Sam is to deal with the students in the class, and, if he sends students to the office, he is to notify the office of the problem and indicate what he has done and what parental contact he expects to make after class.

III. Effective Instruction:

- Sam must plan his class with an introduction, lesson for the day and then concluding questions or a summary that refocuses his students on the purpose for the lesson. The end of the class must be more than just clean-up before the children leave the class.

IV. Promotion of Equity and Appreciation of Diversity:

- Sam must have consistent expectations of all students.

V. Fulfillment of Professional Responsibilities:

A. The teacher constructively initiates interactions with parents and solicits and is receptive to their contributions.

Communication:

- Sam needs to continue his efforts to speak directly to parents when there is a behavioral problem in his class. Direct contact with the parents will ensure an effective resolution to the problem.
- Sam must work to develop a better relationship with the Arts Council. It is problematic to have two art programs functioning in the school. In addition, the Arts Council might be a source of funding when internal funds are limited.

B. Attendance

- Sam must continue the good attendance pattern that he established after his surgery last year. This year's evaluation will focus on the areas noted above, but will assess all seven of the principles of effective teaching.

2. Supports available:

- The art curriculum coordinator is available to provide support upon request.
- The principal and coordinator will help arrange for instructional strategies to be discussed with colleagues in other schools in Brookline.
- Sam is engaged in a master's program at Northeastern University; resources should also be available there.
- I am available for any discussions that will support this process.

3. Monitoring System:

At least one announced observation with appropriate pre-meeting and feedback will occur during the year. At least one unannounced observation will be completed during the year.

Joint observations scheduled (Coordinator and me):

11/18/99   3/3/00

1/13/00   3/5/00 visit same class

_____   _____
Signature of evaluator   date

_____   _____
Signature of teacher   date

Signature signifies receipt of, not concurrence with, this improvement plan.

IMPROVEMENT PLAN FOR JAMES MORGAN AUGUST 1999, SAMPLE SCHOOL

The following document sets forth a plan to support James Morgan in his efforts to address the recommendations made based on my observations and the discussions we had on April 28, 1999 and June 3, 1999. This plan will be implemented during the 1999–2000 academic year.

1.   Areas for Improvement and Related Recommendations

The primary goal is to better integrate the principles of effective teaching (district performance standards) more explicitly into daily practice. The following identifies several specific areas for improvement. The 1999–2000 evaluation will focus on these areas, but will also assess all the principles of effective teaching.

I.   Currency in the Curriculum

To organize and teach the 7/8 mathematics curriculum so it follows a sequence consistent with the district's 7/8 math curriculum and the district's learning expectations for grades 7/8.

II.   Effective Planning, Delivery and Assessment of Curriculum and Instruction

a.   To begin each class with an itinerary of the day's activities and make reference to it as activities change from one to another

b.   To explicitly state the goals or objectives with students for units or lessons studied

c.   To explicitly connect work from the previous day or previous learning to work that will take place that day

d. To spend the end of each class summarizing what has been taught and to foreshadow next steps to come

e. To develop clearer, more comprehensive handouts and other supportive materials which enhance lessons and describe projects or other major assignments

f. To consistently utilize a broad variety of active learning strategies and to incorporate an array of resources and materials in daily instruction to meet the needs of a diverse and heterogeneously grouped student body

g. To work collaboratively with the computer teacher on integrating computer technology into daily practice to enhance student understanding of mathematical concepts and their applications

III. Effective Management of Classroom Environment

a. To fine tune daily classroom management routines to more smoothly transition from activity to activity and to capture students' attention more readily to focus on the learning task at hand

b. To widen the repertoire of behavior management strategies used to better contain students who are unfocused, distractible, chatty or disruptive and thereby help them to learn more successfully

IV. Promotion of High Standards and Expectations for Students' Achievement

To recognize, understand and work more effectively with those students who have a history of lower math achievement or for whom math presents a particular challenge

VII. Fulfillment of Professional Responsibilities

To voluntarily assume at least two additional duties which support the extra-curricular activities of the 7/8 team, such as managing the finances of a fund-raiser for the class trip

In early September, a meeting will take place with the director of personnel, principal, math coordinator, teachers' association representative and James to review and revise this improvement plan.

2. Supports Available to the Evaluatee

To assist James in improving the above-stated areas, the Sample Public Schools is prepared to provide him with a mentor who will work with him on a monthly basis throughout the school year. It will also pay for him to attend the Research for Better Teaching class Understanding Teaching. Alternative or additional supports may be discussed at the September meeting.

3. The Monitoring System

James will be supervised and evaluated by the principal with contributions from the math coordinator for grades 5–8. Both announced and unannounced observations will take place. At least three announced observations will occur between September and January, 2000, all dates to be mutually agreed upon. The first will occur in late September and will be done by the principal. A second announced observation will be conducted in November by the math coordinator, who is scheduled to be at Sample School for that month. In November or December, both the principal and the math coordinator will do a joint, announced observation.

In addition, throughout the September to December period, the principal and the math coordinator each will do at least one unannounced observation. A meeting will take place at the end of November between the principal, math coordinator, mentor and James to discuss progress to date. This will be followed by a meeting in January between the director of personnel, principal, math coordinator, union representative and James to check James's progress, to determine next steps and to set a monitoring schedule for the remainder of the year. The evaluation will be written and submitted by April 30, 2000, and will include a summative assessment of the areas for improvement and the other performance standards.

_____   _____
Signature of evaluator   date

_____   _____
Signature of teacher   date

Signature signifies receipt of, not concurrence with, this improvement plan.

SAMPLE OF A TEACHER WITH MORE THAN 20 YEARS OF EXPERIENCE

Annual Report of Teacher Effectiveness

Teacher: Karen Sullivan
School: Sample
Grade/subject: Reading–Writing Specialist

I.   Currency of Curriculum
II. Effective Planning and Assessment of Curriculum and Instruction
III. Effective Management of Classroom Environment
IV. Effective Instruction
V.   Promotion of High Standards and Expectations for Students' Achievement

VI. Promotion of Equity and Appreciation of Diversity

VII. Fulfillment of Professional Responsibilities

Karen Sullivan has been teaching for a number of years in the Sample Public Schools, in varying capacities. For the past several years at Sample, Karen was responsible for a tutorial and after-school homework program. This seemed to have started out strongly at the time when it was located in one of the public housing communities where many Sample children live.

Over time, however, the program moved back into the Sample building and became less effective, with fewer and fewer children in attendance. In spite of repeated efforts to hold her accountable to a schedule, a procedure for keeping records and attendance, for tracking students' school performance, and for maintaining contact with parents, Karen was not able to develop and stick to a well-articulated plan. Last year, she submitted no attendance reports. While Karen was kind and caring to her students, they knew there was no accountability, and the program lost its impact.

As a result, other homework programs sprang up around the building. Attendance in these programs grew, and it became clear that we would need to identify another role for Karen. In addition, it was obviously not cost-effective to pay a teacher to staff a program that would function very well in the hands of instructional aides. With the retirement of longtime reading specialist Susan Miller, Karen took on responsibility for delivering a reading program to children in grades four through six at Sample and Washington Schools. Karen accepted this in good spirit and with a commitment to do her best.

I.   Currency of Curriculum

In order to prepare Karen for this new job, the language arts coordinator located an excellent summer course at Lesley College to refresh Karen's knowledge of diagnostic and pedagogical techniques for readers in the middle elementary grades. In addition, the language arts coordinator provided some days for Karen to observe and learn from a seasoned reading teacher in another building, had her attend workshops and made herself available for on-site mentoring. Nonetheless, the program has not met our expectations.

Teachers report that Karen is often late for her scheduled meetings with reading groups or misses them altogether. One described the program this way: "It's happening, but it's not dependable or productive. Kids never know whether they'll see her or not, so it undermines their commitment to keep up with their reading."

Teachers at Washington have reported to the principal that the same pattern of lateness and missed appointments has occurred there too. In addition, some of the teachers have had persistent difficulty in arranging a regular schedule with Karen.

It was noteworthy during a reading group observed in February that Karen did not once refer to a student by name. Since there were only four children in the group, it should have been possible to learn and use their names right away, even if this had been the very first time the group met.

The lesson consisted of a preview of Lois Lowry's *The Giver*. By and large, the time was spent having students look at the book's cover and make some predictions, then take turns reading aloud and answer brief questions. While each of these techniques may have merit, in this case the group—which consisted of very bright, motivated children—was lackluster and unenthusiastic. After five minutes of rather aimless discussion, a student was asked, "And what do you think?" She responded, "Well, it's hard to know what you think when you haven't even read the first sentence of the book." Once students began reading, Karen's questions were mostly along the lines of, "How do you feel about this?" or "What do you think about this community?"— questions to which students would likely have far more substantive answers once they'd read a significant part of the text.

II. Effective Planning and Assessment of Curriculum and Instruction and V. Promotion of High Standards and Expectations for Students' Achievement

A couple of weeks before the unit on *The Giver* got underway, the classroom teacher approached me with grave reservations about having Karen teach this beautiful and complex work. The teacher reported that she had been completely frustrated trying to work with Karen, who, as she saw it, took no initiative and showed no evidence of planning. She noted that in one case it was clear that Karen had not even read the book ahead of time.

This teacher told Karen that she wanted her to plan a unit on *The Giver,* but she noted that when Karen showed her the unit plan, it was all work that had been done by her predecessor, Ms. Miller.

For her part, Karen reported being treated disrespectfully by this teacher. She resented being asked to show lesson plans and said that the teacher had resorted to asking her to do busywork, such as copying and laminating. When I spoke to the teacher about this, she acknowledged that these allegations were true, but that she had reached a point of desperation. She felt she could not send her struggling readers to Karen and added that some teachers had begun refusing to send their students to her at all.

I have not been successful in mediating a rapprochement between Karen and this teacher. Unfortunately, the classroom teacher is not alone in finding the reading program wanting. Some teachers have been pleased to have Karen in their classrooms, finding her "helpful" and "cooperative," but they are unanimous in their conviction that a diagnostic, prescriptive program with solid planning, ongoing assessment and well-monitored progress is unavailable to their students.

Teachers at Washington have reported to the principal that they share similar frustration. While she has been helpful with individual students and specific books, there is a perception that she cannot be consistently counted on to deliver an effectively planned program.

III. Effective Management of Classroom Environment

Karen maintains a calm, pleasant classroom. Students are clearly at ease with her and know they will be treated kindly.

The physical environment leaves much to be desired. No student work is on display. Books—the tools of the trade for a reading teacher—are piled untidily here and there, not displayed or stored with care. The one poster on the wall during a March visit is of autumn leaves.

To be fair, Karen shares this space with the grades 3/4 homework center. Still, there is no evident pride in maintaining a bright, inviting space in which to welcome students.

IV. Effective Instruction

One of the most important functions of a reading specialist is conducting diagnostic tests. Given the centrality of reading skills to the success of students in the upper grades, the only means to effective instruction is good, ongoing assessment.

Since this was a new role for Karen, we tried to keep testing demands light in this first year. In late October, however, we received a request from the parent of a fifth grader to test his son in reading. He felt the child was not picking up on the main ideas of things he read, and he was even more deeply worried about higher-level comprehension and inferential skills. For this parent, the matter of getting this testing done and a plan in place was of particular urgency; he is dying of cancer and feels a deep responsibility to attend to his sons' needs and ensure that they will be met in the future.

By mid January, Karen had not yet begun testing this child, although the language arts coordinator had provided specific training in the instrument she needed to use. The father was desperate and angry. Finally, the language arts coordinator tested the child herself and met with the father to review her findings.

The Washington principal reports that in his conversations with Karen she has expressed that diagnostic testing is new to her and that she has found it quite challenging. The principal reports that he is appreciative of her efforts to master the testing but feels he must join with me (Sample School principal) in noting the importance and centrality of diagnostic testing in the reading specialist's role. He further states that it is imperative that she immediately focus on this task and commit all of her personal resources to mastering it.

VI. Promotion of Equity and Appreciation of Diversity

There is no question that Karen cares deeply about children and wants them to succeed. Her work in former years with some of Sample's most economically disadvantaged children is evidence of her belief in the right of every child to equal opportunity through an excellent education.

VII. Fulfillment of Professional Responsibilities

It seems evident that this has not been a happy year for Karen. She knows that many of her colleagues in both buildings are unhappy with her work. The fact that she is often late for school or misses scheduled meeting times with groups or individual children suggests that she has trouble sustaining enthusiasm for the job. It must be very difficult for such a warm, caring person to sense that her performance has been disappointing to people who have been friends and colleagues for many years.

I am deeply concerned that we find a way to break this cycle. The Washington principal and I therefore offer the following recommendations:

- a clearly articulated job description, with well-defined procedures for accountability
- the development of an improvement plan
- a year of intensified support with an evaluation out-of-cycle
- the identification of coursework that will have a direct impact on job effectiveness

_____ This evaluation indicates performance above district standard.

_____ This evaluation indicates performance that meets the district standard

__**X**__ This evaluation indicates performance which is below the standard expected of staff in the Sample Public Schools.

Overall Evaluation: _____ Satisfactory   __**X**__ Unsatisfactory

_____   _____
Signature of evaluator   date

_____   _____
Signature of teacher   date

Signature indicates receipt of, not concurrence with, this evaluation. Teachers Are Encouraged To Submit Comments. (Please make comments on the back of this form or on an attached sheet.)

IMPROVEMENT PLAN FOR KAREN SULLIVAN

Reading–Writing Specialist
1999–2000 School Year

1. **Areas for Improvement and Recommendations**

I. **Currency in the Curriculum (Performance Standard I)**

    In order to effectively plan for, teach and assess student learning, Karen will be familiar with and understand the language arts learning expectations for the specific grade levels of her students.

II. **Effective Planning and Assessment of Curriculum and Instruction Performance Standard II)**

    Karen will provide evidence of planning and preparation for her work with students in small groups and on a one-to-one basis. She will meet with the students' classroom teachers to assess students' needs, plan appropriate materials and plan a focus of instruction. Evidence of this preparation will be documented in her plan book and will indicate that she has:

    - read student books before meeting with her groups
    - outlined objectives for teaching the books, indicating what the students will understand during and after reading
    - developed specific instructional plans for each reading class that address the objectives
    - completed plans for the subsequent week before the start of school on Monday

IV. **Effective Instruction (Performance Standard IV)**

    1. Karen will provide instruction to reteach or reinforce literacy strategies for her students. Strategies will be based on the Learning Expectations for the grade levels of her students. The focus of instructional strategies will be on word knowledge, comprehension and response to literature and writing. Lessons will be developed to meet the specific needs of her students. For example, students who have limited word recognition skills will be provided with direct instruction in structural analysis of words followed by multiple opportunities to practice the skills taught in meaningful text. Students with difficulty in comprehending text will be given graphic organizers to identify important information and will use this information to provide an oral or written summary. Specific instructional interventions and support may include:

        • modeling and demonstration of strategies
        • teacher read-alouds before students read

- preteaching vocabulary
- making predictions and asking questions before reading
- opportunities for students to reread portions of text
- a variety of questions to enhance student understanding
- partially completed graphic organizers
- story frames to support summarization

2. Karen will assess student achievement and progress using specific performance samples based on instruction as well as the Qualitative Reading Inventory. Results of all assessments will be shared with the classroom teacher and, when requested, with the students' parents.

VII. Fulfillment of Professional Responsibilities (Performance Standard VII)

As a reading–writing specialist, Karen has specific responsibilities to students, teachers and parents. This role requires that she

1. develop a schedule during the first month of school and provide the schedule to classroom teachers, the school principal and the language arts coordinator no later than October 15. This schedule will include regular times to meet with the classroom teachers of her students;

2. assesses the literacy skills of low-performing readers and writers recommended for work with her on a pull-out basis. Assessments will be administered at the beginning of the year by October 15 and at the end of the school year by June 1;

3. arrives on time for her small group work with students both in and out of the classroom;

4. attends the monthly meetings of the reading–writing specialists with the language arts coordinator;

5. communicates effectively with parents on the progress of their children (e.g., parent conferences, telephone calls, written progress reports);

6. reviews standardized test results to identify students at risk or in need of extra help.

The focus of this improvement plan is on sections I, II, IV and VII of the performance standards for the Sample Public Schools, however, Karen's evaluations will address and assess her abilities related to all of the performance standards.

II. Support Available

A. The language arts coordinator will meet individually with Karen monthly in the fall and as requested by Karen in the spring to assist her in developing and implementing her program. The meetings will focus on

1. assessing student achievement using the QRI. Karen received one hour of training for this assessment with the other reading–writing specialists in the fall of 1998. Additional training will be provided to Karen and will include demonstrations by the language arts coordinator with several of her students;

2. creating a schedule for work with students and teachers;

3. developing instructional strategies to enhance students' literacy learning;

4. using specific materials to support instructional strategies;

5. discussing the progress of her program;

6. creating a record-keeping system or working with another teacher to develop a record-keeping system.

III. Monitoring System

A. Karen will be observed at least three times by the language arts coordinator and at least twice by the principal during the 1999–2000 school year. At least two of these observations will be announced and at least two of these observations will take place prior to January 1, 2000.

B. Additionally, meetings involving the principal, assistant superintendent for personnel, language arts coordinator, association representative and Karen will be held in October, January and April to assess and discuss Karen's progress.

_____   _____
Signature of evaluator   date

_____   _____
Signature of principal   date

Signature signifies receipt of, not concurrence with, this improvement plan.

Open Book Assessment on Improvement Plans

Define the four major areas of an improvement plan, which are listed below, and explain why each area is an integral part of an improvement plan.

1. Areas for improvement

_____

_____

_____

_____

2. Recommendations for improving these areas

_____

_____

_____

_____

3. Supports available to the evaluatee

_____

_____

_____

_____

4. Monitoring system

_____

_____

_____

_____

SOURCES

American Federation of Teachers and the National Education Association. (1998). *Peer assistance & peer review: An AFT/NEA handbook.* Washington, D. C.

Bridges, E. (1992). *The incompetent teacher: Managerial responses* (2nd ed.). Washington, D. C.: The Falmer Press.

Briggs v. Board of Directors of Hinton Community School District, 282 N.W.2d 740, 743 (Iowa 1979).

Dopazo, J. & Ribas, W. Legal material written specifically for this book.

Finnegan, S. (2000). *MGL 2000: Selected Massachusetts general laws for school committees and personnel.* Boston, MA: Massachusetts Association of School Committees Inc.

Fraser, R. G. (1996, August 18). Untitled handout given at the workshop, *Supervising the marginal teacher,* given by the Massachusetts Association of School Personnel Administrators.

Garner, B. A. (Ed.). (1999). *Black's law dictionary* (7th ed.). St. Paul, MN: West Group.

Levasseur, D. & Ribas, W. Material written on duty of fair representation specifically for this book.

Liacos, P. (1999). *The Massachusetts handbook on evidence* (6th ed.). NY: Aspen Publishers, Inc.

Needham Education Association and Needham School Committee (Needham, Massachusetts). American Arbitration Association case no. 1139–2023–83 (July 30, 1984).

Platt, A., Tripp, C., Ogden, W. & Fraser, R. (2000). *The skillful leader confronting mediocre teaching.* Acton, MA: Ready About Press.

Chapter 6

PROGRESSIVE DISCIPLINE

WHAT IS PROGRESSIVE DISCIPLINE?

The philosophy of formative supervision is one that calls for a cooperative and collegial working relationship. You will recall from chapter 1 that we defined the formative supervision and evaluation process as a positive, supportive and collaborative process designed to improve students' performance and attitudes by increasing the effectiveness and attitudes of a district's teachers.

In addition, much of a school's culture and the norms which motivate staff are predicated on the good will built up between supervisors and the 95% to 98% of the staff members who perform in the satisfactory range as they work together on a day-to-day basis in a mostly formative and collegial manner. It often presents a dilemma for school supervisors when they are faced with a situation that warrants disciplinary action toward a staff member. The definition of discipline, "punishment intended to train or correct" (Soukhanov, 1988) indicates actions which are opposite of the steps supervisors take when developing a school culture based on formative interactions and collegial relationships.

Progressive discipline is the legal and contractual concept that guides employee supervision and evaluation. Most arbitrators, courts and the just cause legal standard for due process require that a public employer follow a pattern of progressive discipline in order to sustain a disciplinary action. The word "discipline" in this term often raises discomfort because it sounds more punitive than corrective. However, progressive discipline is the universally accepted term naming the procedure for situations requiring corrective action by a supervisor. Most important, progressive discipline is a consistent and fair way to treat the people you supervise. We should always remind ourselves that discipline as we use it with staff is intended *to correct*, not to punish, despite the definition of the word in the dictionary. Even the most extreme measure of dismissal is primarily intended to remove the offender from the school house to ensure the well being of others rather than to punish the offender.

Steps in Progressive Discipline

Progressive discipline is a process that works within and parallel to a district's supervision and evaluation processes. Typically, progressive discipline has four steps: verbal warning (or reprimand), written reprimand and warning, suspension without pay (or with pay during investigation) and final warning and discharge. However, I always recommend to supervisors a preliminary step, corrective recommendation, in most situations in which the supervisor feels he/she needs to correct a behavior. A **corrective recommendation** is a private, informal conversation with a staff member about a behavior in question. The staff member should have an opportunity to explain his/her perspective on the behavior. After the discussion, the supervisor should write a brief note to his/her own file indicating date, time and substance of the conversation. Many supervisors keep track of these discussions by writing brief notes on the bottom of their appointment calendars and keeping the calendars from year to year, in case there is a need to refer to the date of earlier discussions. In most cases, they will never need to refer to these notes. However, if at some future point they need to move to a higher level of the progressive discipline process, the notes will be important in jogging the supervisor's memory and/or as evidence that the conversation actually took place.

> Much of a school's culture and the norms which motivate staff are predicated on the goodwill built up between supervisors and the 95% to 98% of the staff members who perform in the satisfactory range as they work together on a day-to-day basis in a mostly formative and collegial manner. It often presents a dilemma for school supervisors when they are faced with a situation that warrants disciplinary action toward a staff member.

The next step should be a **verbal warning (or reprimand).** This kind of warning details the nature of the infraction or the failure to meet an expectation and includes a statement saying that if the same infraction or concern (e.g., yelling at student, arriving at the classroom or work area after the assigned time) occurs again, more serious disciplinary action will result. This should be done at a place and time that allows for adequate opportunity for the employee to give his/her side of the incident in a private area in order to protect the employee's confidentiality. The employee has the right, known as the Weingarten right (see the explanation of the Weingarten right in chapter 5 on page 124), to ask that the discussion be postponed until the employee has representation. The subject matter of the conversation and the fact that a verbal warning has been given should always be documented in the form of a memorandum to the employee. The administrator should ask the employee to initial and return a copy. The decision of whether the copy is placed in the administrator's own file as a memory aide or placed in the personnel file is one the district-level administration should make and ensure it is carried out in a consistent manner by all supervisors. A sample of a memo sent after a verbal warning may be found later in this chapter on page 176.

The next step in the progression is a **written reprimand and warning.** The specific incident or concern is reduced to writing and presented to the employee with the clear understanding that a copy will be placed in the employee's personnel file. The written reprimand and warning should also contain a statement of what the consequences will be if there is a repetition of this or any other disciplinary incident or problem. Many districts require building-level administrators to consult with a member of the central administration prior to issuing a written reprimand and warning. This is done to ensure that there is a common administrative application of these reprimands across the district. It is suggested the written warning be given after a meeting in which the employee has an opportunity to respond to the concern. A copy of the reprimand and warning, signed or initialed by the employee, should be placed in the personnel file at the personnel office. Samples of written reprimands may be found later in this chapter on pages 175 and 178–179.

> At each stage, the supervisor should conduct *a fair and impartial investigation to establish the facts of the case.*

The next step is **suspension without pay (or suspension with pay during investigation)** and **a final written warning** stating that another incident or problem will result in discharge. This step should only be taken by the building principal after consultation with the superintendent or the superintendent's designee. If the principal cannot be reached by the administrator wishing to issue the verbal warning, the administrator should consult directly with the superintendent or the superintendent's designee. When possible, the staff member should be notified in person of the suspension and warning, then sent a written confirmation of the details of the discussion. A copy of the written confirmation, signed or initialed by the employee, should be placed in the employee's official personnel file.

The final step is **discharge.**

At each stage, the supervisor should conduct a fair and impartial investigation to establish the facts of the case. The staff member's employment record should be reviewed, and the handling of other similar cases by this and other supervisors should be considered. It is only after the investigation is completed that official disciplinary action should be taken. At times, the investigation will show clear misbehavior on the part of the employee. At other times, the investigation will completely exonerate the employee. A third possibility is that the investigation will lead to conflicting evidence and no clear determination. For these types of cases, the administrator should write a memo documenting the alleged incident and the fact that a clear finding could not be reached. An example of this type of memo may be found later in this chapter on pages 180–181.

The Exceptional Situation

Not all problems with employees require each step of progressive discipline. Some incidents may be so serious in and of themselves that they justify moving immediately to one of the higher steps or even to discharge. For example, a staff member charged with an assault or other crime directly related to his/her job may be suspended and even, in some cases, discharged before the matter is resolved in the criminal justice system or in arbitration. (The structure of this explanation and some of the content is based on a handout given by Robert Fraser, 1996.)

KNOWING HOW TO USE PROGRESSIVE DISCIPLINE IS OFTEN EASIER THAN ACTUALLY DOING IT

Educators typically have had much more practice and training in the area of student discipline than in the area of staff discipline. This leads to a higher comfort level and experience level with student discipline than with staff discipline. Staff discipline raises an entirely new set of emotions and legal issues. Delgado's work (see page 28 in chapter 2) will help the reader better understand the emotional pitfalls. A review of the legal standards (see chapter 5) will help the evaluator better understand the legal standards and processes. A good way to understand your own *emotional* reaction to staff discipline is to try the following activity.

Completing the following "word splash" will help you to free-associate your initial emotional responses to the concept of staff discipline. It will also give you an opportunity to begin to assess what you know and what you want to know about progressive discipline. To start, close your eyes and think of a time you or someone else had to discipline a teacher. Think of yourself as the disciplinarian. Below the directions, write emotions, questions or comments that come to your mind. Do this activity before moving on in this chapter.

Word Splash

List all the emotions, questions and comments that come to your mind when you think of yourself as being the administrator in a staff discipline case.

_____

_____

_____

_____

_____

DOCUMENTING YOUR PROGRESSIVE DISCIPLINE ACTIONS

The next section presents a description of the components of a memo summarizing an oral warning/reprimand and of a written reprimand. You will note that the differences in the actual documents are minor. However, the *legal* distinction is vast. When a written reprimand is given, the disciplinary action is now proceeding through the required progressive steps, and getting closer to the final resolution of discharge.

The list of components is followed by actual oral reprimands/warnings and written reprimands used in real cases. The last sample, that of Bill Murphy, is neither a reprimand nor a warning. It is documentation of the claim, investigation and the administrator's clarification of the expectation when the administrator could not find direct evidence or a sufficient accumulation of indirect evidence to determine whether or not the infraction did indeed take place.

In the sample reprimands/warnings, the names of the administrators, teachers and schools have been changed to protect confidentiality.

COMPONENTS OF A WRITTEN REPRIMAND
(AND MEMO FOLLOWING AN ORAL REPRIMAND)

The components of a written reprimand and the components of a memo that follows an oral reprimand are very similar. Please note that, for those items where there are differences between the two, the wording for the oral reprimand has been written in parentheses below the language for the written reprimand.

1. The reprimand should state specific facts, such as date, place, witnesses to (or other data) and inappropriate actions of the individual(s).

2. The reprimand should identify the performance standard, policy, contract provision, law, appropriate practice or directive violated or breached.

3. The reprimand should outline all previous corrective recommendations, reprimands or warnings, if any.

4. Avoid making assumptions or using hearsay evidence from a single source. Let the direct data or accumulation of indirect data prove the case.

5. The reprimand should state that this letter constitutes a written reprimand and that it will be placed in the employee's personnel file.

    (*Oral:* The memo should state that this memo is to confirm the oral reprimand given on...)

6. It should state that if there is not sufficient improvement and/or a repeat of the inappropriate behavior the staff member will be subject to further disciplinary action. In some circumstances, it is important to also include the outer extent of the disciplinary action (e.g., including dismissal).

    (*Oral:* It should state that if there is not sufficient improvement and/or if there is a repeat of the inappropriate behavior the staff member will be subject to further disciplinary action.)

7. Give the staff member two copies of the letter and ask that one be signed and returned to you. Indicate in the signature area that the signature signifies receipt of, not concurrence with the letter.

8. Forward a copy of the signed letter to the personnel office to be included in the staff member's file. If he/she refuses to sign it, indicate the date and time you delivered the letter and the staff member's refusal on a copy of the letter and send it to the personnel office.

    (*Oral:* If he/she refuses to sign, indicate the date and time you delivered the memo and the staff member's refusal on a copy of the letter and keep the copy in your file).

PEER CONFERENCING TO HELP YOUR PEERS WITH MEMOS AFTER ORAL REPRIMANDS AND/OR WRITTEN REPRIMANDS

1. Start with an area in the memo that is done well. Be sure to be specific about what is done well and give evidence to support your opinion.
    *   Don't say, "This is really good."
    *   Do say, "You clearly stated the date, place, time and location of the incident."

2. Has the administrator *met with the staff member* and reviewed everything that is stated in the document *in person* prior to writing and delivering the memo?

3. Does the document contain all the items in numbers 1–6 of the Components of a Written Reprimand? If not, help the writer identify what is in his/her document and what is not.

4. Is there a way the writer might revise the document to describe the items in 1–6 of the Components of a Written Reprimand in a way that is more concise, concrete, observable, verifiable or understandable? If so, give a suggestion as to how the writer might do this better.

5. Does the level of disciplinary action taken match the transgression? (Does the "penalty fit the crime"?)

6. Do you, as the reader, have any questions about the content or the intent of the written document? If so, what questions do you have?

STUDY GUIDE ON PROGRESSIVE DISCIPLINE

1. Why do we use the term "progressive discipline" rather than a term that sounds less threatening and more supportive?

2. The process of progressive discipline is widely understood and used by courts, arbitrators and other judiciary boards to make decisions about employee discipline. However, formal progressive discipline procedures with documentation are rarely used by most school administrators. What are the barriers that keep school administrators from using formal progressive discipline?

3. What are the four formal steps of progressive discipline used in legal circles? Is a corrective recommendation one of the formal, legal steps? If not, why is it discussed with progressive discipline and recommended for school administrators?

4. What are the components of a well-written memo summarizing an oral reprimand? What are the components of a written reprimand?

5. Explain the legal standards of *just cause, Weingarten right* and *harassment.*

6. Explain the legal standards of *insubordination* and *conduct unbecoming a teacher.*

SAMPLE HIGH SCHOOL
SCIENCE DEPARTMENT

To: Ms. Mortimer   From: Mr. Department Chair

Re: Verbal warning   Date: January 29, 2000

This memo is to confirm that on Friday, January 26, 2000, I gave you a verbal warning regarding the incident that occurred on the previous Wednesday, January 24, 2000, involving the student Margaret Herrera. The warning was for your insensitive treatment of Margaret. At a time when she was visibly upset (by the account of three adults who were present), and she was in a conversation with an adult, you interrupted and escalated the situation without adequately hearing Margaret's side or hearing from the adult.

As a background to this warning, I made reference to a meeting you and the principal had on November 13, 1999. In that meeting, he referred to two incidents this year involving confrontations between you and students outside of the classroom. His characterization to you at that time was that your manner of handling these incidents tended to "intimidate rather than educate."

Please be aware that further occurrences of this kind will lead to more serious disciplinary action.

Please sign this memo below and return to me. Your signature acknowledges receipt of the verbal warning, not agreement with it. You should feel free to meet with me again to discuss the warning; you may also include whatever comments you wish on the back of this memo.

_____   _____
Mr. Department Chair   date

_____   _____
Ms. Mortimer   date

ANYWHERE PUBLIC SCHOOL
MEMORANDUM

March 12, 2000

To: Joan Doe
From: Mary Principal
Re: Written Reprimand

As I stated in our meeting on March 9, I am giving you this written reprimand for your lack of participation in the "hoe down" on March 7, 2000. Throughout this event you sat in the back of the gym while your fourth grade colleagues assisted the children with the dancing and even participated in the dancing themselves. Your lack of participation increased the burden on the other fourth grade teachers and was a negative example for the children. This event was part of our school-wide theme on the Regions of the United States, a collaborative effort with the parents (performance standards I and VII). On at least six other occasions we discussed that you have a poor reputation with the parent community (as evidenced by the negative letters from parents that I shared with you) and I have directed you to seek opportunities to enhance your reputation with parents. Your failure to assist and participate in this event, with parents attending, is inconsistent with my directive.

I will remind you that on March 1 you did not participate when the Anywhere Square Dance group visited the school. This event was also arranged and attended by the parent coordinators as part of our school-wide theme. At that time you received an oral reprimand from me for your lack of participation. Please be aware that a failure to follow my directives in the future will lead to further disciplinary action.

Please feel free to make an appointment to discuss this further or comment below. Please sign one copy of this memo and return it to me by March 19, 2000. Your signature signifies receipt of, and not concurrence with, this memo.

_____   _____
         Ms. Joan Doe   Ms. Mary Principal

cc Ms. Joan Doe
     Ms. Mary Principal
     Ms. Doe's personnel file

Progressive Discipline and Evaluation

Progressive discipline is primarily a supervisory process. Most instances occur without a direct connection to the teacher's summative evaluation. There are cases, however, in which there is a direct connection to the teacher's evaluation. The following examples of an oral reprimand and a written reprimand are a direct extension of the teachers' evaluation during the previous year.

In this example, the teacher was given a low evaluation and recommended for a second consecutive year of summative evaluation. During the period of time after the completion of the first year's evaluation and before the writing of the second evaluation, the teacher continued to fail to complete reports and other paperwork that were past due. The evaluator moved directly into progressive discipline as a formal written process for addressing the problem, since action could not wait until the following evaluation year was completed.

The Sample School

Office of the Principal

Memorandum

Date: September 23, 2000
To: Ms. Sped Teacher
From: Ms. Principal
Re: Verbal Reprimand

This memo is to confirm that on Wednesday, September 22, 2000, I gave you a verbal reprimand regarding your failure to submit thirty-five overdue IEP reports after repeated requests.

As a background to this reprimand, I made reference to a number of meetings and conversations that we had had regarding this issue.

On April 29, 2000, during a discussion of your final evaluation report, I inquired about the status of your overdue reports and offered assistance in the form of substitute coverage to enable you to complete them. I did provide coverage on more than one occasion, but never received any reports.

On the last day of school, I asked about the status of these reports and told you I needed them by the close of school that day. I neither received the reports nor an explanation from you.

On Tuesday, June 29, I called and asked you for the reports, citing that they were long overdue. You told me you were planning to bring them in on Thursday or Friday of that same week. You never came or called.

On August 31, I again asked for the reports and told you I needed them within forty-eight hours. When I asked for the reports the

---

memo continues

following week, you told me you were working on them but hadn't completed any.

On a memo dated September 7, the special education coordinator cited that you had forty overdue reports that needed to be submitted immediately. During the week of September 13, I provided daily substitute coverage so you could work on these reports. At the end of the week, you had completed five reports, leaving thirty-five incomplete.

On September 17, I asked if you could have ten reports completed by Tuesday, September 21 (long weekend). You said you thought that was reasonable and doable.

On Tuesday, when I came for the reports, you told me that you hadn't completed any of them, because you had things to do over the weekend. You indicated that you needed to work on the reports in school. I explained that these reports were many months overdue and that you had had the summer to complete them. I said that we needed to meet on the following day and would provide substitute coverage.

At our meeting, with the special education coordinator in attendance, you acknowledged that these reports were seriously overdue and that I had asked you on many occasions for them. You explained that your need for additional sleep and family responsibilities make it difficult for you to do work at home.

In addition to agreeing to a schedule for providing these reports, I explained that I would be doing an out-of-cycle evaluation because of your failure to meet Sample District Performance Standards II and VII.

The schedule we agreed to for submitting the thirty-five reports is as follows: On Monday, September 27, you will provided twelve totally completed reports. The following Monday, October 4, you will provide another twelve totally completed reports. The remaining eleven reports will be submitted no later than Tuesday, October 12. (Monday is a holiday.)

Please be aware that failure to comply with any part of this schedule will lead to more serious disciplinary action.

Please sign this memo below and return to it to me by October 5, 2000. Your signature acknowledges receipt of the verbal warning, not agreement with it. You should feel free to meet with me again to discuss the warning. You may also include whatever comments you wish on the back of this memo.

Ms. Principal	date

Ms. Sped Teacher	date

SAMPLE HIGH SCHOOL

October 22, 2000

To: Ms. Sped Teacher
From: Ms. Principal
Re: Written Reprimand

As I stated in our meeting on Tuesday, October 19, 2000, I am giving you this written reprimand for your failure to submit the overdue IEPs and reports that I have requested on at least six different occasions. On Wednesday, September 22, 2000, I gave you a verbal warning regarding your failure, after repeated requests, to submit thirty-five overdue IEPs and reports. The background to this warning, with documented occasions when requests were made for these documents, was included in a subsequent memo that you signed and returned to me on September 26, 2000.

In our discussion on September 22, 2000, you agreed to submit ten completed reports on Monday, September 27, ten completed reports on Monday, October 4, and five completed reports on Tuesday, October 12. As I explained at our meeting on October 19, 2000, you have not appropriately completed all of the IEPs and reports. There are still seven reports that either were not submitted or that have been returned because they were incomplete.

Your professional responsibilities to communicate with parents and colleagues in a timely fashion and to meet mandated state and district deadlines for submitting paperwork are contained in the Principles of Effective Teaching II and VII.

Please be aware that your failure to comply with the following schedule for the submission of overdue paperwork will result in further disciplinary action.

memo continues

Due: Monday, October 25, 2000		Due: Monday, November 1, 2000	
J. H	(review for 3/00–6/00)	M. L	(re-eval 1/00–6/00)
A. G	(IEP)	Ja L	(IEP)
G. L	(progress reports)	B. L	(testing report)
J. L	(IEP)	R. M-Scott	(progress reports)
F. R	(IEP)	A. G	(progress reports)
C. C	(IEP)	Jos. B	(IEP)
D. B	(graduation notice)	M. V	(progress reports)
		D. D	(IEP)
		M. P	(social studies goals)

We have planned a follow-up meeting for Tuesday, December 7, 2000, at 2:00 p.m. that will again include the assistant superintendent and an association representative. Please feel free to make an appointment to discuss this further or to comment in writing below. Please sign one copy of this memo and return it to me by October 26, 2000. Your signature acknowledges receipt of the verbal warning, not agreement with it.

_____   _____
Ms. Principal   date

_____   _____
Ms. Sped Teacher   date

cc Ms. Sped Teacher's personnel file

Confidential

Sample Middle School
M e m o r a n d u m

To: Bill Murphy
Date: 18 June 2000
From: Peter Principal
Re: Expectation Clarification

This memo is to review the meeting we had yesterday, during which I went over with you my notes from a meeting I had with Margie Manning on June 15. Margie asked to see me to discuss some concerns she had about her son Sean's experience in seventh grade math. This was not a meeting Margie had scheduled, so I did not have an opportunity to speak with you first. The following were the points she made.

You recently gave a test in seventh grade math. The period was ending, and Sean and Stephen Fox needed more time. (Sean's IEP specifies that he may have additional time on tests when he needs it.) Sean reported to his mother that there was no problem with his needing more time, but that when Stephen wanted more, you said no. When Stephen asked why, you said, "Because Sean has a learning disability." Margie felt that this was a hurtful and inappropriate comment to make to another child, and an invasion of Sean's privacy.

During her parent conference with you, Margie reported that you spoke entirely about yourself and your son, including his difficulties in school. She found this very inappropriate. Margie noted that she tried to redirect the conversation to focus on Sean, but that you resisted all attempts to do so. She felt that you had little information that was of any use.

When I asked Margie whether she had spoken with you about this, she said that she would feel comfortable going to any other teacher here, but that you are unapproachable. She mentioned that she had tried to work on an issue with you earlier in the year and that you had been rude and defensive. She could not recall exactly what this was about. Margie commented that the kids do not like you, because they feel you show them no respect. She said that all the other teachers take the time to work with kids.

memo continues

When I asked if she could be more specific, Margie mentioned a time in the middle of the year when you called to tell her that Sean was behind in his homework, which was something she appreciated, since this is sometimes a problem for him. You then "launched into a diatribe" about having Sean tested for ADD. This made Margie feel very defensive, since she feels that she and her husband John have been very proactive in addressing Sean's needs and very open to any recommendations from the school. ADD has never been mentioned as a diagnosis for Sean by any of the specialists who have worked with him, in the school or in the medical field.

Margie reported that you said, "I've saved kids before who have had this." The drugs now are wonderful! She felt that this was an inappropriate discussion for a classroom teacher to initiate, and it made her very uncomfortable.

I told Margie that I thought it was very important for teachers to hear this kind of feedback and asked her permission to share it with you, since she was not comfortable approaching you herself. She said that she would not have been willing to have me do so in the middle of the year, but that since it was the end of the year she would give her permission.

When you and I spoke, you took issue with several of these points. I believe it would not be possible at this time to establish whether your account or that of the parent is more accurate. However, please be aware that events such as those described, if they occurred as described by the parent, would be inappropriate behavior for a teacher.

You are welcome to write a response to this memo. Please return a signed copy to me by Monday, June 21.

_____   _____
     Signature of Peter Principal   date

_____   _____
       Signature of teacher   date

Signature indicates receipt of, not concurrence with, this memo.

cc Association Representative
    Math Coordinator

SOURCES

Crew L, Everitt T. & Nunez W. (1985). *Sample written reprimands: A program of corrective discipline for school personnel.* Sacramento, CA: American Association of School Personnel.

Finnegan, S. (2000). *MGL 2000: selected Massachusetts general laws for school committees and personnel.* Boston, MA: Massachusetts Association of School Committees, Inc.

Fraser, R. G. (1996, August 18). Untitled handout passed out at the workshop, *Supervising the marginal teacher,* given by the Massachusetts Association of School Personnel Administrators.

Hirsch, J. (1999). *Labor and employment in Massachusetts: a guide to employment laws, regulations and practices* (2nd ed.). Newark, NJ: Lexis Publishing.

Procedures related to discipline of employees. (1993, September 1). Internal document from the Boston Public Schools, Boston, MA.

Soukhanov, A. H. (Ed.). (1988). *New Riverside university dictionary.* Boston: Houghton Mifflin Company.

Chapter 7

Supervision and Evaluation Documents and Contract Language

All supervision and evaluation documents contain two major components. The first is the **performance standards** section, which focuses on the educational practices. They are used during supervision and evaluation to summatively determine the teacher's level of success and to focus the teacher's formative professional growth activities in ways that maximize student success.

The second major component is the **process** (often called the **evaluation procedures**). In all evaluation documents the process describes how the evaluator assists with the teacher's formative growth and how the evaluator summatively assesses the teacher's implementation of the performance standards. This assessment would include implementation of the district's curriculum if there were a performance standard addressing that topic. In recent years, evaluation documents have increasingly been integrating professional development into a three, four and even five-year cycle. In these documents, the process describes how teachers and administrators work together formatively to improve the teacher's performance through professional development activities in years when the evaluator does not complete a summative evaluation document. In many states, labor laws (*legal*) require that the school board and the teachers' association/union negotiate both the performance standards and the process section. In other states, the bargaining requirements are less demanding, however, involving the teachers through their association is often most beneficial.

This chapter contains performance standards and evaluation processes from two districts. In these examples, the performance standards are called the principles of effective teaching. Example 1, that of Brookline, Massachusetts, is a purely summative evaluation document. Example 2, that of Lexington, Massachusetts, contains both the summative evaluation component and the formative professional development component. The processes in the two sample documents differ in a variety of other ways as well. We will discuss those differences as the chapter progresses.

THE PROBLEM WITH A POORLY FUNCTIONING EVALUATION PROGRAM IS USUALLY NOT THE DOCUMENT!

When a district decides that its evaluation system is not working, it usually concludes immediately that a major cause of the problem is the document. Districts commonly reach this conclusion because there are only two possible reasons for the problems with the district's evaluation system. The first is that the document doesn't work. The second is that the people are not using the document effectively. Consciously and subconsciously, it is easier for districts to conclude that the failure is with the thing (the document) rather than to conclude it's with the people. This is particularly true when the people making these judgments are the *administrators* responsible for ensuring the effective use of the district's document!

> Consciously and subconsciously, it is easier for districts to conclude that the failure is with the thing (the document) rather than to conclude it's with the people. This is particularly true when the people making these judgments are the *administrators* responsible for ensuring the effective use of the district's document!

It's easier, personally and interpersonally, to make changes in documents than it is to change people's practices. In chapter 5, we discussed the myriad of *social–emotional* and *legal* reasons why many evaluators avoid having those difficult, face-to-face conferences when they need to tell a teacher his/her performance must improve. Or, they write the negative information without ever honestly discussing it with the teacher, thus creating an even greater chasm between the administrator and the teacher.

This same reticence is true for the district-level administrators having responsibility for district-wide supervision and evaluation programs. They often have a difficult time confronting their supervisees (the evaluators) about their poor performance in evaluating the teachers. They are uncomfortable confronting teachers or the teachers' association with information about low teacher performance because of the *legal* and *public relations* (*political*) ramifications these discussions may have. Therefore, when district-level administrators are displeased with the effectiveness of their present evaluation systems, they often, due to subconscious, emotional factors, choose the costly and time-consuming direction of gathering together committees and developing and negotiating new supervision and evaluation documents, rather than thoroughly assessing the implementation of their current programs.

Bringing together a committee to develop a new document feels like the right thing to do when we have identified issues with supervision and evaluation in our districts. It allows district administrators an opportunity to work constructively and harmoniously with the evaluators, the teachers and the teachers' association on the *educational standards and processes*. It helps districts to avoid confronting the difficult *social–emotional* and *legal* issues that are the real cause for ineffective supervision and evaluation. The truth is, however, that in most cases changing the documents is unnecessary because the evaluation procedures already have most or all of the necessary components to be successful. The problems with the supervision and evaluation programs are rarely the documents themselves and are most often caused by inadequate implementation by the evaluators or by insufficient training or support for the evaluators and a lack of supervision of the evaluators by the central administrators.

Many districts have spent a year, two years and, in some cases, even longer in developing and collectively bargaining new documents. Shortly after these efforts are complete, there is a flurry of activity and excitement that leads to short term improvements in their evaluation systems. By the second or third year, however, the infatuation with the new documents fades and the supervision and evaluation programs quickly decline to their previous state. The people who passionately developed and implemented the new documents leave or move on to other projects. Over time, people find that in replacing the old documents they've eliminated the problems contained in them, but they have also eliminated many of their strengths. Before very long, the districts wonder again why their supervision and evaluation programs are not working. This is not to say that districts shouldn't assess their documents at some point, however, in ninety percent or more of the cases it should be the *last step* in seeking to improve supervision and evaluation programs.

It is for this reason that I advise districts to start their improvement efforts by addressing the implementation of the present documents. The first step in doing this is to make sure everyone is using the correct documents and using them properly. During the past five years, I've had the opportunity to work with at least ten districts that were unhappy with their evaluation systems. In all of these cases, I found a number of the evaluators were neither using their districts' documents nor using them correctly. People were not being negligent; they had either just fallen out of practice, or hadn't received adequate training in the effective use of the documents when beginning their administrative careers in these districts.

Evaluators first need to be trained in the proper use of the documents. They then need to be required to use the documents correctly. Requiring evaluators to use the documents without training them in their proper use would only lead to frustration for the evaluators and teachers and would feed into the general belief that the documents don't work. Evaluators must be shown the value (to the evaluators, the staff and the students) of using the prescribed documents in the correct way. Chapters 2 and 3 describe how districts might provide the teaching, coaching, assessment and reteaching to evaluators that is necessary to have an effective system of supervision and evaluation.

TALE OF TWO DOCUMENTS

The following documents are both from exemplary school districts, Brookline and Lexington, Massachusetts, with excellent systems of supervision and evaluation. In reviewing the documents, however, you will see that they are quite different, representing the districts' varying approaches to supervision and evaluation. One is not better or worse than the other; they just have different strengths and weaknesses. In both cases, the reason for effectiveness of the districts' evaluation systems is the training, coaching and supervision that evaluators receive, and not the structure of the documents.

The Brookline Document

The first document, Brookline's, contains both contracted components and components developed by management in collaboration with the teachers' association, to effectively implement the collectively bargained performance standards (principles of effective teaching). Contracted components are the items negotiated and agreed upon with the teachers' association through the *legal process* known as collective bargaining. Each state has its own laws that define which parts of the evaluation process and standards must be bargained between the employer and the legal representative (union or association) of the employees. Those evaluation processes and standards not indicated in the law as "mandatory subjects of bargaining" are left for management to determine by policy or other managerial instrument.

Managerial implementation processes need not be collectively bargained because they are outside the mandatory subjects of bargaining outlined in the laws of the state of Massachusetts. Typically, they are designed to ensure that the collectively bargained components are carried out effectively. However, it is important to note that the line between those parts of the evaluation process and standards that are mandatory subjects of bargaining and those areas that are open to managerial implementation processes is often *gray rather than black and white*. In those cases, this line is usually further defined in the case law created by the courts and/or arbitrators.

The Brookline document section begins with the contract articles related to supervision and evaluation that have been collectively bargained. They may be found in the contract between the Brookline Educators Association and the Brookline School Committee. This document includes the procedures, which consist of the Evaluation Criteria and Format on the first five pages, the two forms on the sixth and seventh pages and the Brookline Principles of Effective Teaching (performance standards). These are the parts of the document that have been collectively bargained.

The Timeline for Teacher Evaluations, High School Evaluation Teams and the Evaluation Assignments for Integrated Services are managerial implementation documents designed to ensure that evaluators effectively implement the bargained procedures. The final document, High School Student Comment Sheet, combines the language that has been collectively bargained to govern the use of a form that exists in the School Committee Policy Manual rather than in the contract.

The Lexington Document

The second document, Lexington's, contains all the components within the collectively bargained document. The Lexington document is designed on a four-year cycle that incorporates professional development activities. For those who wish to learn more about the four-year evaluation process that incorporates staff development activities, I recommend Jonathon Saphier's book, *How to Make Supervision and Evaluation Really Work* (1993) and Charlotte Danielson's and Thomas McGreal's book, *Teacher Evaluation to Enhance Professional Practice* (2000). The Lexington document is designed to be both summative and formative. In contrast, the Brookline document operates on a two-year cycle and is primarily a summative evaluation document. Formative professional development is provided outside of the evaluation system but is summatively evaluated through the performance standards.

You will note that the Lexington document contains many of the same components as the Brookline document. Time lines, observation requirements, designations of appropriate evaluators for all positions and the required forms all exist in both documents.

Analyzing the Documents

In the following section, we will analyze the documents and draw conclusions about the strengths and weaknesses of the various components of each document. I believe the best way to do this is for you to read the documents carefully before you read my comments on the strengths and weaknesses of each document. While reading, consider each document's advantages and disadvantages in addressing the E.L.P.S. components of supervision and evaluation.

People's assessments of the documents' effectiveness will vary according to their perspectives. No document can be all things to all people. There is an old truism in politics that says, "Where you sit determines where you stand." This statement is never more true than in its application to people reviewing supervision and evaluation documents. Therefore, as you read, try to assess the documents from each of the following perspectives. Although many people may agree on the educational merits of a document, where a person "sits" typically determines his/her opinion on the legal, public relations (*political*) and social–emotional merits of the documents. There are of course innumerable factors influencing where a person "stands" on any part of any document. However, I have provided the ten perspectives below to give the reader a framework for comparison. I am well aware that two high-performing teachers might feel very differently about a single provision. However, for a number of items in evaluation documents, there is at least a general consensus among the various groups.

1. Which part of each document would a high-performing teacher like? Why?

2. Which part of each document would a low-performing teacher (as described in the case studies in chapter 5) like? Why?

3. Which part of each document would an evaluator of a high-performing teacher like if he/she had less than ten evaluations in a given year? Why?

4. Which part of each document would an evaluator of a high-performing teacher like if he/she had more than twenty evaluations in a given year? Why?

5. Which part of each document would an evaluator of a low-performing teacher (as described in the case studies in chapter 5) like if he/she had less than ten evaluations in a given year? Why?

6. Which part of each document would an evaluator of a low-performing teacher (as described in the case studies in chapter 5) like if he/she had more than twenty evaluations in a given year? Why?

7. Which part of each document would the superintendent or assistant superintendent responsible for system-wide supervision and evaluation like? Why?

8. Which part of each document would a school district's labor attorney (assigned to sustain the dismissal of a teacher evaluated as unsatisfactory) like? Why?

9. Which part of each document would a teachers' association labor attorney (assigned to overturn the dismissal of a teacher evaluated as unsatisfactory) like? Why?

10. Which part of each document would the parents and other outside constituents like? Why?

For example:

Educational: The Brookline Annual Report of Teacher Effectiveness requires that the evaluator check a final designation from the three levels of satisfactory teaching.

Advantage: This enables the teacher to get a quantified understanding of his/her performance that is not readily apparent from the narrative.

Disadvantage: Many teachers become preoccupied with the "final grade" and have difficulty refocusing themselves on the commendations and recommendations contained in the narrative.

Advantage: Teachers who receive the top designation feel their hard work and effort is recognized and appreciated.

Disadvantage: Teachers who receive the third designation often feel very threatened and become negative toward the administrator and the supervision and evaluation process.

Advantage: Administrators working with low-performing teachers find at times that the concrete, objective nature of checking off the third level forces a teacher who has shown denial about declining performance to take a serious look at his/her teaching. The first step a low-performing teacher must take to move toward permanent improvement is "owning the problem."

Disadvantage: Administrators working with low-performing teachers find it difficult at times to refocus the teacher receiving the third level away from improvement for self-preservation (external) and toward improvement for professional fulfillment (internal). The teacher may get stuck in the belief that the problem is with the administrator or the students and fail to "own the problem." The first step a teacher must take to move toward permanent improvement is owning the problem. The angst administrators have about the time and effort it would take to overcome this ownership issue causes some administrators to avoid checking the third level even when it is appropriate.

Joint labor–management committees developing new documents inevitably have long debates on whether the final check-off should be simply a choice between "satisfactory" or "unsatisfactory" or if there should be gradations within the satisfactory level. These debates tend to be caused more by the committee members' personal beliefs (*educational* and *social–emotional*) than by whether or not they are labor or management representatives. As noted above, there are advantages and disadvantages to each structure.

BROOKLINE CONTRACT LANGUAGE ON SUPERVISION AND EVALUATION

Article 6 – Evaluation and Supervision
6.1 Evaluation and Supervision

A. Effectiveness will be based upon the Brookline Principles of Effective Teaching and Examples of Descriptors (appearing later in this chapter). The annual report for nurses will be based upon the Brookline Principles of Effective Nursing and Examples of Descriptors (later in this chapter). The procedure for evaluation shall be as set forth in Article 6.2.

B. Annual Reports and Progress Reports, as described in Article 6.2 (appearing later in this chapter), must be submitted by principals in the Elementary Schools and by secondary curriculum coordinators in the High School (in cases where there is no secondary curriculum coordinator, by the Headmaster). Annual Reports and Progress Reports may be submitted by Curriculum Coordinators, Deans, Headmaster and/or Director of Personnel.

   Deans will cooperate in requested evaluations of pre-professional teachers in accordance with practices followed by housemasters in the past.

   Upon the request of the Headmaster, a Dean will conduct an evaluation of a teacher with professional status following the procedures established in the contract. Absent unforeseen circumstances, the Headmaster will attempt to notify the Deans about such teachers at the beginning of the school year.

C. The Brookline School Committee and the Brookline Educators Association endorse the concept of student/teacher interaction and encourage teachers actively to seek and use student evaluation. All teachers may be required to administer the student evaluation form adopted by the BSC. The completed forms may be reviewed by a teacher with his/her Supervisor at either's request provided that a teacher shall not be required to review or share the completed form with his/her Supervisor.

A committee consisting of an equal number of representatives of the BSC and the BEA, may be convened during the terms of this contract at the request of the BSC, to study the issue of student evaluation of teachers and to make recommendations to the BSC relating to the process of student evaluation. The student evaluation process described herein shall not be changed during the term of the agreement unless otherwise mutually agreed by the BSC and the BEA.

D. The BSC encourages continual peer observation-supervision at all levels for the purpose of mutual sharing, developing and examining of teacher styles, approaches and techniques.

E. When it becomes necessary to engage teachers in the formal evaluative process (by request from Evaluators or the teacher being evaluated), then the following formula should be used:

  i. In the High School, the consensus of the teacher's department shall determine the selection of one peer evaluator, and the consensus of the teacher's house shall determine the selection of additional peer evaluators.

  ii. In the Elementary Schools, the teacher involved in peer evaluation will be determined by a consensus of the building faculty; or in the case of seventh and eighth grade specialist, by a consensus of the Town-Wide Department.

  iii. In both cases the number of peer evaluators and administrators shall be equal.

  iv. For teachers with Professional Status, Supervisors and Evaluators always have the possibility of initiating a request for another Evaluator (administrator or peer).

F. The BSC encourages self-evaluation by teachers with pre-professional status and teachers with professional status. The mechanism for this might be either a checklist filled out by the teacher or an Annual Report of Teacher Effectiveness completed by the teacher. Self-evaluation can be requested by either the teacher or the Supervisor. It may be followed up by a conference if it is desired by either party.

G. It is strongly suggested that Supervisors provide for visitations by teachers within departments, among departments, and among buildings and other school systems. Also, Supervisors are encouraged to provide in-service workshops for teachers.

6.2 Procedure for Evaluation

A. Frequency of Evaluation – Teachers with pre-professional status will be evaluated every year and teachers with professional status will be evaluated every other year. For the remainder of Article 6.2, references

to teachers with professional status refer only during their year
of evaluation.

B. Orientation – In September of each year, all teachers with professional status and teachers with pre-professional status will meet
with Supervisors for an orientation of the evaluation procedures.
It is the intent of this meeting to allow all staff the opportunity to
enter the evaluation process with full and open knowledge of what
the process is.

C. Pre-Evaluation Conference – On or before October 15, Supervisors
shall meet with all teachers with pre-professional status. On or
before December 1, supervisors shall meet with all teachers with
professional status. These pre-evaluation conferences will address
goals for the year, strengths of the teacher, relationships between
current and previous evaluations and support available.

D. Classroom Observations
    i.   There will be one announced, formal classroom observation
         for each teacher with pre-professional status and for each
         teacher with professional status. Each formal classroom observation will be at least thirty (30) minutes in length for elementary
         teachers and a full period for secondary teachers.
    ii. Supervisors may informally observe teachers at any time.

E. Pre-Observation Conference – A pre-observation conference may
take place prior to a formal classroom observation. Requests for these
conferences may be made by either the Supervisor or the teacher.

F. Post-Observation Conference – A post-observation conference shall
be held within seven (7) workdays of the classroom observation,
unless the Supervisor and the teacher agree to waive the seven (7)
day timeline and arrange another mutually convenient date. A classroom
observation report shall be completed at or after the post-observation
conference. A copy of the completed observation form, signed by the
teacher and the supervisor, will be given to the teacher.

G. Staff Progress Report – Each teacher with pre-professional status
shall receive a Staff Progress Report three (3) times a year, normally
every two months. For teachers with professional status, Staff
Progress Reports may be used if desired.

H. Annual Reports of Teacher Effectiveness – An Annual Report of
Teacher Effectiveness will be made prior to February 15 each year
for every teacher with pre-professional status except that the Superintendent can extend the period to a date not later than March 15

when, in his/her judgment, there is good reason for doing so. An Annual Report of Teacher Effectiveness will be made prior to May 1 of each year for every teacher with professional status.

Each teacher shall receive a copy of his/her report and have the right to discuss the report with his/her superior and submit his/her own comments within ten days. It is expected that the evaluator will have conferred periodically with the teacher concerning his/her progress before the submission of the Annual Report of Teacher Effectiveness.

I. Non-renewal of teachers with pre-professional status – A teacher with pre-professional status shall be notified, in writing, on or before April 15 if he/she is not to be employed for the following school year.

J. Out-Of-Cycle Evaluation – Any teacher with professional status may be evaluated out-of-cycle. On or before October 20, the Supervisor will provide the teacher with substantive reasons for undertaking the out-of-cycle evaluation, and it is understood this action does not necessarily imply a negative evaluative finding. This decision to undertake an evaluation out-of-cycle, though grieveable, shall not be subject to arbitration.

When the performance of a teacher with professional status is considered satisfactory after having been evaluated out-of-cycle, that teacher's cycle will begin anew at the time of the satisfactory evaluation.

6.3 Duration of Evaluation System

For the duration of this Agreement, i.e., through August 31, 200__, present system-wide practices concerning evaluations will continue in effect.

6.4 Withholding Salary Increment

The BSC reserves the right to withhold a salary increment from any teacher who has not performed in a satisfactory manner. If a teacher is at the maximum of his/her preparation column and has not performed in a satisfactory manner, the BSC reserves the right to withhold any salary increases.

6.5 Personnel File

Each teacher shall have the right to review and make copies of the contents of his/her personnel file originating after initial employment and to have a representative of the BEA accompany him/her in such review.

6.6 Derogatory Material

Should any material which the BSC shall consider to be derogatory be placed in the teacher's personnel folder, then the teacher involved will be given the opportunity to review same prior to its placement in the personnel folder. The employee shall initial such material prior to its insertion. The employee's initials do not signify agreement with the contents but rather serve as evidence that the employee has seen the material in question. If the teacher chooses to do so, he/she may submit any statement concerning the derogatory material; and if he/she so desires, said statement shall be filed with the alleged derogatory material in the teacher's personnel folder.

If such material may result in discipline or otherwise affect the teacher's status, it shall be sent to the teacher involved within twenty (20) school days. It is understood that the BSC will make an appropriate investigation before inserting derogatory material into an employee's file. In addition, with regard to nurses, any complaint to any school official regarding the performance of a nurse which the school official believes could affect the nurse's employment status, shall be called to the attention of the nurse involved within 7 working days.

THE PUBLIC SCHOOLS OF BROOKLINE, MASSACHUSETTS EVALUATION CRITERIA AND FORMAT

The teacher's central role in the schools is classroom teaching. But the teacher's other roles outside the classroom are important, too; for example, in parent and community relations and as a member of the staff. This evaluation format seeks to identify the most important areas of performance within these roles, yet remain flexible enough for educators to communicate fully and honestly about teaching performance.

The criteria listed in the attached sheets are intended to represent the image of good teaching in Brookline, to serve as an aid for teacher self evaluation, and to establish a standard towards which all members of the professional staff of the Brookline Public Schools can work cooperatively to improve instruction.

ANNUAL REPORT OF TEACHER EFFECTIVENESS

Teacher _____

School _____

Grade/subject _____

Please attach a narrative and recommendations on the following areas as outlined in detail in the Brookline Principles of Effective Teaching.

I.   Currency of Curriculum

II.   Effective Planning and Assessment of Curriculum and Instruction

III.   Effective Management of Classroom Environment

IV.   Effective Instruction

V.   Promotion of High Standards and Expectations for Student Achievement

VI.   Promotion of Equity and Appreciation of Diversity

VII.   Fulfillment of Professional Responsibilities

_____ This evaluation indicates performance with no areas of concern.

_____ This evaluation indicates performance with need for improvement in one or two areas (See recommendations).

_____ This evaluation indicates performance with need for improvement in several areas (See recommendations).

_____ This evaluation indicates performance which is below the standard expected of staff in the Brookline Public Schools (See recommendations).

Overall Evaluation: _____ Satisfactory _____ Unsatisfactory

_____   _____
        Signature of evaluator   date

_____   _____
        Signature of teacher   date

Signature signifies receipt of, not concurrence with, this evaluation. Teachers are encouraged to submit comments. (Please make comments on the back of this form or on an attached sheet.)

STAFF PROGRESS REPORT

TEACHER: _____

SCHOOL: _____

DATE: _____

Please attach the narrative of the observation if report is based on a classroom observation:

_____

_____

_____

_____

_____   _____
Signature of evaluator   date

Teacher's comments:

_____   _____
Signature of teacher   date

Signature signifies receipt of, not concurrence with this evaluation.
Teachers are encouraged to submit comments.

PRINCIPLES OF EFFECTIVE TEACHING
Massachusetts Department of Education

with suggested *Skilful Teacher*, (S.T.) and *Understanding by Design*, (U.D.) connections
adapted by Carol Gregory, Jonathon D. Saphier, and Claire Jackson.

PRINCIPLES	EXAMPLES OF DESCRIPTORS	REFERENCE DOCUMENTS
I. CURRENCY IN THE CURRICULUM A. The teacher is up-to-date regarding curriculum content.	1. Demonstrates working knowledge of the core curriculum of the teacher's assignment	*Massachusetts Department of Education Learning Expectations*
	2. Frames curriculum around essential questions in the discipline that provide opportunities for reasoning, logic, analysis, and synthesis when planning units, lessons, and assessments	U.D. Chapters 7, 8, 9
	3. Keeps current in the field and applies knowledge to the instructional program	S.T. Chapter 18: OVERARCHING OBJECTIVES, 549–560
	4. Contributes to the ongoing evaluation of the curriculum	U.D. Chapters 1, 10, 11
II. EFFECTIVE PLANNING AND ASSESSMENT OF CURRICULUM AND INSTRUCTION A. The teacher plans instruction effectively.	1. Has a personal vision of committed, confident learners and uses that vision to guide learning goals, expectations, and standards for student work	S.T. Chapter 14: OBJECTIVES, 395–422 U.D. Chapters 2, 3
	2. Sets short-term and yearlong goals for curricular units which derive from unifying themes of fundamental importance to students' present and future lives	S.T. Chapter 14: OBJECTIVES, 395–422
	3. Identifies individual and group needs and plans appropriate strategies, including those that involve the use of available up-to-date technologies to meet those needs	S.T. Chapter 15: LEARNING EXPERIENCES, 423–456

PRINCIPLES	EXAMPLES OF DESCRIPTORS	REFERENCE DOCUMENTS
II. EFFECTIVE PLANNING AND ASSESSMENT OF CURRICULUM AND INSTRUCTION (continued)	4. Uses materials and resources, including technologies that are appropriately matched to curricular goals and to students' learning styles	Chapter 15: LEARNING EXPERIENCES, 423–456
	5. Frames curriculum around students' own prior knowledge and experience and identifies prerequisite skills, concepts, and vocabulary that are important for students to know in order to be successful at a task	S.T. Chapter 8: CLARITY [The Big Picture] 210–219 S.T. Chapter 15: LEARNING EXPERIENCES, 423–456
	6. Seeks out and collaborates with school-based specialists, resource personnel, technology specialist, and administrators to better design curricula or instructional modifications to meet the special learning needs of students and to support all students to learn and apply a challenging core curriculum	S.T. Chapter 9: PRINCIPLES OF LEARNING, 235–268 S.T. Chapter 8: CLARITY [Activators] 213–214; [Itinerary & Communicates Objectives] 211–213 S.T. Chapter 15: LEARNING EXPERIENCES [Grouping and Interpersonal Complexity] 442–443 U.D. Chapter 4
	7. Plans engaging ways to introduce each unit of study	S.T. Chapter 18: OVERARCHING OBJECTIVES, 549–560 S.T. Chapter 15: LEARNING EXPERIENCES [Degree of Structure] 436–442; [Supervision] 433
	8. Plans frequent instructional opportunities in which students are interacting with ideas, materials, teachers, and each other	S.T. Chapter 15: LEARNING EXPERIENCES [Sources of Information] 426–427; [Resources] 427; [Sensory Channels] 445–446
	9. Designs curriculum experiences in which students take increasing responsibility for their own learning	S.T. for 1, 2, and 3 see S.T. Chapter 16 on ASSESSMENT for comprehensive treatment of these three items.
	10. Integrates the teaching of reading, listening, writing, speaking, viewing, and the use of appropriate learning tools (e.g. calculators, computers, etc.) within the discipline	S.T. for 1, 2, and 3 see S.T. Chapter 16 on ASSESSMENT for comprehensive treatment of these three items.
B. The teacher plans assessment of student learning effectively.	1. Determines specific and challenging standards for student learning	Brookline Learning Expectations S.T. for 1, 2, and 3 see Chapter 16 on ASSESSMENT for comprehensive treatment of these three items.
	2. Develops and uses authentic assessment which describes a student's learning process as well as his/her learning achievements	U.D. Chapters 5, 6 S.T. Chapter 16: ASSESSMENT
	3. Incorporates time for individual and interactive reflection including response journals, debriefings, and group discussions	S.T. Chapter 8: CLARITY [Checking for Understanding] 190–198

PRINCIPLES	EXAMPLES OF DESCRIPTORS	REFERENCE DOCUMENTS
II. EFFECTIVE PLANNING AND ASSESSMENT OF CURRICULUM AND INSTRUCTION (continued) C. The teacher monitors students' understanding of the curriculum effectively and adjusts instruction, materials, or assessments when appropriate.	1. Regularly uses a variety of formal and informal authentic assessments of students' achievement and progress for instructional revisions and decision making	S.T. Chapter 16: ASSESSMENT S.T. Chapter 8: CLARITY [Checking for Understanding] 190–198
	2. Implements evaluation procedures which appropriately assess the objectives taught	S.T. Chapter 16: ASSESSMENT [Records] 492–503
	3. Communicates student progress to parents, students, and staff members in a timely fashion using a range of information including portfolios, anecdotal records and other artifacts	S.T. Chapter 16: ASSESSMENT [Records] 492–503
	4. Prepares and maintains accurate and efficient record keeping systems of the quality and quantity of student work	S.T. Chapter 16: ASSESSMENT
	5. Uses individual and group data appropriately; maintains confidentiality concerning individual student data and achievement	S.T. Chapter 13: CLASSROOM CLIMATE, 355–394
III. EFFECTIVE MANAGEMENT OF CLASSROOM ENVIRONMENT A. The teacher creates an environment that is positive for student learning and involvement.	1. Implements instructional opportunities in which students are interacting with ideas, materials, teachers, and each other	S.T. Chapter 9: PRINCIPLES OF LEARNING [Active Participation] 244–245 S.T. Chapter 10: MODELS OF TEACHING, 269–292
	2. Implements curriculum experiences in which students take increasing responsibility for their own learning	S.T. Chapter 18: OVERARCHING OBJECTIVES, 549–560 S.T. Chapter 15: LEARNING EXPERIENCES [Structuring] 436–442
	3. Demonstrates an openness to student challenges and questions about information and ideas	S.T. Chapter 8: CLARITY [Students' Own Thinking] 196–198 S.T. Chapter 13: CLASSROOM CLIMATE [Influence] 374–385
	4. Uses classroom time and classroom space to promote optimal learning	S.T. Chapter 4: SPACE, 47–60 S.T. Chapter 5: TIME, 61–84
	5. Understands principles and patterns of child growth and development and uses this knowledge in working with students	"Matching" concept around which the entire book is organized
	6. Establishes classroom procedures that maintain a high level of students' time-on-task and that ensure smooth transitions from one activity to another	S.T. Chapter 6: ROUTINES, 85–186 S.T. Chapter 3: MOMENTUM, 29–46
B. The teacher maintains appropriate standards of behavior, mutual respect, and safety.	1. Maintains systematic approach to discipline by establishing and administering a consistent and fair set of rules supporting appropriate expectations	S.T. Chapter 11 : EXPECTATIONS [Expectations for Behavior] 293–304 S.T. Chapter 7: DISCIPLINE, 103–186

PRINCIPLES	EXAMPLES OF DESCRIPTORS	REFERENCE DOCUMENTS
III. EFFECTIVE MANAGEMENT OF CLASSROOM ENVIRONMENT (continued)	2. Manages routines effectively	S.T. Chapter 6: ROUTINES, 85–102
	3. Maintains appropriate professional boundaries with students	S.T. Chapter 12: PERSONAL RELATIONSHIP BUILDING
IV. EFFECTIVE INSTRUCTION	4. Serves as a positive role model for students	S.T. Chapter 11: EXPECTATIONS [Modeling] 298–299
A. The teacher makes learning goals clear to students.	1. Makes connections between concepts taught and students' prior knowledge and experiences	S.T. Chapter 8: CLARITY [Makes Connections] 215–216
	2. Regularly checks for students' understanding of content, concepts and progress on skill	S.T. Chapter 8: CLARITY [Checking] 190–196
	3. Identifies confusions and misconceptions as indicated by student responses and regular assessment strategies; remediates, reteaches, or extends teaching to meet individual and/or group need	S.T. Chapter 8: CLARITY [Misconceptions/ Unscrambling Confusions] 194–198
	4. Communicates clearly in writing and speaking using precise language	S.T. Chapter 8: CLARITY [Speech] 204–206 [Explicitness] 206–210
	5. Understands and shows students the relevance of the subject to lifelong learning	S.T. Chapter 15: LEARNING EXPERIENCES [Personal Relevance] 428–429
B. The teacher uses appropriate instructional techniques.	1. Uses a variety of teaching strategies, including cooperative, peer and project-based learning, audio-visual presentations, lecture discussions and inquiry, practice and application, and the teaching of others	S.T. Chapter 8: CLARITY [Explanatory Devices] 198–204 S.T. Chapter 10: MODELS OF TEACHING, 269–292
	2. Provides options for students to demonstrate competency and mastery of new material, including written work, plays, art work, oratory, visual presentations, exhibitions, and portfolios	S.T. Chapter 16: ASSESSMENT [Means of Gathering] 482–492
	3. Uses a variety of appropriate materials in order to reinforce and extend skills, accommodate learning styles and match instructional objectives	S.T. Chapter 15: LEARNING EXPERIENCES [Sensory Channels] 445–446; [Sources of Information] 426–427; [Resources Used] 427; [Scale] 446;
	4. Causes students to become cognitively active in summarizing important learning and integrating them with prior knowledge	S.T. Chapter 9: PRINCIPLES OF LEARNING [Application in Setting; Teach for Transfer; Concrete, Semi-abstract, Abstract; Say-Do]
	5. Demonstrates working knowledge of current research on optimum means for learning a particular discipline	S.T. Chapter 8: CLARITY [Summarizing] 218–219 Chapter 9: PRINCIPLES OF LEARNING [Active Participation] 244–245

PRINCIPLES	EXAMPLES OF DESCRIPTORS	REFERENCE DOCUMENTS
IV. EFFECTIVE INSTRUCTION (continued) C. The teacher uses appropriate questioning techniques.	1. Uses a variety of questioning techniques, including those which encourage and guide critical and independent thinking and the development of ideas 2. Presents information recognizing multiple points of view; encourages students to assess the accuracy of information presented	S.T. Chapter 8: CLARITY [Checking] 190–196 S.T. Chapter 15: LEARNING EXPERIENCES [Degree of Abstraction and Cognitive Level] 434–436 S.T. Chapter 15: LEARNING EXPERIENCES [Information Complexity] 444–445
D. The teacher evaluates, tries innovative approaches, and refines instructional strategies, including the effective use of technologies, to increase student learning and confidence to learn.	1. Regularly tries innovative approaches to improve instructional practices 2. Conscientiously evaluates, tries innovative approaches and refines instructional strategies, including the effective use of technologies, to increase student learning and confidence about learning 3. Assesses instructional strategies in authentic ways by comparing intended and actual learning outcomes	S.T. Chapter 10: MODELS OF TEACHING, 269–292 S.T. Chapter 15: LEARNING EXPERIENCES S.T. Chapter 1: 3–4 S.T. Chapter 11: EXPECTATIONS [Students Who Don't Get It Yet] 322–324 S.T. Chapter 16: ASSESSMENT
V. PROMOTION OF HIGH STANDARDS AND EXPECTATIONS FOR STUDENTS' ACHIEVEMENT A. The teacher communicates learning goals and high standards and expectations to students.	1. Regularly communicates objectives or learning outcomes to students 2. Regularly provides feedback to students on their progress on goals and objectives 3. Communicates standards, expectations, and guidelines regarding quality and quantity of students' work, work procedures and interpersonal behavior to students and parents 4. Responds to students' answers and work so as to keep students open, thinking, and willing to take risks and to persevere with challenging tasks 5. Models the skills, attitudes, values and processes central to the subject being taught	S.T. Chapter 8: CLARITY [Communicates Objectives] 211–213 S.T. Chapter 9: PRINCIPLES OF LEARNING [Knowledge of Results] 247 S.T. Chapter 16: ASSESSMENT [Clear Criteria for Success] 463–475 S.T. Chapter 11: EXPECTATIONS, 295–304 S.T. Chapter 11: EXPECTATIONS [Response to Student Answers] 307–315 S.T. Chapter 11: EXPECTATIONS [Modeling] 298

PRINCIPLES	EXAMPLES OF DESCRIPTORS	REFERENCE DOCUMENTS
V. PROMOTION OF HIGH STANDARDS AND EXPECTATIONS FOR STUDENTS' ACHIEVEMENT (continued) B. The teacher promotes confidence and perseverance in the student that stimulate increased personal student responsibility for achieving the goals of the curriculum.	1. Uses prompt feedback and student goal setting in order to increase student motivation and ownership of learning	S.T. Chapter 9: PRINCIPLES OF LEARNING [Knowledge of Results] 247; [Goal Setting] 251–252
	2. Develops and supports students' awareness of themselves as learners and their ability to overcome self-doubts associated with learning and taking risks	S.T. Chapter 13: CLASSROOM CLIMATE [Confidence and Risk Taking] 368–574; [Teaches Students to Use Principles of Learning]; [Learning Style and Choices] 377–381
	3. Nurtures students' eagerness to do challenging work and provides incentive, interest and support for students to take responsibility to complete such tasks successfully	S.T. Chapter 11: EXPECTATIONS [10 Arenas] 305–330
	4. Acts on the belief that all students can learn and that virtually all can master a challenging core curriculum with appropriate modifications of instruction	S.T. Chapter 11: EXPECTATIONS [3 Key Messages] 295–296; [10 Arenas] 304–330
	5. Encourages and supports students to believe that effort is a key to high achievement and acknowledges and values student work, study and inquiry	S.T. Chapter 11: EXPECTATIONS [3 Key Messages] 295–296; [10 Arenas] 304–330 S.T. Chapter 13: CLASSROOM CLIMATE [Risk Taking and Confidence] 368–574
	6. Regularly identifies students needing extra help and secures student cooperation and participation in extra help sessions	S.T. Chapter 11: EXPECTATIONS [3 Key Messages] 295–296; [10 Arenas] 304–330 Chapter 13: CLASSROOM CLIMATE [Risk Taking S.T. and Confidence] 368–574
	7. Identifies students who are not meeting expectations and develops a plan that designates the teacher's and the student's responsibilities regarding learning	S.T. Chapter 11: EXPECTATIONS [Students Who Don't Get It Yet] 322–324
	8. Demonstrates attitudes of fairness, courtesy and respect that encourage students' active participation and commitment to learning	S.T. Chapter 11: EXPECTATIONS [Students Who Don't Get It Yet] 322–324 S.T. Chapter 9: PRINCIPLES OF LEARNING [Goal Setting] 251–252
	9. Builds positive relationships with students and parents to enhance students' abilities to learn effectively	S.T. Chapter 12: PERSONAL RELATIONSHIP BUILDING 343–354 S.T. Chapter 12: PERSONAL RELATIONSHIP BUILDING, 343–354
	10. Recognizes and responds appropriately when an individual student is having social and/or emotional difficulties which interfere with learning and/or participating in class	S.T. Chapter 7: DISCIPLINE [Matching] 163–173 Chapter 12: PERSONAL RELATIONSHIP BUILDING [Active Listening] 349

PRINCIPLES	EXAMPLES OF DESCRIPTORS	REFERENCE DOCUMENTS
VI. PROMOTION OF EQUITY AND APPRECIATION OF DIVERSITY A. The teacher strives to ensure equitable opportunities for student learning.	1. Provides opportunities to include all students in the full range of academic programs and activities and extracurricular activities 2. Addresses the needs of diverse student populations by applying and adapting constitutional and statutory laws, state regulations and Board of Education policies and guidelines	S.T. Chapter 13: CLASSROOM CLIMATE [Community and Mutual Support] 359–368 [Matching] S.T. Chapter 13: CLASSROOM CLIMATE [Students and Their Communities as Sources of Knowledge] 382–385
B. The teacher demonstrates appreciation for and sensitivity to the diversity among individuals.	1. Demonstrates sensitivity to differences in abilities, modes of contributions, and social and cultural backgrounds 2. Develops and implements educational and organizational strategies that are effective in meeting the needs of a diverse student body 3. Functions effectively in a multilingual, multicultural and economically diverse society	S.T. Chapter 13: CLASSROOM CLIMATE [Personal Efficacy] 374–385 [Matching] concept throughout book S.T. Chapter 10: MODELS OF TEACHING S.T. Chapter 15: LEARNING EXPERIENCES S.T. Chapter 9: PRINCIPLES OF LEARNING S.T. Chapter 13: CLASSROOM CLIMATE [Personal Efficacy] 374–385
VII. FULFILLMENT OF PROFESSIONAL RESPONSIBILITIES A. The teacher constructively initiates interactions with parents and solicits and is receptive to their contributions.	1. The teacher approaches the parent as a positive collaborator in the process of educating the student 2. Keeps parents informed of student's progress and works with them to aid in the total development of the student	
B. The teacher shares responsibility for accomplishing the goals and priorities of his/her grade, team, department, building, and school district by participating on committees and in activities related to school community.	1. Works constructively with others to identify school problems and to develop and implement solutions 2. Works collaboratively with other staff in planning and implementing interdisciplinary curriculum, instruction, and other school programs, and shares expertise and new ideas with colleagues	

PRINCIPLES	EXAMPLES OF DESCRIPTORS	REFERENCE DOCUMENTS
VII. FULFILLMENT OF PROFESSIONAL RESPONSIBILITIES (continued)	3. Participates in school, student, faculty, and staff activities (e.g. administering "sunshine" fund, presenting at faculty meetings, beautifying school); participates in professional organizations (e.g. NCTM), teacher support groups (e.g. BEA) and system-wide committees (e.g. TATF)	
	4. Leads student organizations (e.g. student councils, math league, student newspapers, clubs, school plays)	
	5. Cooperates with other teachers about students' overall workload	
	6. Demonstrates a willingness to provide after-school academic support for students	
	7. Writes evaluations and recommendations for students as appropriate	
C. The teacher is a reflective and continuous learner.	1. Reflects about and acts on what students need to know and be able to do and about what the teacher can do to foster learning	Chapter 20 (TST): TEACHER BELIEFS, 577–586
	2. Uses available resources to analyze, expand, and refine professional knowledge and skills; resources can include professional organizations, academic course work, school-based staff, administrative and community resources, and other colleagues	
	3. Participates in activities that demonstrate a commitment to the teaching profession	
	4. Seeks out information in order to grow and improve as a professional	

PRINCIPLES	EXAMPLES OF DESCRIPTORS	REFERENCE DOCUMENTS
VII. FULFILLMENT OF PROFESSIONAL RESPONSIBILITIES (continued)	5. Is receptive to suggestions for growth and improvement	Chapter 20: TEACHER BELIEFS, 577–586 Chapter 12: PERSONAL RELATIONSHIP BUILDING
D. Maintains professional boundaries with parents and staff by behaving with mutual respect and discretion		

Sources:
Saphier & Gower. *The Skillful Teacher.* Carlisle, MA: Research for Better Teaching, 1997.
McTighe & Wiggins. *Understanding by Design.* A.S.C.D. 1999

Brookline High School Student Comment Sheet

Teacher's Name: _____

Course: _____

Date: _____

This evaluation is designed to help teachers plan courses and to improve the quality of their classes. To be used in this way, the questionnaire must be taken seriously. Please give careful consideration to your answers. Specific comments are most helpful.

Section I

Each question contains a statement. Consider the statement and decide where along the scale below the answer lies for you. Mark your response in the blank at the end of the statement. Space is provided below each question for optional comments.

Scale

1. Strongly Agree   4. Somewhat Disagree
2. Somewhat Agree   5. Strongly Disagree
3. Neither Agree nor Disagree   6. Does Not Apply to this course

1. The teacher appears to know the subject well. _____

Comment:_____

_____

_____

2. The teacher is well prepared for class. _____

Comment:_____

_____

_____

3. Class sessions are well organized. _____

Comment:_____

_____

_____

4.   The teacher gives a clear explanation of the material. _____

Comment:_____

_____

_____

5.   The teacher makes me feel free to ask questions, disagree, express ideas, etc. _____

Comment:_____

_____

_____

6.   The teacher responds effectively to questions. _____

Comment:_____

_____

_____

7.   The work outside of class is relevant to class sessions. _____

Comment:_____

_____

_____

8.   The work required outside of class is appropriate in quantity and quality. _____

Comment:_____

_____

_____

9.   The textbooks are a useful part of this course. _____

Comment:_____

_____

_____

10. The assigned reading helps me understand the subject matter of this course. _____

Comment:_____

_____

_____

11. The teacher is available for individual help. _____

Comment:_____

_____

_____

12. The teacher is interested in trying to help students. _____

Comment:_____

_____

_____

13. The teacher is fair and impartial in dealing with students. _____

Comment:_____

_____

_____

14. The grading system is reasonable. _____

Comment:_____

_____

_____

15. This course has increased my interest in the subject matter. _____

Comment:_____

_____

_____

16. This course has made a real contribution to my knowledge and understanding. _____

    Comment:_____

    _____

    _____

Section II

Please check the response that most accurately reflects your answer.

1. Overall, this course is: Outstanding   Good   Fair   Poor

2. Does the teacher teach this course at the appropriate level for you?

    Yes   No, too simple   No, too difficult

3. Why are you taking this course?

    __ School Requirement __ College Requirement

    __ Interest in Subject   __ Other

4. I do all of my assignments.

    __ Most   __ Some   __ None

Section III

Please use the space below for any additional comments you may have regarding the strengths, needs, recommendations for this course. Additional paper may be used if necessary.

HIGH SCHOOL EVALUATION TEAMS

Headmaster

Assistant Headmaster
Coordinator of School Within a School
Coordinator of Opportunity for Change
Coordinator of Integrated Services
Coordinator of Special Education 9–12
Coordinator of Differentiated Instruction
Coordinator of International Students
Coordinator for Time and Learning
Director of Athletics
Coordinator for Winthrop House

Dean of Mathematics, Science and Technology

Coordinator for Career Education
Coordinator for Health and Physical Education
Coordinator for Mathematics
Coordinator for Science
Associate Dean Grade 9
Associate Dean Grade 11

Dean of Humanities

Coordinator of English
Coordinator of Social Studies
Coordinator of World Languages
Coordinator of Visual Arts
Coordinator of Performing Arts
Associate Dean Grade 10
Associate Dean Grade 12

EVALUATION ASSIGNMENTS FOR INTEGRATED SERVICES STAFF

School Psychologists in the elementary schools based in only one school building will be evaluated by the Principal or his/her designee. Psychologists in the elementary schools who serve in more than one building will be evaluated by the Assistant Superintendent for Integrated Services. Psychologists assigned to the high school will be evaluated by the Coordinator of Integrated Services.

Guidance Counselors in the elementary schools assigned to only one building will be evaluated by the building Principal or his/her designee. Guidance counselors assigned to more than one building will be evaluated by the Assistant Superintendent for Integrated Services or his designee. Guidance counselors assigned to the high school will be evaluated by the Coordinator of Integrated Services.

Social Workers at the high school will be evaluated by the Principal or his/her designee. Social workers for Early Childhood will be evaluated by the Coordinator of Early Childhood Education. Elementary social workers will be evaluated by the building Principal.

Bilingual/E.S.L. teachers at BHS will be evaluated by the Coordinator of Bilingual/E.S.L. Elementary Bilingual/ESL teachers who are assigned to only one building will be evaluated by the building Principal or his/her designee. Elementary Bilingual/ESL teachers assigned to more than one building will be evaluated by the Coordinator of Bilingual/ESL.

Special Education Teachers in elementary schools assigned to one building will be evaluated by the building Principal or his/her designee. High school special education teachers will be evaluated by the Secondary Curriculum Coordinator for Special Education. At the high school the Program Coordinator for Winthrop House will evaluate all Winthrop House Staff. The Coordinator of Differentiated Instruction will evaluate the Learning Skills Staff and contribute to the evaluations of classroom and special education teachers. Special education teachers assigned to more than one building will be evaluated by the appropriate Curriculum Coordinator for Special Education or his/her designee.

Speech and Language Therapists in the elementary schools assigned to only one building will be evaluated by the building Principal. Speech and language therapists assigned to more than one building will be evaluated by the Coordinator of Special Education. Speech and language therapists assigned only to the Early Childhood program will be evaluated by the Coordinator of Early Childhood Education or his/her designee.

Occupational Therapists: Early Childhood O.T.s will be evaluated by the Coordinator of Early Childhood Education or designee. All other O.T.s will be evaluated by the Coordinator of Special Education.

Physical Therapists will be evaluated by the Early Childhood Education Coordinator, the school physician or the Curriculum Coordinator for Special Education.

Adaptive Physical Education teachers will be evaluated by the appropriate Coordinator of Special Education.

Visual Consultant will be evaluated by the Appropriate Curriculum Coordinator for Special Education.

Attendance Officer will be evaluated by the Assistant Superintendent for Integrated Services.

Home Instruction and **Early Childhood Teachers** will be evaluated by the Elementary Curriculum Coordinator for Special Education.

Coordinator of Outside Placements will be evaluated by the Elementary Coordinator of Special Education.

Lesley Interns will be evaluated by the Lesley College Intern Coordinator and the teacher to whom they are assigned.

School Nurses will be evaluated by the school pediatrician.

Timelines for Teacher Evaluations

The following timeline is provided for your information in connection with the implementation of the evaluation procedures as established by the Brookline School Committee. In any case when the date falls on a weekend or holiday, the Evaluator should use the prior work day as the final date. The timelines are consistent with the contract between the Brookline Educators Association and the Brookline School Committee:

September of each year – On or before this date, please discuss evaluation procedures with staff and give each staff member a copy of the Principles of Effective Teaching.

October 15 of each year – On or before this date, evaluators should meet with all preprofessional status teachers to address goals for the year, strengths of the teacher, relationships between current and previous evaluations, the Brookline Principles of Effective Teaching and the support available.

October 20 of each year – Out of Cycle Evaluation: On or before this date, any teacher with "professional teacher status" may be evaluated out-of-cycle. On or before this date, the evaluator should provide the teacher with substantive reasons for undertaking the out-of-cycle evaluation. Possible reasons are:

    a) the teacher is new to your school,
    b) previous problems,
    c) recent developments.

October 31 of each year – There are to be three staff progress reports issued annually to pre-professional status teachers. It is suggested that the first of these be issued by this date.

December 1 of each year – On or before this date, please meet with each teacher with "professional teacher status" who is to be evaluated. The purpose of this meeting is to discuss goals for the year, strengths, relationships between current and previous evaluations, the Brookline Principles of Effective Teaching and support available.

December 2 of each year – It is suggested that you issue the second staff progress reports to the pre-professional status teachers.

January 31 of each year – On or before this date, it is suggested you issue the third staff progress reports to pre-professional status teachers and the first of two progress reports to PTS teachers.

Evaluators should notify the Principal and Assistant Superintendent for Personnel of any pre-professional status teacher whose renewal is questionable and of any professional teacher status teacher who may receive a final check that is unsatisfactory or in the lowest satisfactory category.

February 14 of each year – On or before this date, you should have issued the Annual Report of Teacher Effectiveness to pre-professional status teachers. It is suggested that you issue these as early in February as possible. Please hand deliver unfavorable Annual Reports and those which contain serious reservations. Please call the Director of Personnel if you wish not to recommend a person for reappointment or if you have any doubt about there being a position for him. Kindly send the completed package, together with a cover memo listing the enclosures to this office by February 28.

March 1 of each year – Evaluators must notify the Assistant Superintendent for Personnel in writing of all pre-professional status teachers whose renewal is questionable so a non-renewal letter can be written. The teacher's name should be given even in those cases in which a decision may be made to renew the teacher prior to the April 15 date.

Evaluators must notify the Assistant Superintendent for Personnel of any professional teacher status teacher who may receive a final check that is unsatisfactory or in the lowest satisfactory category.

April 15 of each year – On or before this date all pre-professional teacher status teachers who will not be renewed for the upcoming year must be hand delivered by his/her Evaluator the letter of non-renewal.

April 30 of each year – On or before this date, Annual Reports of Teacher Effectiveness must be issued to teachers with "professional teacher status" by this date. The completed package, together with a cover memo listing the enclosures, should be sent to the personnel office by June 1, 200_. BHS Administrators should also send a copy of each package to the appropriate evaluation team leader indicated on the back. Vice/Assistant Principals should also send a copy of each package to the Principal.

Lexington Public Schools

Article 10–Evaluation and Supervision

A. The philosophy of the Lexington Public Schools supervision and evaluation process emerges directly from the Lexington Public Schools core values: ***Individuality and Diversity, Shared Responsibility, and Continuous Improvement.***

A diverse professional staff, by definition, comprises individuals with different backgrounds, needs, interests, and aspirations. Lexington Public Schools should afford the professional staff opportunities to explore and express their individuality and to appreciate the individuality of colleagues. Hence, the supervision and evaluation process should address the gifts, talents, and special needs of every member of the professional staff. Supervisors and evaluators should practice diverse methodologies in an effort to challenge all staff members, whatever their experience or areas of expertise. Professional excellence can only be achieved when all members of the professional staff know the high, realistic and explicitly stated expectations for them.

Members of the professional staff and administrators must work together within the supervision and evaluation process to harness the power of community, collaboration, and communication. Partnerships which maximize our professional potential, enhance our professional practices, and overcome the defensiveness which sometimes hampers our professional relationships must be developed. A collegial, supportive, non-threatening climate should be promoted by all.

Regardless of the current level of attainment, professional performance should always be improving. An environment that fosters experimentation, persistent innovation, risk taking, and continuing growth leads to a healthy school culture which in turn produces a positive place in which to teach and learn. Professional staff should be lifelong learners who develop the habit of inquiry, try new approaches to problem solving, and understand that some experiments will not work. Alternative assessments to measure the efficacy of professional performance are essential to provide professional staff with the best possible feedback so that they can continuously improve their performance. Feedback loops and constant communication among members of the school community are necessary to help guide all improvement efforts.

With these core values in mind, the purpose of a supervisory system is to provide professional staff with frequent, high quality feedback on their practice. The purpose of an evaluative system is to produce judgments about the performance level and job status of professional staff and whether or not they are performing up to district standards.

B. In accordance with state regulations, the principal or the assistant principal designee will serve as the primary evaluator for all staff assigned to a building. This evaluation will be conducted and completed in collaboration with the designated coordinator or department head as indicated on the chart below. Multi-building staff will be evaluated by the principal of the building where they have the majority of their teaching responsibilities.

CHART OF EVALUATIVE RESPONSIBILITIES

Elementary
Classroom Teachers   Principal

Teaching Specialists   Principal/Coordinator
(Music, Art, Physical Education,
Foreign Languages)

Elementary Subject Specialists K–5 Director of Curriculum and
(Mathematics, Science,   Instruction/Coordinator
Language Arts, Social Studies)

Middle School
Teachers

English, Science, Mathematics, Principal/Assistant Principal/
Social Studies   Department Head

Foreign Language, Art, Music,   Principal/Assistant Principal/
Physical Education, Industrial   Coordinator
Technology, Business, Home
Economics, Guidance

High School
Teachers   Principal/Assistant Principal/
Department Head

Drama   Principal/Coordinator

Counselors
Elementary   Principal
Middle School   Principal
High School   Principal/High School Department
Head

Librarians   Principal/Coordinator of Libraries
and Instructional Materials

Cable Program Supervisor   Principal/Coordinator of Libraries
                                      and Instructional Materials

Social Workers
   High School   Principal/Guidance Department Head
   Middle School   Principal
   Elementary   Principal

Metco Staff   Principal/Coordinator

Reading
   High School   Principal/Department Head
   Middle School   Principal/Department Head
   Elementary School   Principal

Nurses   Principal/Chairperson of Nurses

Chairpersons
   Language Arts/Reading K–5   Director of Curriculum and
                                      Instruction
   Nurses   Coordinator of Health Education
   Guidance K–8   Principal

Special Needs Specialists
   Adaptive Physical Education   Principal
   Integration Specialists   Principal
   Occupational Therapists   Principal
   Psychologists   Principal
   Resource   Principal
   Self-contained Classroom Teachers Principal
   Speech and Language   Principal

Department Heads
   Mathematics and English   Principal/Director of Curriculum
                                      and Instruction

Coordinators   Superintendent/Director of
                                      Curriculum and Instruction

C. Observation Reports

1. The observation of the work performance of a staff member will be conducted openly and with full knowledge of the staff member. Frequency of observation should be a function of perceived performance. Observation of unsatisfactory performance should lead to more frequent observations and conferences.

2. Each observation will be followed by a post conference within 3 school days of the observation. A written observation report will be provided to the staff member within 15 school days after the observation. If a staff member is to be observed more than once before a written observation report is prepared, the reason must be recorded in writing on the observation report. The staff member and the evaluator will mutually agree on the dates and the number of observations.

3. Classroom observations for the purpose of collecting data for evaluation reports shall be no less than thirty (30) minutes in duration at the elementary level and one full instructional period at the middle schools and the high school. Any exception will be mutually agreed to by the staff member and the evaluator.

4. Individual observations shall not be subject to the grievance procedure except as part of a grievance concerning an evaluation. Evaluation shall be subject to the grievance and arbitration procedures, both procedurally and substantively.

5. The Superintendent, Director of Curriculum and Instruction, or the Director of Personnel and Administration may visit a staff member's classroom/workplace to assess the observation skills of an evaluator, to investigate a complaint, or for administrative purposes other than evaluation. The Superintendent, Director of Curriculum and Instruction, or the Director of Personnel and Administration may be visiting staff members' classrooms/workplaces in the course of doing a general review of teaching or they might visit staff members' classrooms/workplaces to follow up after receiving an evaluation report. They will be going into a staff member's classroom/workplace at the specific request of either the staff member or the evaluator, and they will be going into staff members' classrooms/workplaces during the professional status process.

D. Evaluation Reports

1. Normally, evaluation reports will be based on one to three observation reports.

2. Commendations and recommendations relating to Lexington's performance standards are considered to be a routine part of an evaluation report. Adverse or negative comments or conclusions can only appear in an

evaluation report if they have already appeared in an observation report or have otherwise been documented and placed in the staff member's personnel file.

3. The superintendent, director of curriculum and instruction, or the director of personnel and administration can be involved in the evaluation of a staff member.

4. One week prior to the evaluation conference, the evaluator will provide the staff member with a copy of the evaluation report. The staff member's signature on the final evaluation does not necessarily indicate agreement with the final report. Staff members shall have the right to object in writing to anything included therein; this written commentary should be attached to the evaluation report.

5. At the end of a staff member's evaluation cycle, one final evaluation report will be written. Where designated on the chart of evaluation responsibilities, the principal, assistant principal, coordinator, or department head will collaborate in writing the final evaluation report.

6. A staff member may attach a written reply to any evaluation which shall be in his/her personnel file.

E. Non-professional Status Staff Members

1. Non-professional status staff members should be observed at least twice during the school year. The interim observation is to be completed prior to December 15 and the final observation is to be completed prior to May 15. The final evaluation will be written and presented to the non-professional status staff member by May 25.

2. A non-professional status employee who is not reappointed will receive from the Administration a written statement of reasons for non-reappointment.

F. Professional Status Staff Members

1. Important dates in the evaluation process of professional status staff members are as follows:

   October 1: Observation cycle can begin. Normally, the entire evaluation process will be completed within four months of the first observation.

   May 1: The observation cycle ends.

   June 1: Final evaluations are due at the Personnel Office.

2. A comprehensive system of professional growth must give professional staff frequent, high quality feedback on their practice (supervision), and must also produce judgments about their performance level and job

status, and most importantly, whether or not they are performing up to district standards (evaluation). Therefore, a four-year cycle of evaluation and supervision has been designed to meet the needs of the professional staff and the school system:

Year 1: Comprehensive Evaluation

During this year, the staff member will be evaluated on all district performance standards and according to the principles and practices of evaluation as stated elsewhere in this article. At the end of the evaluation period (no later than May 31), the evaluator(s) will confer with the staff member and discuss the final, written evaluation. The evaluation will include a written summary of commendations and recommendations. (See model forms.)

Year 2: Collaborative Year

The purpose of the collaborative year is not only to promote professional growth but also to encourage collaboration and sharing among staff members. Staff members may also collaborate with other professionals. At some time after the comprehensive evaluation has been completed, but prior to October 1 of the collaborative year, the staff member and the evaluator(s) will confer to establish professional growth goal(s) based on the commendations and recommendations made in the comprehensive evaluation. Prior to October 15, the staff member will develop and submit a Professional Growth Plan (see model) which contains the following information:

> Therefore, a four-year cycle of evaluation and supervision has been designed to meet the needs of the professional staff and the school system . . .

- the proposal (see list of suggestions)
- the goals of the proposal which contribute to professional knowledge and/or skill and which are based on commendations/recommendations of the comprehensive evaluation
- the actions or procedures the staff member will follow to accomplish the goal
- a time line
- what evidence the staff member will provide to show completion of the proposal
- staff member or other participants and their roles and responsibilities
- what type of support, if any, might be needed to complete the proposal (materials, time, staff development meetings)

During the course of the collaborative professional growth activities, the evaluator(s) may make observations and hold conferences. When the activities have been completed, the staff member will confer with the primary evaluator(s) and submit a final written report (see model) by May 31. The Professional Growth Plan and the Final Report will be placed in the staff member's personnel file.

In the unlikely event that there is an unresolvable disagreement between the staff member and the evaluator(s) over the Professional Growth Plan, each may select a colleague to participate in the resolution of the disagreement.

Should the disagreement still not be resolved, the director of curriculum and the LEA president will participate in a final resolution.

Year 3: Focused Evaluation

During this year, the staff member will be evaluated on selected district performance standards and according to the principles and practices of evaluation as stated elsewhere in this article. This focus of this evaluation will be determined in a conference between the staff member and the evaluator(s). It should grow out of the goals and outcomes of both the comprehensive evaluation (year 1) and the collaborative year (year 2). At the end of the evaluation period (no later than May 31), the evaluator(s) will confer with the staff member and discuss the final, written evaluation. The evaluation will include a written summary of commendations and recommendations. (See model forms.)

Year 4: Individual Study

This is a year in which the staff member may select a professional growth activity. The staff member will confer with the evaluator(s) and develop a Professional Growth Plan by October 15 with all of the information as listed in Year 2 with one exception: the plan may or may not include other staff member participants. The goal(s) of the plan do not have to be linked to previous evaluations, but the activity must be substantial and should contribute to one's professional knowledge or skill. At the end of the year, the staff member will submit a final report on or before May 31 and confer with his/her evaluator(s). The Professional Growth Plan and the Final Report will be placed in the staff member's personnel file.

Student Feedback

Teachers of grades 6–12 will annually solicit feedback from students in all their classes. However, those special area teachers who teach a large percentage of the student body will solicit feedback from a number of students comparable to a core subject area teacher at their school. This should occur sometime after the midpoint of the course, leaving sufficient time to allow for consultation with the peer reviewer and evaluator(s)/supervisor(s). The purpose of this feedback is to gather information that students are in a position to know which can then be used by the staff member for self-assessment and professional growth. The instrument(s) used to obtain this feedback will be created by an individual teacher or a team of teachers subject to the review of the evaluator(s)/supervisor(s) or their designees. The instruments should seek feedback in the following areas: curriculum, teaching methods, classroom management, assessment and grading, homework, classroom climate, and the teacher/student relationship.

Student completed feedback forms are the sole property of the teacher who issued them. However, the forms are to be shared with at least one of the teacher's peers in a collaborative effort to analyze the findings. The peer reviewer will hold all data and findings in confidence. The issuing teacher will discuss the findings with his/her supervisor(s)/evaluator(s) and, whenever appropriate, should use the data in goal setting activities for the coming year.

Termination of a Professional Growth Plan

If the evaluator(s) personally observes performance of a staff member participating in the Collaborative Year or the Independent Study Year that is adversely affecting the delivery of educational services, the evaluator may call for a conference with the staff member. The intent of the conference will be to address the performance issue and allow the Collaborative Year or the Independent Study Year to continue. If the issue is not resolved, the evaluator may begin a Comprehensive or Focused Evaluation Year after written notification detailing the reasons for this decision has been given to the staff member. This written notification will be placed in the Central Office personnel file.

G. Tier Two Regulations (Professional Status)

1. Normally, a staff member is placed on tier two if there are observed and documented deficiencies in more than one performance standard on the instrument; however, in unusual circumstances, which the evaluator(s) would need to define and defend, a staff member might be placed on tier two on the basis of a severe deficiency in a single category. Placement on tier two presumes that unless the reason for placement is satisfactorily remediated, recommendation for dismissal would be the result.

2. At the end of the second year on tier two, the staff member may be restored to tier one or shall be dismissed. In the second year of tier two, the staff member's increment and/or negotiated salary increase may be withheld. Any staff member restored to tier one shall be placed on the appropriate step as if he/she had never been on tier two.

3. Tier two can begin only in September of the following school year and will last no longer than two school years. No employee shall be dismissed after one year on tier two unless that employee has received a tier two warning letter on or before December 15. Placement on tier two can

only be based upon an evaluation report which includes at least three observations.

The notification of possible placement on tier two can occur at any time and must be based on an evaluator's personal observations of staff member performance. The evaluator(s) must document the observations and review them with the staff member before the issuance of a notification letter. The primary evaluator shall not notify any staff member of possible placement on tier two unless there have first been at least three observations, which the evaluator(s) will have documented and reviewed with the employee.

4. Staff members who have been notified of potential placement on tier two may employ a range of activities or services in the school system including, but not limited to the following: peer consultation, peer observation, use of curriculum support personnel. The activities will not be part of the evaluation record.

5. If a professional status staff member is notified that he/she will be placed on tier two, during the period between the notification (example, May 1) and the placement, (example, September 1) there will be no additional evaluator(s), but coordinators, department heads, department chairs, assistant principals, etc., can provide support and consultation. Once a staff member is on tier two, if there is a subject-related problem, the appropriate curriculum administrator(s) must be involved as a supplementary evaluator(s). Any evaluation conclusion reached by a supplementary evaluator shall be based on observation reports.

6. Within ten school days of the tier two warning or notice placing a staff member on tier two, the staff member and all evaluators shall meet to discuss an improvement plan which shall include: an identification of the aspects of performance which are in need of improvement; the evaluators' specific expectations; the indicators of satisfactory improvement; how the evaluators will assist the staff member, where applicable, in meeting these expectations; the time which will be allowed for improvement; and, the date by which another evaluation report will be completed.

The follow-up evaluation will be completed within two to four months, unless both the staff member and the evaluator(s) agree to a change in this time frame. The LEA president (or his/her designee) and the superintendent (or his/her designee) will have to agree to this change.

If the improvement plan does not identify one or more evaluators, or does not describe the role of any evaluator, the improvement plan shall be amended to identify any such evaluator(s) and to describe such evaluator's role in the improvement plan. This will occur within ten (10) school days from the date of the improvement plan. The staff member shall be given a copy of each amendment. The staff member and all evaluators named in the improvement plan shall meet to discuss the amendment within ten (10) school days of incorporation of the amendment to the plan. Any subsequent amendments must be agreed to by the primary evaluator, the staff member, the superintendent (or his/her designee) and the LEA president (or his/her designee).

An evaluator from the Central Office may be a supplementary evaluator and shall be governed by the provisions relating to supplementary evaluators and their evaluations. The staff member may request a particular evaluator from the Central Office.

Before any evaluator performs any formal observation for the purpose of preparing a follow-up evaluation, pursuant to the improvement plan, he/she shall hold a pre-observation conference with the staff member. There will be a post-observation conference following the observation.

7. The primary evaluator will prepare a draft of the improvement plan and circulate copies to the staff member and all involved evaluators. Each will sign and return the tier-two improvement plan within five (5) school days to the primary evaluator. Any involved person can append suggestions or recommendations. The primary evaluator may or may not incorporate written suggestions in the final plan.

8. Copies of the final improvement plan and any subsequent amendments will be hand delivered by the primary evaluator (or his/her designee) to the superintendent and the president of the LEA each of whom will have five (5) school days in which to raise an objection to the plan and notify all of the other parties in writing of his/her concern(s).

    The superintendent (or his/her designee) shall respond in writing to any written objections of the LEA president (or his/her designee). The LEA president (or his/her designee) shall respond in writing to any written objections of the superintendent (or his/her designee). Responses to objections shall be made within five (5) school days of their receipt.

    The parties shall meet within seven (7) school days of the receipt of objections to resolve said objections. In the event that the parties cannot agree within five (5) school days, they shall meet with a mediator, chosen by mutual agreement, to resolve any outstanding issues. If, after an additional meeting with a mediator, they are unable to resolve any outstanding disagreements, the mediator shall resolve the disagreements. The decision of the mediator is not grieveable.

9. If a tier two warning plan is successfully completed as evidenced by the subsequent evaluation, the staff member shall not be placed on tier two.

10. Placement on tier two is grieveable. There will be an expedited grievance procedure with only one level of management review, that is the superintendent's level. The immediate step thereafter is arbitration.

PROFESSIONAL GROWTH PLAN

Name _____

School _____ Date _____

Check one: _____ Year 2 – Collaborative Year

                 _____ Year 4 – Individual Study

The PROPOSAL _____

_____

_____

_____

GOALS: State the goals of the proposal as related to the comprehensive evaluation. (**Note:** During Year 4, the goals need not be directly linked to the comprehensive evaluation.)

ACTIONS: State the actions or procedures planned to accomplish the goals.

TIME LINE: State the time line for completion.

EVIDENCE: Describe the evidence to be provided to demonstrate completion. _____

_____

_____

_____

COLLABORATING PROFESSIONALS: Identify the collaborating teachers or other professionals involved in the proposal. Describe their roles and responsibilities. (**Note:** Collaboration is optional during Year 4 Individual Study)

ADMINISTRATIVE SUPPORT: Indicate, if any, the type of support (materials, time, staff development meetings) which might be needed from the administration to complete the proposal.

Date of conference: _____

(form continued)

_____   _____
Signature of evaluator   date

_____   _____
Signature of staff menber   date

FINAL REPORT ON PROFESSIONAL GROWTH PLAN

Name _____

School _____ Date _____

Check one: _____ Year 2 – Collaborative Year

                  _____ Year 4 – Individual Study

Report on your professional growth by commenting on the relevant aspects of your Professional Growth Plan. For example: Did you achieve your goals? Did the actions/procedures go according to plan? Have you provided the evidence required? How did the planned collaboration actually work? Was there sufficient time and support?

After addressing the implementation of the plan, make an assessment of the knowledge and/or skills you gained during the year. You might consider questions such as these: What did you learn and how will this knowledge impact on your professional performance? How will the year's professional growth activities affect future goal setting? What new or improved skills will make you a better professional, and how might you share them in future collaborative roles?

N.B.   The staff member and the evaluator(s) should sign and date this final report which will be attached to the Professional Growth Plan and placed in the staff member's personnel file.

Date of conference _____

_____   _____
Signature of evaluator   date

_____   _____
Signature of teacher   date

SUGGESTIONS FOR A PROFESSIONAL GROWTH PLAN

Note: Most of these suggestions can be tailored to fit staff members' needs and desires, and to satisfy the requirements of either a Collaborative Year or an Individual Study Year.

- **Peer Observation:** Teachers agree to observe each other's classes several times during the year and provide and receive feedback important to their goals.

- **Study Groups:** Teachers meet with colleagues in groups to learn new strategies, experiment with these strategies and share the results of their experiments, and to problem solve. Study groups can be developed to feature content which would support a teacher's goals.

- **Field Based Research:** A teacher develops a hypothesis and a research project to test that hypothesis. A teacher might propose the hypothesis that the use of cooperative learning strategies will improve student achievement in U.S. history. The teacher can then identify a section or sections in which to use the strategy and measure student achievement. Findings could be briefly presented in a paper and discussed with other teachers.

- **Analysis of a Portfolio of Artifacts:** A teacher could develop a file of appropriate artifacts/documents in order to analyze certain relationships, such as between the instructional strategies used and student achievement. A final report could be prepared and shared with other teachers.

- **Preparing and Presenting a Staff Development Program:** A teacher with interest and expertise in a particular area of instruction could develop and present a program on the topic to other interested staff. The presentation should include what participants will know or be able to do as a result of participating in the program, why it is important to learn it, and how it relates to student learning.

- **Preparing and Presenting a Parent Education Program:** This is similar to the development of a staff development program, but specifically designed to attract parents. Topics such as how to help children with their homework or how to help children become better readers are only two of many possibilities.

- **Team Teaching with an Administrator, Principal, or Another Professional:** The "team" would create, teach, and evaluate an integrated unit of instruction. All involved share responsibility and work together to assess the unit by identifying its problems and successes.

- **Self-Analysis of Videotapes:** A teacher could videotape several lessons during the course of the year, analyze the lessons, and write up an assessment on the effectiveness of each.

- **Mentoring:** A teacher could develop and/or extend mentoring relationships throughout the school. The mentoring process should include observing the new teacher at several points during the year, providing feedback, being observed by the new teacher, and holding frequent discussions about teaching.

- **Curriculum or Instructional Strategy Development:** A group of teachers could develop and then pilot a substantively new curriculum based on state and/or local goals or requirements. A thorough process of assessing the pilot program must be prepared, implemented, and written up. Or the teachers could apply an instructional strategy such as cooperative learning to a new curriculum or to where it has not been previously used. A plan to assess the effectiveness must be prepared, implemented, and written up.

- **Course Work:** A teacher could participate in substantive in-service professional development and/or take a course.

- **Submission of Articles for Publication:** A teacher could prepare and present one or more articles on instruction and/or curriculum for publication in professional journals.

- **Other:** (Subject to administrative review and approval).

TEACHER PERFORMANCE STANDARDS

I. Currency in the Curriculum

The teacher demonstrates competency in subject area(s).

1. Has an appropriate in-depth knowledge of subject matter

2. Acts as a subject area resource person for students

3. Contributes to the ongoing evaluation of the curriculum

4. Keeps current in the field and applies knowledge to the instructional program

II. Effective Planning and Assessment of Curriculum and Instruction

A. The teacher plans instruction effectively.

1. Sets short-term and year-long goals for curricular units

2. Identifies individual and group needs and plans the use of appropriate instructional strategies

3. Uses materials and resources, including technologies, that are appropriately matched to curricular goals and to individual student needs and learning styles.

4. Seeks out and collaborates with school based specialists and administrators to better design curricula or instructional modifications to meet the special learning needs of students

5. Plans frequent instructional opportunities where students are interacting with teachers and one another while assuming increasing responsibility for their own learning

B. The teacher provides effective assessment of student learning.

1. Determines specific and challenging standards for student learning; compares intended and actual learning outcomes

2. Schedules time for individual and interactive reflection on student progress with the student

3. Regularly provides feedback to students on their progress

4. Implements innovative approaches to assessment

5. Keeps parents informed of student's progress and works with them to aid in the total development of the student

III. Effective Instruction

A. The teacher communicates effectively with students.

1. Implements clear lesson objectives and communicates these to students

2. Promotes students' independence as learners

3. Stimulates students' thinking through classroom discussion and writing activities

4. Identifies confusions and misconceptions as indicated by student responses and regular assessment strategies. Remediates, reteaches, or extends teaching to meet individual and/or group needs

5. Has enthusiasm for subject matter and makes significant efforts to communicate that enthusiasm to students and colleagues

6. Communicates clearly in writing and speaking, using precise language

7. Understands and demonstrates to students the relevance of the subject matter to life-long learning and the inter-relationship of various curricula

B. The teacher uses appropriate instructional techniques.

1. Uses a variety of teaching strategies such as cooperative learning, peer tutoring, project based learning, lecture, discussions, and technologies

2. Provides options for students to demonstrate competency and mastery of new material, such as written work, plays, artwork, oratory, visual presentations, and portfolios

3. Uses a variety of appropriate materials to reinforce and extend skills, accommodate learning styles, and match instructional objectives

4. Encourages students to summarize important learnings and to integrate them with prior knowledge

5. Demonstrates a working knowledge of current educational research

6. Refines instructional strategies to increase student learning and foster confidence in a student's ability to learn

7. Provides opportunities for creativity

8. Uses a variety of questioning techniques to stimulate student participation, including those which encourage and guide critical and independent thinking and the development of ideas

9. Presents information recognizing multiple points of view; encourages students to assess the accuracy of information presented

IV. Effective Classroom Management

A. The teacher applies classroom management techniques to establish a positive and productive learning environment.

1. Uses time and classroom space productively and efficiently in order to promote optimal learning

2. Maintains a high level of student participation and engagement with appropriate time on task

3. Establishes classroom procedures that ensure smooth transition from one activity to another

B. The teacher maintains and models appropriate standards of behavior, mutual respect, and safety.

1. Encourages student achievement and responsibility by reinforcing desired student behaviors that demonstrate attitudes of fairness and respect

2. Establishes and carries out reasonable and routine classroom rules and procedures

3. Maintains appropriate professional boundaries with students

V. Promotion of High Standards and Expectations for Student Achievement

A. The teacher promotes high standards and expectations for student achievement.

1. Communicates standards, expectations, and guidelines regarding the quality and quantity of students' work to students and parents

2. Responds to students' answers and work in a timely and appropriate way

3. Encourages students to take risks and to persevere with challenging tasks

VI. **Promotion of Equity and Appreciation of Diversity**

The teacher promotes equitable opportunities for student learning.

1. Provides opportunities for all students to participate in the classroom

2. Demonstrates sensitivity to differences in abilities, gender, learning style, social and cultural background

3. Develops and implements educational and organizational strategies that are effective in meeting the needs of a diverse student body

VII. **Fulfillment of Professional Responsibilities**

The teacher demonstrates continuing concern for professionalism.

1. Seeks out information and is receptive to suggestions for growth and improvement

2. Works collaboratively with other staff members to implement appropriate curricular and school related programs

3. Shares expertise and new ideas with colleagues

4. Works constructively with others to identify school problems and suggest possible solutions

5. Meets deadlines and fulfills routine responsibilities

6. Observes established school system policies and procedures

7. Participates in appropriate self development activities such as conferences, in-service training and professional study

8. Maintains appropriate professional behaviors in all interactions with students, parents, and colleagues

SCHOOL NURSE PERFORMANCE STANDARDS

I. Currency in School Health

1. The school nurse demonstrates competency in the area of school health. Has an appropriate in-depth knowledge of school nursing practice

2. Acts as a health resource person for students, colleagues, and parents

3. Contributes to the ongoing evaluation of the health services

4. Keeps current in the field and applies knowledge to the health care of students and staff

5. Demonstrates an interest in and concern for the prevention of disease and promotion of health

II. **Effective Planning and Assessment of Student Health Status**
    A. The school nurse plans for health care needs effectively.

1. Sets short-term and year-long goals for health care needs of students

2. Identifies individual needs and plans for the use of appropriate nursing care

3. Uses resources, including technologies, that are appropriately matched to nursing interventions and to individual student health needs

4. Seeks out and collaborates with other school based nurses, specialists, and administrators to better design modifications to meet the special health needs of students

5. Plans for students to increase responsibility for their own health needs

B. The nurse provides effective assessment of student health status.

1. Compares intended and actual health outcomes

2. Schedules time for interaction with the student regarding health issues

3. Regularly provides feedback to students on their progress

4. Implements innovative approaches to health assessment

5. Keeps parents informed of student's health status and works with them to meet the total health needs of the student

III. **Effective Instruction**
    A. The school nurse communicates effectively with students.

1. Implements clear health care objectives and communicates these to students

2. Promotes students' independence as learners with regard to health issues

3. Identifies confusions and misconceptions as indicated by student responses and regular assessment strategies to health care. Remediates, reteaches, or extends teaching to meet individual and/or group health needs

4. Has enthusiasm for school nursing and preventive health care and makes significant efforts to communicate that enthusiasm to students and colleagues

5. Communicates clearly in writing and speaking, using precise language

6. Understands and demonstrates to students the relevance of their health status to their life

B. The school nurse uses appropriate instructional techniques.

1. Uses a variety of strategies for individualized health teaching

2. Uses appropriate materials to reinforce health care needs to accommodate learning styles

3. Encourages students to summarize important health knowledge and to integrate it with prior knowledge

4. Demonstrates a working knowledge of current school nursing research

5. Uses a variety of questioning techniques to encourage student participation, including those which encourage self care and independent evaluation of their health issues

IV. Effective Health Room Management

A. The school nurse establishes a positive health room environment.

1. Uses time and health room space productively and efficiently

2. Maintains a high level of student participation and engagement in their own health care

B. The school nurse maintains and models appropriate standards of behavior, mutual respect, and safety.

1. Encourages student responsibility by reinforcing desired student behaviors that demonstrate attitudes of fairness and respect

2. Establishes and carries out reasonable and routine health room rules and procedures

3   Maintains appropriate professional boundaries with students

4. Handles sensitive information with discretion

V. Promotion of Equity and Appreciation of Diversity
The school nurse strives to ensure equitable treatment and care of all students.

1. Demonstrates sensitivity to differences in gender, social and cultural backgrounds

2. Develops and implements health programs that are effective in meeting the needs of a diverse student body

VI. Fulfillment of Professional Responsibilities
The school nurse demonstrates continuing concern for professionalism.

1. Seeks out information and is receptive to suggestions for growth and improvement

2. Works collaboratively with other staff members to implement appropriate nursing programs

3. Shares expertise and new ideas with colleagues

4. Works constructively with others to identify school health problems and suggest possible solutions.

5. Meets deadlines and fulfills routine responsibilities

6. Observes established school system policies and procedures

7. Participates in appropriate self development activities such as conferences, in-service training and professional study

8. Maintains appropriate professional behaviors in all interactions with students, parents, and colleagues

SPECIAL EDUCATION TEACHER PERFORMANCE STANDARDS

I. Currency in the Curriculum
The teacher demonstrates competency in special education practices.

1. Has an appropriate in-depth knowledge of special education practices

2. Acts as a resource person for students, colleagues and parents in special education matters

3. Keeps current in the field through professional development activities

II. **Effective Planning and Assessment of Curriculum and Instruction for Special Needs Students**

A. **The special needs teacher plans instruction effectively.**

1. Sets short term and year long goals for special education students through the education plan

2. Identifies and plans the use of appropriate instructional strategies

3. Uses materials and resources, including technologies that enhance learning

B. **The teacher provides effective assessment of student learning.**

1. Regularly provides feedback to students on their progress

2. Implements varied approaches to classroom assessments

3. Keeps parents informed of student's progress and works with them to aid in the development of the student

4. Is familiar with relevant information from student records and consults with appropriate personnel

5. Observes and describes student behavior as needed

C. **Participates on the school evaluation team.**

1. Selects appropriate tests and measures as part of the evaluation process

2. Provides written documentation of testing

3. Contributes to education plans, semi-annual reports and parent conferences as appropriate

III. **Effective Instruction**

A. **The teacher communicates effectively with students.**

1. Implements clear lesson objectives and communicates these to students

2. Promotes students' independence as learners

3. Stimulates students' thinking through classroom discussion and activities, when appropriate

4. Remediates, reteaches or extends teaching to meet individual and/or group needs

5. Communicates clearly

B. **The teacher uses appropriate instructional techniques, materials and resources to assist students in achieving Individual Education Plan (IEP) objectives.**

1. Provides for individual differences in student learning rates, styles, abilities and interests by such means as differentiating instruction, grouping, materials and assignments

2. Refers students to appropriate support personnel as needed

3. Uses a variety of instructional materials and strategies

4. Consults with classroom teachers about curriculum modifications

5. Provides recommendations to staff and parents to improve students' strategies in dealing with academic and/or behavioral issues

6. When appropriate, encourages creativity and independent thinking

IV. **Effective Classroom Management**

A. **The teacher applies classroom management techniques to establish a positive and productive learning environment.**

1. Uses time productively and efficiently

2. Reinforces desired student behaviors

3. Establishes and carries out reasonable rules and procedures

4. Uses available space effectively

B. **The teacher maintains and models appropriate standards of behavior, mutual respect, and safety.**

1. Encourages student attitudes of fairness and respect

2. Maintains appropriate professional boundaries with students

V. **Promotion of High Standards and Expectations for Individual Student Achievement Based on Student's Learning Profile and Educational Plan**

The teacher promotes high standards and expectations for student achievement based on the student's learning profile and educational plan.

1. Communicates standards, expectations, and guidelines regarding the quality of student's work

2. Responds to student's answers and work in a timely and appropriate way

3. Encourages student to take risks

VI. Promotion of Equity and Appreciation of Diversity
The teacher promotes equitable opportunities for student learning.

1. Provides opportunities for all students to participate in the classroom

2. Demonstrates sensitivity to differences in abilities, gender, learning style, social and cultural background

3. Develops and implements educational and organizational strategies that are effective in meeting the needs of a diverse student body

VII. Fulfillment of Professional Responsibilities
The teacher demonstrates continuing concern for professionalism.

1. Seeks out information and is receptive to suggestions

2. Works collaboratively with other staff members

3. Shares expertise and new ideas with colleagues

4. Meets deadlines and fulfills routine responsibilities

5. Observes established school system policies and procedures

6. Participates in appropriate self development activities such as conferences, in-service training and professional study

7. Maintains appropriate professional behaviors in all interactions with students, parents and colleagues

LANGUAGE ARTS/READING SPECIALIST PERFORMANCE STANDARDS

I. Currency in the Curriculum
The specialist demonstrates competency in subject area(s).

1. Has an appropriate, in-depth knowledge of literacy development and instructional strategies in all areas of the language arts

2. Acts as a subject area resource person for teachers, curriculum personnel, principals, and parents

3. Contributes to the ongoing evaluation of the curriculum

4. Keeps current in the field and applies knowledge to consultations with teachers, and to the instructional program

II. Effective Planning and Assessment of Curriculum and Instruction

A. The specialist plans instruction effectively.

1. Sets short-term and year-long goals for curricular units

2. Identifies individual and group needs and plans the use of appropriate instructional strategies

3. Uses materials and resources, including technologies, that are appropriately matched to curricular goals and to individual student needs and learning styles

4. Seeks out and collaborates with other school based specialists and administrators to better design curricula or instructional modifications to meet the special learning needs of students

5. Plans frequent instructional opportunities where students are interacting with teachers and one another while assuming increasing responsibility for their own learning

B. The teacher provides effective assessment of student learning.

1. Determines specific and challenging standards for student learning; compares intended and actual learning outcomes

2. Schedules time for individual and interactive reflection on student progress with the student

3. Regularly provides feedback to students on their progress

4. Implements innovative approaches to assessment

5. Keeps parents informed of student's progress and works with them to aid in the total development of the student

III. Effective Instruction

A. The specialist communicates effectively with students.

1. Implements clear lesson objectives and communicates these to students

2. Promotes students' independence as learners through application of a modeling/guided practice/independent practice instructional model, and other appropriate instructional models

3. Stimulates students' thinking through classroom discussion and writing activities

4. Identifies confusions and misconceptions as indicated by student responses and regular assessment strategies. Retouches or extends teaching to meet individual and/or group needs

5. Has enthusiasm for subject matter and makes significant efforts to communicate that enthusiasm to students and colleagues

6. Communicates clearly in writing and speaking, using precise language

7. Understands and demonstrates to students the relevance of the subject matter to life-long learning and the inter-relationship of various curricula

B. The specialist uses appropriate instructional techniques.

1. Uses a variety of teaching strategies such as cooperative learning, peer tutoring, project based learning, lecture, discussions, and technologies

2. Provides options for students to demonstrate competency and mastery of new material, such as written work, plays, artwork, oratory, visual presentations, and portfolios

3. Uses a variety of appropriate materials to reinforce and extend skills, accommodate learning styles, and match instructional objectives

4. Encourages students to summarize important learnings and to integrate them with prior knowledge

5. Demonstrates a working knowledge of current educational research

6. Refines instructional strategies to increase student learning and foster confidence in a student's ability to learn

7. Provides opportunities for creativity

8. Uses a variety of questioning techniques to stimulate student participation, including those which encourage and guide critical and independent thinking and the development of ideas

9. Presents information recognizing multiple points of view; encourages students to assess the accuracy of information presented

C. The specialist consults effectively with teachers, principals, and other curriculum specialists.

1. Listens well and responds appropriately

2. Communicates positively in all interactions with teachers

3. Works effectively with teachers in a consulting capacity

4. Is available for consultation with teachers at times that are mutually convenient for both

IV. **Effective Classroom Management**

   A. **The specialist applies classroom management techniques to establish a positive and productive learning environment.**

   1. Uses time and classroom space productively and efficiently in order to promote optimal learning

   2. Maintains a high level of student participation and engagement with appropriate time on task

   3. Establishes classroom procedures that ensure smooth transition from one activity to another

   B. **The specialist maintains and models appropriate standards of behavior, mutual respect, and safety.**

   1. Encourages student achievement and responsibility by reinforcing desired student behaviors that demonstrate attitudes of fairness and respect

   2. Establishes and carries out reasonable and routine classroom rules and procedures

   3. Maintains appropriate professional boundaries with students

V. **Promotion of High Standards and Expectations for Student Achievement**
   The specialist promotes high standards and expectations for student achievement.

   1. Communicates standards, expectations, and guidelines regarding the quality and quantity of students' work to students and parents

   2. Responds to students' answers and work in a timely and appropriate way

   3. Encourages students to take risks and to persevere with challenging tasks

VI. **Promotion of Equity and Appreciation of Diversity**
   The specialist promotes equitable opportunities for student learning.

   1. Provides opportunities for all students to participate in the classroom

   2. Demonstrates sensitivity to differences in abilities, gender, learning style, social and cultural background

   3. Develops and implements educational and organizational strategies that are effective in meeting the needs of a diverse student body

VII. Fulfillment of Professional Responsibilities
The specialist demonstrates continuing concern for professionalism.

1. Seeks out information and is receptive to suggestions for growth and improvement

2. Works collaboratively with other staff members to implement appropriate curricular and school related programs

3. Shares expertise and new ideas with colleagues

4. Works constructively with others to identify school problems and suggest possible solutions

5. Meets deadlines and fulfills routine responsibilities

6. Observes established school system policies and procedures

7. Participates in appropriate self development activities such as conferences, in-service training and professional study

8. Maintains appropriate professional behaviors in all interactions with students, parents, and colleagues

PSYCHOLOGIST PERFORMANCE STANDARDS

I. Currency in the Professional Area
The psychologist demonstrates competency in professional areas.

1. Has an appropriate in-depth knowledge of psychology

2. Exhibits current awareness of sound psychological principles and practices in evaluation, consultation and counseling

3. Acts as a resource person for students, colleagues and parents in psychological matters

4. Contributes to ongoing evaluation of educational practices

II. Effective Planning and Assessment
A. The psychologist selects appropriate materials, methods, and resources to assist students in achieving learning and behavioral objectives.

1. Refers students to appropriate in-school support personnel as needed

2. Provides recommendations to staff and parents to improve students' strategies in dealing with academic and behavioral issues

3. Where appropriate, refers students and their families to outside resources

B. **The psychologist establishes psychological objectives consistent with student needs.**

1. Uses currently available psychological findings to make appropriate recommendations for provision of services to students

2. States objectives clearly and conveys the meaning of these objectives

3. Demonstrates concern for the affective, behavioral, and medical as well as the cognitive aspects of student learning

C. **The psychologist assesses, describes, and communicates effectively student needs, strengths, weaknesses, interests, and progress.**

1. Communicates clearly to students the standards and evaluative methods that will be used

2. Applies relevant information from student records

3. Consults with appropriate school personnel, parents, and other agencies and individuals outside the school in planning for students

4. Is perceptive in observing and specific in describing student behavior

5. Effectively evaluates and communicates student functioning to students, parents, staff and other appropriate liaisons

6. Provides written comprehensive documentation of testing

III. **Effective Communication**

A. **The psychologist interacts and communicates positively and productively with students in groups and individual settings.**

1. Explains importance of assessments and employs positive expectations to achieve desired outcomes

2. Provides students opportunities to meet for review of evaluations and follow-up as needed

3. Listens and responds appropriately to students

4. Maintains appropriate professional boundaries with students

B. **The psychologist interacts and communicates positively and productively with parents and staff in groups and individual settings.**

1. Listens and responds appropriately to staff, parents, and outside contacts

2. Communicates psychological findings clearly in writing and speaking, using precise language

IV. **Effective Management**

The psychologist demonstrates effective practices.

1. Employs and/or adopts appropriate psychological material and practices in evaluation, consultation, and counseling

2. Deals sensitively and effectively with the perceptions and reactions of the student, the parents, the staff, and other professionals

3. Uses time productively and efficiently

V. **Promotion of High Standards and Expectations for Student Achievement**

The psychologist promotes high standards and expectations for student functioning.

1. Communicates standards, expectations, and guidelines regarding the quality and quantity of student achievement and behavior

2. Encourages students to take risks and persevere with challenging tasks

VI. **Promotion of Equity and Appreciation of Diversity**

The psychologist promotes equitable opportunities and appreciation of diversity for all students.

1. Demonstrates sensitivity to differences in abilities, gender, learning styles, social and cultural background

2. Develops and implements educational and psychological strategies that are effective in meeting the needs of a diverse student body

3. Encourages student responsibility by reinforcing desired student behaviors that demonstrate attitudes of fairness and respect

VI. **Fulfillment of Professional Responsibilities**

The psychologist demonstrates continuing concern for professionalism.

1. Participates in appropriate professional development activities such as conferences, in-service training and study of journals, etc

2. Observes established school system policies and procedures

3. Meets deadlines and fulfills routine responsibilities

4. Works cooperatively with colleagues and supervisors

5. Demonstrates appropriate awareness of school program and policies in interactions with parents

6. Maintains appropriate professional behavior in all interactions with students, parents, and colleagues

SPEECH AND LANGUAGE PATHOLOGIST PERFORMANCE STANDARDS

I. **Currency in the Curriculum**
    The speech/language pathologist demonstrates competency in subject areas.

    1. Has in-depth knowledge in the field of speech/language pathology

    2. Is aware of current developments in speech/language pathology and applies this awareness in working with students and staff

    3. Acts as a subject area resource person for students, teachers, curriculum personnel, principals, and parents

II. **Effective Planning and Assessment of Curriculum and Instruction**
    A. The speech/language pathologist plans instruction effectively.

    1. Sets and writes goals and objectives for annual Individual Educational Plans and informs classroom teachers of them

    2. Assists teachers in planning for adjustment in instruction as needed, and in selecting appropriate instructional materials and strategies

    3. Uses materials and resources, including technologies, that are appropriately matched to student needs

    B. The speech/language pathologist provides effective assessment of student learning.

    1. Administers individual, diagnostic assessments of students' speech and language skills, and uses current, established testing practices and procedures, as well as innovative approaches to assessment

    2. Makes appropriate referrals for further evaluation

    3. Is specific in describing student strengths, weaknesses, and therapeutic/instructional needs in written reports

    4. Correctly interprets and effectively communicates testing data to parents and staff

5. Continuously evaluates students' progress to adjust therapeutic procedures and goals; and provides opportunities for students to reflect on progress

C. Participates on the school evaluation team.

1. Selects appropriate tests and measures as part of the evaluation process

2. Provides written documentation of testing

3. Contributes to education plans, semi-annual reports and parent conferences as appropriate

III. Effective Instruction

A. The speech/language pathologist communicates effectively with students.

1. Implements clear lesson objectives and communicates these to students

2. Encourages students' independence as learners and makes repeated efforts to support them in achieving their learning goals

3. Communicates clearly in writing and speaking, using language appropriately matched to student needs

4. Communicates positive expectations in all interactions with students, classroom teachers, and parents

5. Has enthusiasm for subject matter and makes efforts to communicate that enthusiasm to students and colleagues

B. The speech/language pathologist uses appropriate instructional techniques.

1. Employs sound therapeutic practice, as well as varied instructional strategies in small group and individual settings

2. Promotes students' independence as learners through application of instructional models

3. Stimulates students' thinking and creativity through all communication channels as appropriate to the communication disorder

4. Assists classroom teachers in providing options for students with communication disorders to demonstrate competency and mastery of new material in a variety of ways

5. Demonstrates a working knowledge of current research

6. Uses varied and effective communication strategies to stimulate student participation

7. Deals effectively with student questions, responses, and confusions

8. Remediates, reteaches or extends teaching to meet individual needs

9. Encourages students to summarize important learnings when possible, and to integrate them with prior knowledge

10. Presents information recognizing multiple points of view, and encourages students to assess the accuracy of information presented

IV. Effective Classroom Management

A. The speech/language pathologist applies classroom management techniques to establish a positive and productive learning environment.

1. Uses available instructional time productively and efficiently

2. Arranges and uses available instructional space, furnishings and display areas to facilitate and enhance learning as physical circumstances permit

3. Encourages student achievement and responsibility by reinforcing desired student behaviors to promote a high level of student participation and appropriate time on task

4. Establishes procedures that ensure smooth transitions from one activity to another

5. Is available and prepared for staffing and screenings as needed

6. Maintains accurate records of student progress

B. The speech/language pathologist maintains and models appropriate standards of behavior, mutual respect, and safety.

1. Encourages student achievement and responsibility by reinforcing desired student behaviors which demonstrate attitudes of fairness and respect

2. Establishes and carries out reasonable rules and procedures

3. Maintains appropriate professional boundaries with students

V. **Promotion of High Standards and Expectations for Student Achievement**

The speech/language pathologist promotes high standards and expectations for student achievement.

1. Communicates standards, expectations, and guidelines regarding the quality and quantity of students' work to students and parents

2. Is receptive to student concerns and responds appropriately

3. Encourages students to take risks and to persevere with challenging tasks

VI. **Displays Promotion of Equity and Appreciation of Diversity**

The speech/language pathologist promotes equitable opportunities for student learning.

1. Provides opportunities for all students to participate in the classroom

2. Demonstrates sensitivity to differences in abilities, gender, learning style, social and cultural backgrounds

3. Develops and implements educational and organizational strategies that are effective in meeting the needs of a diverse student body

VII. **Fulfillment of Professional Responsibilities**

The speech/language pathologist demonstrates continuing concern for professionalism.

1. Seeks out information and is receptive to suggestions for growth and improvement

2. Works collaboratively with other staff members to implement appropriate curricular and school related programs

3. Shares expertise and new ideas with colleagues

4. Works constructively with others to identify school problems and suggest possible solutions

5. Meets deadlines and completes routine responsibilities

6. Engages in appropriate self development activities such as conferences, in-service training, and professional study to maintain and extend subject area expertise

7. Observes established school system policies and procedures

8. Maintains appropriate professional behavior in all interactions with students, parents, and colleagues

LIBRARY MEDIA SPECIALIST PERFORMANCE STANDARDS

I.   **Currency in the Curriculum**

The library media specialist demonstrates competency in subject area(s).

1. Has an appropriate in-depth knowledge of subject matters

2. Acts as a subject area resource person for students and teachers

3. Contributes to the ongoing evaluation of the curriculum

4. Keeps current in the field and applies knowledge to the instructional program

II. **Effective Planning and Assessment of Curriculum and Instruction**

A. **The library media specialist collaborates with classroom teachers to plan effective instruction in library related units.**

1. Sets short-term and year-long goals within curricular units

2. Identifies individual and group needs and plans the use of appropriate instructional strategies

3. Identifies, demonstrates and uses materials and resources, including technologies, that are appropriately matched to curricular goals and to individual student needs and learning styles

4. Seeks out and collaborates with classroom teachers, specialists and administrators to help them design curriculum, assessment strategies, and/or instructional modifications to meet the special learning needs of students

5. Plans frequent instructional opportunities where students are interacting with teachers and one another while assuming increasing responsibility for their own learning

B. **The library media specialist evaluates the library program in relation to changing needs and technology.**

III. **Effective Instruction**

A. **The library media specialist communicates effectively with students.**

1. Implements clear lesson objectives and communicates these to students and teachers

2. Promotes students' independence as learners

3. Stimulates students' thinking through classroom discussion and research activities

4. Identifies students' misconceptions and reteaches or extends teaching to meet individual and/or group needs

5. Has enthusiasm for subject matter and makes significant efforts to communicate that enthusiasm to students and colleagues

6. Communicates clearly in writing and speaking, using precise language

7. Understands and demonstrates to students the relevance of the subject matter to life-long learning and inter-relationship of various curricula

B. The library media specialist uses appropriate instructional techniques.

1. Uses a variety of teaching strategies such as project based learning, discussions, and technologies

2. Helps students plan strategies for acquiring, selecting, and evaluating information and demonstrating competency and mastery of new material

3. Uses a variety of appropriate materials to reinforce and extend skills, accommodate learning styles, and match instructional objectives

4. Encourages students to summarize important learnings and to integrate them with prior knowledge

5. Demonstrates a working knowledge of current educational research and information technology

6. Refines instructional strategies to increase student learning and foster confidence in a student's ability to learn

7. Provides opportunities for creativity

8. Uses a variety of questioning techniques to stimulate student participation, including those which encourage and guide critical and independent thinking and the development of ideas

9. Presents information recognizing multiple points of view; encourages students to assess the accuracy of information presented

IV. Effective Management

A. The library media specialist applies classroom management techniques to establish a positive and productive learning environment.

1. Uses time and space productively and efficiently in order to promote optimal learning

2. Maintains a high level of student participation and engagement with appropriate time on task

3. Establishes procedures that ensure smooth transition from one activity to another

B. The library media specialist maintains and models appropriate standards of behavior, mutual respect, and safety.

1. Encourages student achievement and responsibility by reinforcing desired student behaviors that demonstrate attitudes of fairness and respect

2. Establishes and carries out reasonable and routine classroom rules and procedures

3. Maintains appropriate professional boundaries with students

V. **Promotion of High Standards and Expectations for Student Achievement**

The library media specialist works with the teacher to promote high standards and expectations for student achievement.

1. Communicates standards, expectations, and guidelines regarding the quality and quantity of students' work

2. Responds to students' answers in a timely and appropriate way

3. Encourages students to take risks and to persevere with challenging tasks

VI. **Promotion of Equity and Appreciation of Diversity**

The library media specialist promotes equitable opportunities for student learning.

1. Provides opportunities for all students to participate in the library media center's activities

2. Demonstrates sensitivity to differences in abilities, gender, learning style, social and cultural backgrounds

3. Develops and implements educational and organizational strategies that are effective in meeting the needs of a diverse student body

VII. **Fulfillment of Professional Responsibilities**
The library media specialist demonstrates a concern for professionalism.

1. Seeks out information and is receptive to suggestions for growth and improvement

2. Works collaboratively with other staff members to implement appropriate curricular and school related programs

3. Shares expertise and new ideas with students, colleagues and parents

4. Works constructively with others to identify school problems and suggest possible solutions

5. Meets deadlines and fulfills routine responsibilities

6. Observes established school system policies and procedures

7. Participates in appropriate self development activities such as conferences, in-service training and professional study

8 Maintains appropriate professional behaviors in all interactions with students, parents, and colleagues

9. Articulates and models a vision of the library program that is integrated with all the school's instructional programs, provides intellectual and physical access to materials, emphasizes higher order thinking skills, manages networks of information resources and accommodates emerging information technologies

VIII. Effective Administration of the Library Media Center
The library media specialist administers the Library Media Center effectively.

1. Manages systems necessary for effective operation of the Library Media Center

2. Trains and supervises Library Media Center staff

3. Develops and administers budgets

4. Maintains information for the community about school policies, curricula and programs

5. Collaborates with Cary Memorial Library staff

COUNSELOR/SOCIAL WORKER PERFORMANCE STANDARDS

I.   Currency in the Professional Area
The counselor/social worker demonstrates competency in the professional area.

1. Has appropriate in-depth knowledge of guidance and counseling practices

2. Exhibits awareness of current guidance and counseling practices

3. Employs and/or adapts sound guidance and counseling materials and practices

4. Acts as a resource person for students, parents, and staff in matters of guidance and counseling

II. **Planning and Assessment of Guidance and Counseling Interventions**
The counselor/social worker plans and assesses effectively.

1. Formulates objectives and appropriate strategies to assure continuity of effective guidance and counseling services

2. Identifies individual and group needs and plans the use of appropriate counseling intervention

3. Acquires pertinent information from a variety of sources:

   – Student Records

   – Consultation with appropriate school personnel

   – Consultation with students, parents, and other appropriate agencies or individuals outside of school

4. Assesses the effectiveness of intervention strategies

III. **Guidance/Counseling Practices**
The counselor/social worker communicates and interacts effectively.

1. Interacts positively and productively with students, parents, and teachers

2. Listens well, responds appropriately, and encourages student participation in discussion by effective counseling strategies

3. Communicates positive expectations for all students and reinforces positive behavior

IV. **Effective Management**
The counselor/social worker utilizes effective group techniques and activities to establish a productive learning environment.

A. The counselor/social worker applies effective group management techniques.

1. Uses time and space productively and efficiently in order to support optimal learning

2. Maintains a high level of student participation and engagement with appropriate time on task

3. Establishes procedures that ensure transition from one activity to another

B. The counselor/social worker meets individual and group case load responsibilities.

1. Attends to referrals in a timely and responsive manner

2. Refers students to appropriate support personnel as needed

3. Is available at reasonable times outside scheduled appointments

4. Employs strategies for crisis intervention

5. Actively reaches out to contact students

V. Promotion of Standards and Expectations for Personal Growth and Development

The counselor/social worker promotes high standards and expectations for personal growth and development.

1. Stimulates student's self-awareness and involvement in the learning process

2. Provides individual and group opportunities for students to develop critical and reflective skills and resourcefulness

3. Provides opportunities for parents to develop insight and understanding of students' development and appropriate parenting strategies

4. Elicits student involvement in selecting goals for personal change, selecting activities and evaluating progress consistent with age and ability levels of students

5. Helps students develop group and/or individual decision making skills

6. Assists students in learning how to assess their strengths and weaknesses

7. Encourages students to develop personal standards and methods to assess their own efforts and achievements

VI. Promotion of Equity and Appreciation of Diversity

The counselor/social worker promotes equitable opportunities and appreciation of diversity of all students.

1. Provides opportunities for all students to participate in guidance and counseling programs

2. Demonstrates sensitivity to differences in abilities, gender, race, and ethnicity learning style, social and cultural backgrounds

3 Develops and implements strategies that are effective in meeting the needs of a diverse student body

VII. Fulfillment of Professional Responsibilities

The counselor/social worker demonstrates concern for professionalism.

1. Seeks out information and is receptive to suggestions for growth and improvement

2. Works collaboratively with other staff members to implement appropriate guidance and school related programs

3. Shares expertise and new ideas with colleagues

4. Works constructively with others to identify school problems and suggest possible solutions

5. Meets deadlines and fulfills routine responsibilities

6. Observes established school system policies and procedures

7. Participates in appropriate self development activities such as conferences, in-service training, and professional study

8. Maintains appropriate level of confidentiality and professional behaviors in all interactions with students, parents, and colleagues

OCCUPATIONAL THERAPIST PERFORMANCE STANDARDS

I. Currency in the Curriculum

The occupational therapist demonstrates competency in professional area.

1. Has in-depth knowledge in the field of occupational therapy

2. Is aware of current developments in occupational therapy and applies this in working with students and staff

3. Acts as a resource person for all students, staff and parents

II. Effective Planning and Assessment

A. The occupational therapist plans instruction effectively.

1. Administers individual diagnostic assessments for varied purposes

2. Uses current established testing practices and procedures

3. Makes appropriate referrals for further evaluation

4. Observes and specifically describes student strengths, weaknesses, and therapeutic/instructional needs

5   Develops clearly stated measurable occupational therapy goals and objectives based on appropriate assessments and observations in accordance with the I.E.P.

6. Assists teachers as needed in selecting appropriate instructional materials and strategies

B. The occupational therapist provides effective assessment.

1. Correctly interprets and effectively communicates diagnostic assessments, testing data and relevant information on student progress to parents and staff

2. Continuously evaluates students' progress to adjust therapy procedures and goals

3. Assists teachers in adjusting instruction as needed

4. Provides opportunities for students to reflect on progress

III. Effective Instruction

A. The occupational therapist communicates effectively with students.

1. Implements clear lesson objectives and communicates these to students

2. Promotes students' independence as learners through application of appropriate instructional models

3. Stimulates students' thinking and creativity through discussion and, where appropriate, writing activities

4. Uses effective questioning strategies to stimulate student participation

5. Deals effectively with student questions, responses, and confusions and remediates, reteaches or extends teaching to meet individual and/or group needs

6. Communicates clearly in writing and in speaking using precise language. Has enthusiasm for subject matter and makes significant efforts to communicate that enthusiasm to students and colleagues

7. Interacts positively and productively with all students and teachers

B. The occupational therapist uses appropriate instructional techniques.

1. Uses a variety of appropriate material to reinforce and extend skills, accommodate learning styles and match I.E.P. objectives.

2. Sets short-term and year-long goals for mastery of goals and objectives

3. Encourages students to summarize important learnings and to integrate them with prior knowledge

4. Recognizes multiple points of view and encourages students to assess the accuracy of information presented

5. Identifies individual and group needs and plans the use of appropriate instructional strategies, materials and resources

IV. **Effective Occupational Therapy Management**

   A. The occupational therapist applies appropriate management techniques to establish a positive and productive learning environment.

1. Uses time and space productively and efficiently in order to promote optimal learning. Maintains a high level of student participation and engagement with appropriate time on task. Establishes procedures that ensure smooth transition from one activity to another

   B. The occupational therapist maintains and models appropriate standards of behavior, mutual respect, and safety.

1. Establishes and carries out reasonable rules and procedures

2. Maintains appropriate professional boundaries with students

V. **Promotion of High Standards and Expectations for Student Achievement**

   The occupational therapist promotes high standards and expectations for student achievement.

1. Communicates standards, expectations, and guidelines regarding the quality and quantity of students' work to students, parents, and teachers

2. Accepts students' concerns and responds appropriately

3. Encourages students to take risks and to persevere with challenging tasks

VI. Promotion of Equity and Appreciation of Diversity

The occupational therapist promotes equitable opportunities for student learning.

1. Provides opportunities for all students to participate in the classroom

3. Demonstrates sensitivity to differences in abilities, gender, learning style, social and cultural background

3. Develops and implements therapeutic, educational, and organizational strategies that are effective in meeting the needs of a diverse student body

VII. Fulfillment of Professional Responsibilities

The occupational therapist demonstrates continuing concern for professionalism.

1. Actively engages in appropriate self development activities such as conferences, in-service training and professional study

2. Works cooperatively with colleagues and supervisors

3. Demonstrates an appropriate awareness of school programs and policies

4. Works constructively with others to identify school problems and suggest possible solutions

5. Meets deadlines and fulfills routine responsibilities

6. Observes established school system policies and procedures

7. Participates in appropriate self development activities such as conferences, in-service training and professional study

8. Maintains appropriate professional behaviors in all interactions with students, parents, and colleagues

ELEMENTARY CONSULTING SPECIALIST

I.   **Currency in the Curriculum**

The elementary consulting specialist demonstrates competency in the subject area.

   1.   Has an appropriate in-depth knowledge of the subject area

   2.   Keeps current with and understands and evaluates current research literature and practice in the curriculum area to ascertain the most effective teaching/learning paradigms and practices

   3.   Acts as a subject area resource person for staff and colleagues

II. **Effective Planning and Assessment of Curriculum and Instruction**

A. The elementary consulting specialist plans instruction effectively.

   1.   Sets short term and long term goals for design, development, implementation and evaluation of curriculum, based upon National Standards and State Frameworks and systemic core values

   2.   Formulates and coordinates curriculum objectives, ensuring that there is meaningful sequence to the program goals and interrelation with other areas of curriculum wherever possible

   3.   Works collaboratively with principals and colleagues to develop, design and implement school organizational models, curriculum, teaching strategies and assessment techniques needed by schools to prepare students to meet the demands of the 21st century

   4.   Helps teachers and principals engage in systematic planning to improve curriculum and achieve coherence

B. The elementary consulting specialist provides effective assessment of curriculum, curriculum implementation, instruction and student learning.

   1.   Works with system administrators and teachers to determine standards for student learning and methods of assessing this learning

   2.   Assumes responsibility for organizing a style of curriculum design, development, implementation and assessment toward the goal of continuous improvement of curriculum and instruction

   3.   Promotes innovative and developmental approaches to assessment to help teachers and students reflect on learning and progress

III. **Effective Instruction**

The elementary consulting specialist promotes effective instruction through communication, provision of resources, and staff collaboration.

1. Works with staff to articulate a vision and standard of excellence for curriculum and pedagogy

2. Promotes a stimulating professional environment for staff which supports and encourages their own continuous learning

3. Helps teachers stay abreast of relevant research and the knowledge base related to teaching, learning, and the discipline(s)

4. Provides encouragement, models, and opportunities to help staff members develop a broad repertoire to support the engagement and achievement of all students

5. Provides colleagues with opportunities for sharing that will nurture "best practice"

6   Submit budget proposals for resources and provisions to support quality instruction

IV. **Promotion of Equity and Appreciation of Diversity**

The elementary consulting specialist promotes equitable opportunities for learning.

1. Works with staff to develop and implement educational and organizational strategies that are effective in meeting the needs of a diverse student body

2. Cultivates understanding of issues related to equity, diversity, and excellence so that differences are understood and accommodated, but quality of program and expectations for excellence are uniformly high

V. **Fulfillment of Professional Responsibilities**

The elementary consulting specialist demonstrates a continuing concern for professionalism.

1. Seeks out information and is receptive to suggestions for growth and improvement

2. Works collaboratively with other staff members to implement appropriate curricular and school related programs

3. Shares expertise and new ideas with colleagues

4. Works constructively with others to identify school/system problems and suggest possible solutions

5. Meets deadlines and fulfills routine responsibilities

6. Observes established school system policies and procedures

7. Participates in appropriate self development

8. Maintains appropriate professional behaviors in all interactions with students, parents, and colleagues

CURRICULUM LEADER PERFORMANCE STANDARDS

I. **Currency in the Curriculum**
   The curriculum leader demonstrates competency in the subject area.

   1. Has an appropriate in-depth knowledge of the subject area

   2. Acts as a subject area resource person for staff and colleagues

   3. Understands and evaluates current research, literature, and practice in curriculum and applies knowledge to the instructional program

   4. Keeps current in the field and translates that expertise into developmentally appropriate curriculum and learning environments for children

II. **Effective Planning and Assessment of Curriculum and Instruction**
    A. The curriculum leader plans instruction effectively.

   1. Addresses system core values and priorities, and solicits support and input of administrators, teachers, staff, parents and students

   2. Sets short term and long term goals for design, development, implementation and evaluation of curriculum and instruction

   3. Formulates and coordinates curriculum objectives, ensuring meaningful sequence of program goals and meaningful interrelationship with other areas of the curriculum

   4. Develops, designs and implements school organizational models, curriculum, teaching strategies and assessment techniques to prepare students for 21st century challenges

   5. Works with teachers and principals to identify individual and group needs and to plan the use of appropriate instructional strategies

6. Collaborates with specialists, administrators, and appropriate staff to design curriculum and instructional modifications to meet the special learning needs of students

B. The curriculum leader provides effective assessment of curriculum, curriculum implementation, instruction, and student learning.

1. Works with system administrators and teachers to determine specific challenging standards for student learning, to design and implement appropriate assessments, and to communicate results and recommendations to appropriate constituencies

2. Assumes responsibility for organizing a cycle of curriculum design, development, implementation and assessment toward the goal of improvement of curriculum and instruction

3. Promotes innovative and developmental approaches to assessment to help teachers and students reflect on learning and progress

4. Collaborates with system leaders to acquire and portray to the community a comprehensive overview of progress for the system

5. Helps teachers and principals engage in systematic planning to improve curriculum, instruction, and assessment

III. Effective Instruction

The curriculum leader promotes effective instruction through communication, provision of resources, and staff collaboration.

1. Works with staff to articulate a vision and standard of excellence for curriculum and pedagogy

2. Helps teachers balance interconnected responsibilities to the individual student, the group, school, and larger community

3. Promotes a stimulating professional environment for staff

4. Helps teachers stay abreast of relevant research and the knowledge base related to teaching, learning, and the disciplines

5. Ensures that staff members have opportunities to acquire and develop new materials, approaches, and pedagogical skills

6. Ensures that teachers have adequate resources and provisions for their students and their daily work

7. Provides encouragement, examples, and opportunities to help staff members develop a broad repertoire to support the engagement and achievement of all students

8. Provides opportunities for sharing and collegiality that nurture "best practice"

IV. **Supervision and Evaluation**

The curriculum leader supports curriculum, instruction, teacher effectiveness and student learning through quality supervision and evaluation.

1. Provides a context for supervision and evaluation by ensuring that staff understand system core values and priorities, as well as short term and long range goals of the curriculum/instruction area

2. Communicates clearly to staff about the process, timeliness and expectations related to supervision and evaluation in the Lexington Public Schools, and in their school/curriculum context

3. Creates a positive atmosphere, process and dialogue which allows the staff member to reflect on strengths and achievements, and on areas for inquiry and improvement

4. Provides opportunities for pre- and post-discussion

5. Respects staff members' reflections analysis and recommendations as major contributions in the supervision/evaluation process

6. Approaches supervision and evaluation as an opportunity to encourage self reflection and personal growth of the teacher

7. Completes observation and evaluation reports in a timely manner as specified by contract

V. **Promotion of High Standards and Expectations for Student Achievement**

The curriculum leader promotes high standards and expectations for student achievement.

1. Works with teachers and administrators to broadly communicate standards, expectations, and guidelines regarding the quality and quantity of students' work

2. Establishes and sustains a process to engage teachers, departments, and individual schools in meaningful conversation about assessment of students' work and development

3. Provides information that allows the public to understand standards and expectations for student achievement, and methods of assessment

4. Encourages teachers and students to take risks and to persevere with challenging tasks

VI. Promotion of Equity and Appreciation of Diversity

The curriculum leader promotes equitable opportunities for learning.

1. Promotes professional awareness and competence to ensure that all students feel welcome and affirmed in the classroom, and become full participants and active successful learners

2. Demonstrates, cultivates, and insists upon sensitivity to difference in abilities, gender, learning style, social and cultural background

3. Works with staff to develop and implement educational and organizational strategies that are effective in meeting the needs of a diverse student body

4. Cultivates understanding of issues related to equity, diversity, and excellence so that differences are understood and addressed as part of the process in maintaining quality programs

5 Cooperates with Personnel Office, system administrators and hiring committees to recruit and maintain a staff that reflects and promotes equity and appreciation of diversity

VII. Fulfillment of Professional Responsibilities

The curriculum leader demonstrates continuing concern for professionalism.

1. Seeks out information and is receptive to suggestions for growth and improvement

2. Works collaboratively with other staff members to implement appropriate curricular and school related programs

3. Shares expertise and new ideas with colleagues

4 Works constructively with others to identify school/system problems and suggest possible solutions

5. Meets deadlines and fulfills routine responsibilities

6. Observes established school system policies and procedures

7. Participates in appropriate self development

8. Maintains appropriate professional behaviors in all interactions with students, parents, and colleagues

LEXINGTON PUBLIC SCHOOLS OBSERVATION FORM

Name: _____

School: _____

Subject: _____ Grade Level: _____

Date and Time of Observation: _____

Location/setting: _____

No. of Students: _____ No. of I.E.P.'s: _____

Observation Record:

Commendations and/or Recommendations:

Dates and Duration of Conferences: _____

_____

_____   _____
Signature of evaluator   date

_____   _____
Signature of evaluatee   date

LEXINGTON PUBLIC SCHOOLS FINAL EVALUATION FORM

Name: _____

School: _____

Subject: _____ Grade Level: _____

Evaluator: _____

Total No. of Observations: _____

No. of Years in Lexington: _____ In Present Position: _____

Pre-professional Status: Year 1 _____ Year 2_____ Year 3 _____

Professional Status: Tier 1: _____ Comprehensive _____

Focused _____ Tier 2: _____

I.   Currency In The Curriculum
Commendations and/or Recommendations

II.   Effective Planning and Assessment of Curriculum and Instruction
Commendations and/or Recommendations:

III. Effective Instruction
Commendations and/or Recommendations:

IV. Effective Classroom Management
Commendations and/or Recommendations:

V.   Promotion of High Standards and Expectations for Student Achievement
Commendations and/or Recommendations:

VI. Promotion of Equity and Appreciation of Diversity
Commendations and/or Recommendations:

VII. Fulfillment of Professional Responsibilities
Commendations and/or Recommendations:

Recommendation:

<table>
<tr><td>**Pre-professional Status**</td><td>**Professional Status**</td></tr>
<tr><td>Second Appointment _____</td><td>Tier 1_____ Tier 2 _____</td></tr>
<tr><td>Third Appointment _____</td><td>Normal Increment/Increase _____</td></tr>
<tr><td>Professional Status _____</td><td>Recommend to Tier 2 ___ Year 2____</td></tr>
<tr><td>Non-reappointment _____</td><td>Withhold increment/increase _____</td></tr>
<tr><td></td><td>Restore to Tier 1 ___ Dismissal ___</td></tr>
</table>

_____   _____
      Signature of evaluator   date

Teacher's Comments: (optional)

I have read this evaluation, a conference has been held with the evaluator, and the stated number of visits and hours are correct.

_____   _____
      Signature of staff member   date

The staff member's signature does not imply agreement with the evaluation. The teacher has the right and is encouraged to comment on this evaluation.

SO WHAT ARE THE CORRECT ANSWERS?

In actuality, the answer to all four questions posed in the section before the Brookline and Lexington documents is dependent upon the evaluator and the teacher. The Brookline document is significantly shorter and, therefore, leaves a great deal open to interpretation. This brevity gives it the ability to bend and change to fit varying needs. In some situations, this is an advantage, but in others it is a disadvantage. The second document is the inverse. It is much more specific in its requirements, providing different advantages and disadvantages than the first document. Below is an analysis of one example in each of the E.L.P.S. dimensions of how parts of each document serve as an advantage in some circumstances and as a disadvantage in others. This analysis illustrates the point that there are no perfect documents and that there rarely are unusable documents. More often the key to success lies in the training and supervision of the evaluators, not in the structure of the documents.

> . . . there are no perfect documents and . . . rarely are . . . unusable documents. More often the key to success lies in the training and supervision of the evaluators, not in the structure of the documents.

BROOKLINE DOCUMENT

Educational: The document requires only a single observation of teachers with tenure in the evaluation year. This enables evaluators with large evaluation loads to focus their observation time on those teachers that need the most attention.[1] The disadvantage to this language is that some evaluators may let their practice decline to the lowest required level, thereby not observing more often, even when it is appropriate or necessary.

Legal: The document allows administrators to recommend an out-of-cycle evaluation up to October 20 of the following year. This enables administrators to reassess a teacher's performance during the first six weeks of the next school year before making a decision about whether or not to evaluate that teacher again. The disadvantage of this language is the October 20 date. In some cases, it may be too early and, in other cases, too late. The date may be too late because in some circumstances the administrator may not have enough time to decide whether or not there has been sufficient improvement. In other cases, a date in the new school year may be too late because an administrator may be tempted to delay a decision on evaluating a teacher for a second year, even though he/she has all the information needed to make the decision at the end of the previous school year. Decisions like these are best made as soon as the necessary information is available.

---

[1] This is only advised when a district has other assessment options for teachers, such as peer coaching and/or self-assessment.

Public Relations (Political): The public's primary concern about supervision and evaluation is how the process addresses low-performing teachers. The document itself offers little or no direct information about the process for improving or removing low-performing teachers. A community member who reads the document might conclude that no such procedures exist. However, all such implementation procedures are addressed in Brookline's evaluator training and in the evaluation guide designed for Brookline's administrators. This enables the district to update and improve administrators' implementation as the general performance of the administrators improves, without creating the anxiety among the teaching staff that inevitably occurs when a district seeks to change the contracted document.

Social–Emotional: The document requires a post-observation conference within seven working days of the observation. The possible seven-day delay permits an administrator to reflect on the observation, so he/she might offer helpful comments and suggestions. On the other hand, seven days might feel like a lifetime to a teacher who is anxious to hear the administrator's assessment of his/her performance.

LEXINGTON DOCUMENT

Educational: The document contains eight separate sets of principles of effective teaching (performance standards). Each set is individualized to the specific needs of the eight different categories of "teaching" positions to be evaluated. Having these separate performance standards enables administrators to better tailor their observation comments and recommendations to the specific positions. It also gives non classroom teachers a better assessment of their performance in relation to the unique characteristics of their jobs. However, it does require a significant amount of training and studying on the part of evaluators new to the district to learn eight sets of criteria. If sufficient training and discussion is not available to these evaluators to help them learn and remember the eight sets, they may be less inclined to use the principles in their write-ups and conferences.

> The internal process allows for more objective parties to review the positions of both the teacher and the evaluator, increasing the likelihood of a mutually acceptable plan.

Legal: The document has an easily implemented process to resolve differences between the evaluator and the teacher in the content of the improvement plan in the district. *The internal process allows for more objective parties to review the positions of both the teacher and the evaluator, increasing the likelihood of a mutually acceptable plan.* The document also has a provision for expedited arbitration to resolve differences in improvement plans. Resolving differences between management and the union through arbitration, prior to implementing the plan, ensures that the validity of the plan will not be an issue in the future, if the final evaluation is challenged. However, the cost of an arbitrator's time is $700 (or more) per day. A district with several plans in arbitration is forced to use scarce funds to resolve the plans rather than using them for something more productive, like mentoring or staff development opportunities for the low-performing teachers.

The next example shows the close interconnection between the E.L.P.S. dimensions. A public relations advantage in the document might also be a legal disadvantage.

Public Relations (Political): The comprehensiveness of the contracted process for addressing low-performing teachers will impress any member of the public who reads the document. However, the complexity of this procedure increases the potential for procedural errors by the evaluating administrators unless there is adequate ongoing training and coaching for administrators in the implementation of this process. As mentioned in chapter 5, if an evaluation has serious procedural flaws, a teachers' association may feel it must continue to defend a teacher whose performance has been documented as unsatisfactory to avoid being sued for failure to meet its duty of fair representation.

Social–Emotional: The post-observation conference takes place within three school days of the observation. This provides the teacher with prompt feedback and limits the period of anxiety that might exist for the teacher between the observation and the observation conference. However, teachers and administrators have busy schedules. It is not unusual for an administrator with fifteen or twenty evaluations to complete two or three observations in a single week. Finding mutually convenient times to discuss the observations within three days may be a difficult and stress-producing requirement for the administrator.

SUMMARY

The issues noted in the preceding discussion are just a few of those related to these documents and similar ones which are inherent in every district's document. As noted in the examples, many decisions about the structure of documents lead to advantages in some circumstances and disadvantages in others. Many elements may be advantages for evaluators, but disadvantages for teachers or vice versa. Because of these dynamics, the process of developing documents is usually very time-consuming. What starts off as an effort to develop a document that better meets the needs of everyone in every situation, often ends up as an unfinished document or a document that in time proves to be only as effective as (or less effective than) the previous document. One way to avoid this problem is to initially devote your supervision and evaluation improvement efforts to training evaluators and improving the implementation of the present document. Once you have maximized the implementation of your present document, you may then assess the document from the perspective of teachers and evaluators and through the lens of the four E.L.P.S. dimensions. Having followed these recommendations, you will then be in a much better position to determine which (if any) improvements are needed to maximize the effectiveness of your supervision and evaluation program.

SOURCES

Danielson C. & McGreal, T. (2000). Teacher evaluation to enhance professional practice. Alexandria, VA: Association for Supervision and Curriculum Development and Educational Testing Service.

McTighe, J. & Wiggins, G. (1999). *Understanding by design.* Alexandria, VA: Association for Supervision and Curriculum Development.

Saphier, J. (1993). *How to make supervision and evaluation really work.* Carlisle, MA: Research for Better Teaching.

Saphier, J. & Gower, R. (1997). *The skillful teacher.* Carlisle, MA: Research for Better Teaching.

Chapter 8

ENSURING INTER-RATER RELIABILITY AND PERMANENT, POSITIVE CHANGE IN YOUR DISTRICT'S SUPERVISION AND EVALUATION SYSTEM

The *final* and *most important standard* for assessing how well a program has been implemented in a district is the extent to which the program continues to effectively function after the key person (or people) responsible for the program's development and implementation leaves the district.

People come and go, but school districts endure forever. For this reason, it is important that programs be designed so they will continue to operate successfully as some people leave and others arrive. "Operating successfully" means that a district's supervision and evaluation program maintains a high level of individual evaluator competency and a high level of inter-rater reliability. This is best achieved by designing structures that

1. *teach* the concepts and skills needed to successfully operate the program

2. *coach* new and veteran evaluators in the implementation of those concepts and skills to create and maintain mastery

3. *assess,* at least annually, the evaluators' implementation of those concepts to ensure continued mastery and inter-rater reliability

4. *re-teach* the skills and concepts to those who need to improve and also to those who need to refresh their levels of mastery

5. *teach* new concepts and skills as they evolve in the changing educational, legal and political environment in which evaluators work

This book has provided the reader with documents and activities for the continuous assessment of supervision and evaluation. These documents include

1. The twelve competencies districts should require of their supervision and evaluation trainer(s) (pages 20–22)

2. The five skill components (pages 16–19) that need to be taught, coached, assessed and re-taught, which, as stated in chapter 4, require an *exceptional level of skill and awareness* whenever an evaluator is evaluating a below-standard teacher or one that barely meets the standard

   a. knowledge of the district's performance standards for successful teaching
   b. ability to analyze teachers' and students' behavior (as impacted by the teacher) and determine if the performance standards are met or exceeded
   c. ability to talk with teachers honestly and openly about their performance on the standards
   d. ability to document in writing teachers' levels of performance on the standards
   e. ability to assess teachers' performance using numerous sources of information in addition to classroom observations

3. The Survey of Potential Supervision and Evaluation Topics for Next Year's Administrator Training

4. The Teacher's Assessment of His/Her Evaluator's Performance as a Supervisor and Evaluator (page 37)

5. The Characteristics of Excellent Evaluators documents (both the self-assessment [pages 41–45J] and the one for those assessing evaluators [pages 46–47])

The use of these activities also maintains the common level of practice throughout a district that ensures inter-rater reliability. Later in this chapter, I have included some sample lessons that also improve and maintain the level of inter-rater reliability.

Please Don't Make Me Train the Administrators![1]

In chapter 2, I spoke about the importance of good training, listing twelve characteristics of a good trainer and training program for supervision and evaluation. During my career, I have taught elementary students, middle school students, high school students, graduate students, in-service teachers and in-service administrators. I found the last group to be the most difficult to keep interested and involved. This is especially true when I'm teaching about supervision and evaluation. The reasons for this are probably many, however, here are two of the more obvious ones.

First, administrators hate to leave their buildings or districts, because they are never sure what they will find when they return. When teachers go to workshops, it is true that substitute teachers cannot really replace the regular teacher. However, a good substitute can keep the classroom running at a reasonable level and can at least correct some papers or teach some of the curriculum. There will be some clean up for the teacher, but the contracted day is completed by the substitute and need not be made up by the teacher. There are no substitutes for administrators. All of the work they

> The final and most important standard for assessing how well a program has been implemented in a district is the extent to which the program continues to effectively function after the key person (or people) responsible for the program's development and implementation leaves the district.

are not doing while attending a workshop is piling up back at the office. No one else will write those evaluations, handle the discipline problems, plan the faculty meetings, return the parents' calls or be certain that the custodians are cleaning the bathrooms. This may make administrators unwilling and even angry workshop participants at worst and distracted attendees at best.

Second, supervision and evaluation is a time-consuming, difficult and emotionally charged responsibility. Inevitably, the content of the workshop will include training in activities which evaluators don't do well and would prefer to avoid. I find this dynamic most apparent when teaching about supervising and evaluating low-performing teachers. For the reasons discussed in chapter 5, many evaluators avoid this task. They have learned to work around the low-performing teacher, rather than address the issues. Teaching administrators the skills to address these issues and challenging them to do so often causes a great deal of angst and defensiveness in the workshops.

---

1 In some of the most progressive districts, teachers are becoming evaluators of low-performing teachers. (See the section on peer evaluation in chapter 3 on page 94.) At this point, however, the vast majority of evaluators nationally are administrators and so my comments reflect that reality.

For these reasons, supervision and evaluation workshops for administrators must employ the very best teaching techniques. The trainer must keep administrators actively involved and constantly feeling that the content is useful and supportive of their work.

Keep Them Interested

Below I have provided some sample lessons for teaching the standards and processes described in this book in a way that will keep administrators interested. I have specifically chosen lessons that will increase administrators' collaboration when dealing with difficult issues, thereby increasing inter-rater reliability. The activities chosen are in no way an all-inclusive group. I typically spend ten to fifteen full days[2] in a district over a two- to three-year period when implementing the E.L.P.S. program. In that time, I use a minimum of forty to sixty activities.

> Supervision and evaluation workshops for administrators must employ the very best teaching techniques. The trainer must keep administrators actively involved and constantly feeling that the content is useful and supportive of their work.

The order in which the activities are presented in this chapter is just one possible sequence. Districts should arrange and/or rearrange the order, rewrite the activities and/or write their own activities based on the specific needs of the participants and their districts. The sample activities may be easily revised to match the configuration of your local performance standards, curriculum standards and evaluation procedures.

Creating Training Groups

Good training requires a mix of teaching configurations. Whole class, large group, small group, pairs and independent work should all be part of the teaching repertoire. Before beginning group or pair work, the trainer should decide whether he/she wants to construct the groups, randomly make them or have the participants pick the groups themselves. There are times when any one of these choices is preferable to the others. However, more times than not, careful structuring of the groups will enhance the training experience. For example, in districts where there has not been much previous training, it is often advantageous early in the training program to have evaluators with similar jobs and expectations grouped together. This enables the administrators to begin the process of understanding their colleagues' practice and work toward common expectations (increasing inter-rater reliability). At other times, however, the trainer may determine that one group of administrators has skills from which

---

2 I spend this amount of time in districts with approximately 6,000 students, with more days in larger districts and fewer in smaller districts.

the others may learn. In this case, it may make sense to arrange the groups by mixed skill level, rather than by job similarity. Group structure may have a significant impact on a session's level of success.

Consider the example of one large high school with 1800 students, 230 teachers, 21 evaluators and 6 non-evaluating administrators. The evaluators were divided for the first year of training into three groups based on the school's administrative structure. The school had a headmaster who supervised and evaluated one group of administrators, an assistant headmaster for the humanities and an assistant headmaster for math, science and technology, each of whom supervised and evaluated their own group of department heads, who in turn evaluated the teachers. The high school supervision and evaluation workshops during the first year of E.L.P.S. training were done with six groups made by dividing each of the three groups in half. During the course of the year, the three recombined groups met with their leaders each quarter for coaching support. The district's trainer would attend these meetings as needed to answer questions and provide assistance.

During the second year, the groups continued to have their quarterly meetings. However, for workshop sessions, the trainer varied the groups throughout the year. When re-teaching, the trainer would often mix the groups to increase the inter-rater reliability among them. When new information was presented, the trainer had the evaluators work in their original support/coaching groups. (See chapter 2 for a discussion about the need for group and partner support for evaluators.)

Changing the Groups When Confronted With a Negative Dynamic

Even the most carefully crafted groups may result in a poor mix of members due to factors that were unknown or not anticipated. In these situations, transition times are a good point to change the membership in the groups. A shift in activity that coincides with a break is often a good transition period. It enables a change without signaling that the change is due to some participants' "misbehavior."

I was once hired by a superintendent to train the administrators in a district. The district had about seventy administrators. Each training day was given twice with approximately thirty-five administrators in each session. The first day of training was for the elementary administrators and the second day was for the high school administrators and sixth to twelfth grade administrators. The elementary day went without a hitch. The superintendent introduced the workshop and two of the assistant superintendents stayed for the day. The principals, assistant principals and elementary curriculum people were all eager and positive participants. As a result, I kept principals and assistants together and rotated the district-wide curriculum people to promote inter-rater reliability in the buildings and K–8 throughout the district.

The high school was a different story. People wandered in late and no central administrators came that day. Fifteen minutes into the workshop, the high school principal, who was the ranking administrator in the room, announced that he did not want to be there and did not want his administrators there because there were more important things they should be doing back at the building. "His" administrators were only there because the superintendent required their attendance.

I had originally put together groups of people with the same responsibilities (job-alike). During the first two hours, it became obvious to me which people were following the principal's lead by functioning minimally, looking for opportunities to be oppositional or using the group work times to conduct other business. At the break, I restructured the groups, as I explained, "to provide people with different jobs the opportunity to work together." In addition, I tried to place no more than one discontented participant in each group. I made this change to ensure the groups stayed on the assigned task rather than conducting other business during the group work times or just complaining about being in the workshop rather than back at the building.

Assigning Tasks to Group Members

Once the groups are made, another strategy for groups is assigning tasks to the various members. Typically, at a minimum, groups need a **leader, scribe** and **reporter**. The leader's job is to see that the group completes the task in the time allotted. The leader also makes sure that the ideas of all the group members are heard and that no one member monopolizes the discussions. The scribe keeps notes of the key points in the discussion. The reporter presents these points to the larger group. These assignments may be given in a variety of ways.

1. Let the group choose the roles.
2. The trainer assigns the roles.
3. The trainer assigns the leader and then the leader assigns the other roles.
4. Assign the roles through a random selection such as by using the following criteria.

    leader: person who has lived in the place farthest from the district
    reporter: person who has lived in the state for the longest amount of time
    scribe: person who has lived in the state for the least amount of time

Assigning jobs using criteria number 4 may have the positive side effect of helping the group members to better know one another on a personal level.

5.   This is a variation of the criteria used in number 4 to assign roles. Assign them initially by using the preceding criteria. Then rotate the jobs for each activity, as indicated below:

	Activity 1	Activity 2	Activity 3
lives farthest from	leader	scribe	reporter
longest in state	reporter	leader	scribe
least in state	scribe	reporter	leader

Getting Started

It is usually good practice to begin your first session with some type of ice-breaker or community builder. This helps participants become acquainted (or better acquainted) and prepares people for the content area discussions to come. It is easier to be open and honest with someone you know and trust than with a "stranger." The following are examples of the many conversation starters that may serve this purpose.

Why Am I Here? (Think, Pair, Share)

- How long have you been a supervisor and/or evaluator of teachers?
- Why did you become a supervisor/evaluator of teachers?[3]
- What is the most significant similarity between teaching students and supervising/evaluating teachers?
- What is the most significant difference between teaching students and supervising/evaluating teachers?
- What do you want to learn about supervision and evaluation?
- What age students and/or which curriculum areas have you taught?

The participants share the information above with a partner. The partner then tells the larger group about his/her partner. The need to share about a partner forces participants to listen actively, an important skill for all evaluators to have.

Each group makes a list and reports to the entire training group the two most important things they want to learn about supervision and evaluation. This exercise serves two purposes. First, it gives the trainer a sense of the group's priorities and needs. Second, it illustrates to the group the varied priorities

---

3 This is a great question for stimulating a more personal discussion and connection among the group members. However, it may be too personal for use at the early stages of the group's work and, therefore, may be better left for later in the workshop series. The decision is dependent upon the trainer's interpretation of the group's level of readiness for looking at some of their own social–emotional motivations.

that exist among the participants. This enhances each participant's willingness to be supportive of the trainer's work in teaching concepts that not all participants might personally consider to be a priority.

The trainer should limit each ice-breaker to two questions in addition to the question asking participants "What do you want to learn?" so as not to take too much time from the day's curriculum.

SAMPLE INTRODUCTORY ACTIVITY

The following sample introductory activity is designed to assess the group's previous learning about the educational, legal, public relations and social–emotional standards and processes of supervision and evaluation.

1. It allows the group's collective knowledge on the subject to be brought forward for all to see and learn.

2. It is a pre-assessment that gives the trainer information on the accuracy of the group's present knowledge.

3. It enables the administrators to learn from one another and examine their own beliefs. Information and techniques the participants are helped to discover for themselves or learn from one another, often have *greater credibility* and, therefore, are *retained longer* than those described directly by the trainer.

A side effect of using techniques of this type when training administrators is that they may use some of them when they run their own staff meetings. One of the biggest complaints I get from teachers and teachers' associations about principals and department heads (a.k.a. secondary curriculum coordinators) is that meetings are often presented with the talking head approach to administrator presentation. This is boring to staff because it does not take into account the varied level of knowledge teachers already have on the topic of discussion or the teachers' different learning styles. Throughout supervision and evaluation training, the trainer should remind the administrators of the importance of using varied teaching techniques in their own meetings. Varying their meeting style would demonstrate to teachers the administrators' willingness to walk the walk and not just talk the talk.

> Throughout supervision and evaluation training, the trainer should remind the administrators of the importance of using varied teaching techniques in their own meetings. Varying their meeting style would demonstrate to teachers the administrators' willingness to walk the walk and not just talk the talk.

Procedures

1. Divide the participants into four groups. Setting the room up cafeteria style will help facilitate group work. However, if the room is set up as a theater, participants may turn their chairs into circles. In large groups, people may be asked to partner rather than work in groups and the four assignments may be given out based on the area of the room where people are sitting.

2. Refer to the overhead (sample below) and have each group follow the steps to answer questions 1 through 4. Each group should be assigned one question. The extension for those groups that finish early is to discuss the other questions. Additional extension activities can be found later in this chapter.

Handouts

Adult learners, like children and adolescents, need directions presented in more than one modality to maximize their retention and understanding. Some administrators follow directions best when presented orally, some when presented visually and some when the activity is demonstrated. Make an overhead or wall chart of the steps of each activity. Use the overhead while giving the directions orally. The various graphs and lists in this book can easily be copied and made into overheads on a copy machine or typed into presentation software such as Power-Point®. It is suggested that you give the participants a handout packet containing a copy of all the overheads you use. (Trainers using this book as a text will not need to duplicate in a handout packet those charts and lists

> Information and techniques the participants are helped to discover for themselves or learn from one another, often have *greater credibility* and, therefore, are *retained longer* than those described directly by the trainer.

that are found in the book.) Most presentation software has a function that allows you to put the text of several overheads on a single sheet of paper. Doing this will allow the participants to take notes directly on the handout while you are speaking, saving them time, keeping their notes organized and limiting the amount of content they might miss while hurrying to write notes.

These ideas and the following ones are just a few of the considerations when developing and providing training for groups of in-service evaluators. For those who are interested in learning more about giving interesting and helpful training presentations, I strongly recommend you read the book by Robert Garmston, entitled *The Presenter's Fieldbook: A Practical Guide* (1997).

INTER-RATER RELIABILITY ACTIVITY 1: CLIMBING THE E.L.P.S.

Objective: The following activity is designed to assess the group's previous learning about the educational, legal, public relations and social–emotional standards and processes of supervision and evaluation. It allows the group's collective knowledge on the subject to be brought forward and connects to the group's previous learning in clinical supervision and evaluation. The activity enables members of the group to learn from one another and examine their own beliefs about the processes and standards of teacher supervision and evaluation. This is the first step toward creating common understanding and increasing the level of common practice.

Educational processes and standards of supervision and evaluation

Legal processes and standards of supervision and evaluation

Public relations (political) processes and standards of supervision and evaluation

Social–Emotional processes of supervision and evaluation

1. What are the educational processes and standards of teacher supervision and evaluation?

2. What are the legal processes and standards of teacher supervision and evaluation?

3. What are the public relations (political) processes and standards of teacher supervision and evaluation?

4. What are the social–emotional processes of teacher supervision and evaluation?

Steps of the Lesson

1. In your group, compare and contrast the definition of standard and the definition of process as found in the introduction to this book.

2. In your group, discuss the question (from preceding questions 1 through 4) assigned to your group. The leader should keep the discussion moving and ensure that everyone participates.

3. Your group's scribe should write the answers to your question on the chart paper and tape it to the wall.

4. When all the groups have hung up their papers, the groups will stand by their charts. The groups will then carousel clockwise around the room, reading the answers on each chart and adding any additional answers they may have for the questions on the chart papers.

5. When the groups have completed the carousel, the reporter from each group will report on the answers from the chart that was initially assigned to that group.

You will note that the design of the activity is to get the participants standing, moving and interacting soon after the start of the workshop. This sets the stage for a period of presentation by the trainer. It is important that the participants receive an overview of the educational, legal, public relations (political) and social–emotional dimensions in order to create a context for more in-depth learning about each area. It is recommended that any lecture period be kept to no more than thirty-six minutes, with two minutes at the end of each ten minutes of lecture for processing, questions and comments. The questions and comments will stimulate the group and enable the trainer to assess the group's level of understanding.

Sample overhead for assigning group tasks:

> **leader:** traveled to the farthest destination in the last twelve months
> **scribe:** most years in public education
> **reporter:** fewest years in public education

INCREASING INTER-RATER RELIABILITY USING YOUR DISTRICT'S PERFORMANCE AND CURRICULUM STANDARDS

The following activities are designed to increase inter-rater reliability in the district by focusing participants on the use of the district's performance standards and curriculum standards in their evaluations. Participants begin the process of discussing and defining which observable teaching practices represent each of the standards. They also develop their skills and willingness to talk with teachers about the "hard-to-hear" information. The assumption in the activities is that the participants have all been taught how to observe, script and write using claims, evidence, interpretations and judgments or some similar format that uses objective evidence to support inferred conclusions. (See page 50 in chapter 3.) These skills should be fairly well internalized before moving to the more difficult task of teaching the participants to use the district's performance and curriculum standards. The next three activities focus on the use of the performance standards.

The first inter-rater reliability activity begins with the application of the standards to high-performing teachers. I have purposely started with high-performing teachers because this is psychologically easier for most evaluators. In many groups, the evaluators are uncomfortable admitting in front of their peers and/or supervisors that they have low-performing teachers in their buildings or departments until a certain level of trust has been established. They often feel guilty or embarrassed they haven't dealt with the low performer effectively up to this point.

The second inter-rater reliability activity uses the trainer's teaching to introduce the discussion of low performance. It sensitizes the participants to talking about less successful or unsuccessful performance in an environment that can be safer than talking about their own staff before they are ready. Activity 4 begins the discussion about the evaluator's own low performers. Be prepared for resistance from some during this activity for the reasons mentioned above.

INTER-RATER RELIABILITY ACTIVITY 2: HIGH-PERFORMING TEACHERS AND THE DISTRICT'S TEACHER PERFORMANCE STANDARDS

Visual Imagery

1. Close your eyes and take three deep, slow breaths. Picture your staff as a group (pause). Picture an excellent teacher . . . (pause), picture a teacher who is performing fine, but is one that you would like to move toward excellence . . . (pause), picture a marginal teacher . . . (pause), and, lastly, picture your lowest-performing teacher . . . (pause). First, we will focus on the excellent teacher.

2. Open your eyes and list the behaviors that make this teacher successful. Now connect one or more of these behaviors to the district's performance standards. Describe the behavior you have connected in the language of the district's performance standards and as much as possible in terms of observable behaviors. Write this description in paragraph form and be ready to share it with your group.

3. Each member of the group should share his/her example. While sharing, be sure to explain the following: Why is this example representative of the standard you chose? Does it demonstrate more than one standard? Can you determine this practice is successful from watching the students? If so, how? Why do you believe this practice is successful? How does this standard positively impact student learning?

4. Choose one of the examples from your group and be ready to share it with the larger group in a way that at least covers the five questions posed in number 3.

INTER-RATER RELIABILITY ACTIVITY 3: RECOMMENDATIONS FOR IMPROVEMENT ARE HARD TO HEAR! OR SAYING THE "HARD-TO-SAY STUFF" VERBALLY AND IN WRITING!

The following activity is designed to get evaluators to write about poor performance and to watch and/or participate in a post-conference in which the evaluator needs to talk about poor performance[4]. The activity uses the trainer as "the teacher" to provide practice in a safe yet authentic environment. Conferencing with teachers about performance that needs improvement and writing evaluation reports to teachers about this type of performance are two of the most difficult tasks for evaluators.

1. Think about the teaching you have observed thus far in this workshop. Apply one of the performance standards to what you have observed. Write an evaluation paragraph making a claim, judgment and interpretation, supported by evidence, about one aspect of the teaching that should be improved. (For help, see the description of these concepts on page 50 in chapter 3.)

2. Write a recommendation for improving the teaching of that aspect of the workshop based on one of the performance standards.

3. Be prepared to give oral feedback to the trainer about an area of success and the area for improvement, as you would to a teacher after a classroom observation.

   The trainer should bring one participant from each group to the front of the room to have a post-conference about something in the teaching the trainer should improve. During and after the conferences, the following four points should be emphasized.

> Always say the "hard to hear stuff" to the teacher before you give it to him/her in writing.

Important Rules for Giving Suggestions and Negative Feedback

1. Always say the "hard to hear stuff" to the teacher before you give it to him/her in writing.

2. Consider whether you are a mama bear, papa bear, or baby bear, and then be sure you give the feedback with the right balance of sensitivity and clarity. (See the explanation of the Goldilocks Effect on pages 134 and 144 in chapter 5.)

3. Always begin with something positive.

4. Good questioning and good listening is as important or more important than good advice.

---

4 As noted in the Characteristics of Effective Evaluators, it is important that the areas for improvement be stated orally to the teacher before putting them in writing. Saying the "hard to say stuff" before writing it is more respectful of the teacher. It enhances the school climate by increasing the respect the teachers feel and increasing the level of trust between the evaluator and the teacher he/she evaluates.

Chapter 3 (pages 73–76) discusses the use of good listening skills in difficult situations. It includes sample questions that evaluators can use in a post-conference to address the teacher's use of assessment. Similar questions can be applied to all areas of instruction.

ASSIGNING HOMEWORK

The following sample homework assignment uses work the participants have already completed or need to complete as part of their regular responsibilities prior to the next workshop. Busy administrators are reluctant to do homework that is not readily connected to their responsibilities.

There is also an implicit objective built into the assignment. The implicit objective is asking the administrators to begin to classify their teachers' performance as top third, middle third or bottom third. This is a new and often difficult concept for many evaluators to accept and implement. It is a summative, standards-based concept that measures teachers' performance against a district standard. Many administrators have become accustomed to and are more comfortable with solely formative supervision and evaluation that is devoid of judgments that in any way indicate that one teacher's performance on a standard may be better than that of another teacher's. You will note that the definitions of formative and summative are written on the homework sheet as a reminder to evaluators that both roles are important.

In my work with districts, I have found a significant disconnect between the way evaluators conduct evaluation conferences and write observation and evaluation reports and the language of the documents themselves on which they write their final evaluation reports. In many districts the conferences, observation write-ups and final evaluation narratives are solely formative. However, the districts' documents require that evaluators check one of three or more summative judgments of performance level. In these cases, the districts' evaluation processes often suffer from two big issues. The first is rampant grade inflation; the vast majority of teachers (as many as ninety-nine percent) receive the highest rating. The second is that when teachers do not receive the highest rating, they are justifiably shocked and angered at what appears to be a disconnect between what they have been hearing all year and the judgment checked-off on their evaluations.

SAMPLE HOMEWORK SHEET
HOMEWORK FOR THE NEXT WORKSHOP

Date: TBA
Time: TBA
Place: TBA

Formative supervision and evaluation is a positive, supportive and collaborative process designed to improve students' performance and attitudes by increasing the effectiveness and attitudes of a district's teachers.

Bring three observation write-ups you completed during the school year (or previous school year if this assignment is being done in the summer or early fall). One write-up should be for a teacher performing in the top third of your school/department, the second should be for a teacher performing in the middle third of your school/department and the third should be for your lowest-performing teacher. *Remember, this is your lowest-performing teacher. The teacher need not be considered a low-performing teacher in the district.*[5] You need not be self-conscious about the quality of the write-ups. We all come with different levels of skill attainment in this area and are here to learn how to improve our write-ups and other supervision and evaluation skills.

Be sure to use opaquing liquid or black marker to cover the names of the teachers. The write-ups will only be used in the privacy of the workshop. Covering the names and following the confidentiality instructions the trainer will give on the day of the workshop will ensure the teachers' privacy.

Summative supervision and evaluation is a process designed to measure the teachers' levels of success s as compared to the district's curriculum and performance standards.

INTER-RATER RELIABILITY ACTIVITY 4:
LOW-PERFORMING TEACHERS AND THE
DISTRICT'S TEACHER PERFORMANCE STANDARDS

1. Picture your staff again as a group. Picture the lowest-performing teacher in your building/department for whom you brought the write-up . . . List the behaviors that need to be improved and connect one of these behaviors to one of the district's performance standards. Identify the

---

5 Even though the directions ask participants to bring an evaluation for the lowest performer in your school/department, in every case in which I have given this assignment several administrators raise their hands and say they have no low-performing teachers. The trainer may need to repeat the directions several times and emphasize the fact that everyone has someone who is at the bottom of the school/department. Even if the administrator's lowest teacher is in the top third of the district, the teacher is still that administrator's bottom performer and warrants more time and attention than others in the building/department.

teaching technique using the language of the performance standard as much as possible (claim). Provide objective evidence supporting the claim, in terms of observable and or verifiable behaviors. Remember, verifiable behavior can come from many sources other than classroom observations. Indicate the impact of the teaching technique on student learning (interpretation). Finally, include a value judgment that indicates whether the teaching technique is below, barely meets, meets or exceeds the district's standard.

2. Write this description in paragraph form. If you have a good example in the write-up you brought, you may use it by rewriting the paragraph in the C.E.I.J. form. Make the claim in the language of one of the district's performance standards.

3. Write an evaluation recommendation for the teacher that is related to the behavior. To the extent possible, indicate the impact the recommendation will have on student learning.

4. Share the paragraph and recommendation with your partner and give and receive feedback using the peer-edit sheet found on page 72.

5. Each pair should choose one of their examples and share it with the group. Please do not use the teacher's name. While sharing, be sure to answer the following questions.

   a. Why is this example representative of the standard you chose?
   b. Does it demonstrate more than one standard?
   c. Can you determine that this practice is not successful from watching the students? If so, how?
   d. Why do you believe that this practice is not successful?
   e. How will your recommendation improve student learning?

INTER-RATER RELIABILITY ACTIVITY 5: THE WAY WE WANT SUPERVISION AND EVALUATION TO HAPPEN VERSUS THE WAY IT REALLY HAPPENS

The importance of contract and labor law increases exponentially when evaluating a low-performing teacher. Unfortunately, many administrators overestimate or underestimate the requirements of the law because they lack sufficient training in the standards and processes articulated in labor and contract law. When you combine this lack of knowledge with the administrators' varying predispositions toward addressing low performance (the Goldilocks effect), you often end up with one of two outcomes.

Some administrators act too quickly and skip steps because of their frustration with the time and effort needed to complete the process correctly. Others act too slowly so they may avoid the final steps for a teacher who does not adequately improve (i.e., a "last chance year" or dismissal). As I often tell my workshop participants, typically there are only two mistakes an evaluator can make. The first is going too fast through the steps. The second is going too slowly through the steps.

This activity is intended to identify both the misconceptions and the accurate prior knowledge of the participants concerning the factors that increase the complexity of evaluating a low-performing teacher. It also begins the process of evaluators' identifying their own varied levels of willingness to address low-performing teachers. The participants' understanding of those differences is the first step toward district-wide amelioration of the differences in their supervision and evaluation of low-performing teachers.

1. Picture again the lowest-performing teacher in your building/department from the previous activity.

2. Imagine you are in a perfect world where you are not encumbered by factors such as time constraints, contract or labor law, the impact on other staff, emotional reactions, etc. List your goals for this teacher's improvement, and briefly develop a professional development or improvement plan and time line for achieving these goals.

3. Now look at your goals and time line in the context of the real world full of all of the educational, legal, public relations (political) and social–emotional factors (challenges?) that come into play when you evaluate a below-standard teacher. List the factors that keep you from carrying out your perfect world plan for achieving your goals for this person. Be prepared to explain how these factors impede your ability to implement your goals from item 2.

4. When you finish, share the information with your partner and brainstorm strategies for overcoming the real life challenges faced by your plan. Please do not use the teacher's name.

5. Share with your group the goals, time line, list of challenges and any strategies you and your partner developed for overcoming the challenges.

6. The group recorder should list the challenges discussed that increase the complexity of evaluating a low-performing teacher and any corresponding strategies for overcoming these challenges.

INTER-RATER RELIABILITY ACTIVITY 6: LEARNING FROM OUR MISTAKES AND OUR SUCCESSES

This activity is best used after the participants have completed the case study activity on pages 143–144 and learned the format for an improvement plan.

Think about a difficult evaluation you've done in the past. Now, think about the teacher in terms of the questions that appear on pages 143–144 after the Jeff Doe case study.[6] Be prepared to explain to your group your answers to the following questions:

1. What about the evaluation went well?

2. Why did that part go well?

3. What did not go well?

4. What would you do differently if you had the chance to do that evaluation again?

5. What supports would have been helpful for you when doing this evaluation?

Share your answers to questions 1 through 5 with a partner. What additional suggestions does your partner have for the next time you face a similar situation?

INTER-RATER RELIABILITY ACTIVITY 7: DEVELOPING AN IMPROVEMENT PLAN

1. Skim chapter 5. (This chapter should have been read at an earlier point.)

2. Closely review the final evaluation and improvement plan for Karen Sullivan, beginning on page 156. Compare that improvement plan to the section that describes the components of an improvement plan on pages 148–150.

3. List those components that exist in Karen Sullivan's plan and those that are missing. Be prepared to share this list with your group.

4. Think about how the components of the improvement plan apply to the lowest-performing teacher in your specific building/department. Remember, evaluation is a problem-solving process and one that requires situational leadership. Many of the strategies can be modified to match

---

6 One of the most difficult areas for an evaluator to assess is the impact his/her intensive work with a low-performing teacher has on the other staff members and the school culture. One technique some evaluators use is to visualize each of their teachers individually. (This is best done in a quiet setting such as in the car during the commute to or from work.) They then do a brief assessment of each teacher's response to the evaluator's work with the low-performing teacher and try to place the teacher in one of the following categories: believes the evaluator is not addressing the issue sufficiently; is pleased that the issue is being addressed and fully supportive of the actions; is pleased that the issue is being addressed, but feels a bit threatened; believes that the evaluator is pushing too hard; believes that the evaluator is pushing too hard and feels threatened; believes that the evaluator's actions are inappropriate and unwarranted.

specific situations. Write an improvement plan for the lowest-performing teacher in your building/department. Use a pseudonym for the teacher when you share the plan with your working group.

5. Below, make a list of the questions that arose as you wrote the improvement plan. Be prepared to share these questions with your group.

6. Share the questions in the group and try together to answer as many as possible.

7. Make a group list of the questions that remain.

INTER-RATER RELIABILITY ACTIVITY 8:
AN INTRODUCTION TO TEACHING SAMPLE LESSONS TO CREATE A SCHOOL/DEPARTMENT CULTURE IN WHICH PEOPLE ARE OPEN TO TALKING ABOUT STRATEGIES FOR IMPROVING THEIR TEACHING

Teaching sample lessons is an important technique evaluators can use to get teachers to talk openly and honestly about their practice. The trainer should help the participants realize that the intent of model teaching is to generate a conversation with the teacher about what he/she observed that went well or did not go well. The evaluator does not have to teach an expert lesson. There still is great value to the teacher in observing and discussing the evaluator's teaching of a less-than-perfect lesson. In fact, one would hope that an evaluator who is a full time administrator would not be able to teach as well as a full time teacher. Except in rare circumstances or very specific situations, we should expect that an experienced teacher, teaching a familiar curriculum to a class he/she knows well, should be able to teach a lesson in that class better than an administrator would.

Teaching sample lessons on the legal concepts is also a good way to get the participants to better internalize these concepts and the practices they will need to be successful evaluators of low-performing teachers. Reading a document with the knowledge that they may have to teach it will increase the participants' comprehension. Preparing and teaching a lesson will create a deeper level of understanding.

1. Each participant should reread the section on teaching sample lessons on pages 77–79. Each set of partners should discuss these ideas and generate a list of questions for the trainer.

2. Each pair is assigned one of the legal concepts from chapter 5. A suggestion of how the assignments can be made follows these instructions.

3. Each pair should read their document and make a list of any questions they have about the document. Discuss the group's questions and generate answers. If you get stuck, ask the trainer for help.

4. The pair should plan an approximately fifteen minute lesson using their best instructional practices and addressing more than one learning style in presenting the material. Each lesson will be followed by a question and answer period when the trainer and the presenting group will answer the class's questions about the document just taught.

5. When each pair is teaching their lesson, the other participants in the workshop should listen with the goal of learning the content of the document and thinking about how it applies to their specific lowest-performing teacher. Remember, evaluation is a problem-solving process. Many of the strategies below can be modified to match a particular situation.

Sample Assignments

Pairs 1–7: just cause and due process (assign each pair one of the seven standards)

Pair 8: duty of fair representation

Pair 9: harassment

Pair 10: direct evidence through classroom observation

Pair 11: direct evidence from sources other than classroom observations

Pair 12: indirect evidence from parents

Pair 13: indirect evidence from students

Pair 14: indirect evidence from other staff

INTER-RATER RELIABILITY ACTIVITY 9:
THE SOCIAL–EMOTIONAL COMPONENTS OF STONE SOUP

The workshop begins by asking participants to listen carefully to the story, *Stone Soup* (1993), published by Troll Associates and illustrated by Diane Paterson. *Stone Soup* is a French folktale that is excellent for starting discussions with children or adults about group dynamics. Other trainers may have other stories or discussion starters that work equally well.

It is recommended that the trainer have at least two copies of the big book version so the participants can follow the story while it is being read. If possible, it is good for each participant or group to have the small book version as well so they can refer to it during the activity. I usually have one of the participants read the story and two others hold the big books and show the pictures. This enables the trainer to quickly assess each participant's awareness of the impact of supervision and evaluation on a school's culture. The discussion about the questions below can then be tailored to the needs of the group. While the story is being read, the participants should think about the following questions.

1. In which ways are the social–emotional relationships in the story *Stone Soup* the same as those that occur between evaluators and teachers in their buildings/departments during the supervision and evaluation process?

2. In which ways are the social–emotional relationships in *Stone Soup* different from those between evaluators and teachers in their buildings/departments during the supervision and evaluation process?

   The trainer works to move the discussion toward an examination of the social–emotional factors in the story that are similar to supervision and evaluation. For example:

   a. If an evaluator sees the villagers as the teachers and the soldiers as the supervisors and evaluators, the story indicates that you get more from teachers when you engage them as partners in the process and make evaluation something you do with teachers rather than to them. The story is a good example of how supervisors who use "expert power" (Hershey & Blanchard, 1982, p. 176) rather than "coercive power"[7] (Hershey & Blanchard, p.186) build a collaborative school culture in which the whole is greater than the sum of the parts.

   b. Some evaluators initially see the villagers as the evaluators and the soldiers as the teachers protected by their union. These evaluators often verbalize that they are powerless to address low teacher performance because of coercive behavior by the union (see pages 113–115 in chapter 4). Trainers should remember that this response from evaluators may be caused by a union that uses strong-arm tactics, by the evaluators themselves who hide behind the "threat" of the union as the reason they don't address low performance or by both of these factors. In this scenario, the trainer should try to get more information from the senior administration and/or the union about the reason evaluators feel it is difficult to address low performance.

   c. Reading the story initiates a discussion that allows the trainer to refer to many of the social–emotional components inherent in earlier activities.

---

7 Hershey and Blanchard define expert power as based on the leader's possession of expertise, skill and knowledge, which, through respect, influence others. They define coercive power as based on fear that a failure to comply will lead to punishment.

EXTENSION ACTIVITIES

The movement away from homogeneous grouping by ability in classrooms has made them increasingly diverse academically. Academic diversity increases the difficulty of timing lessons so that all students remain productively on task and continue learning at their own levels throughout the work period. This challenge may be even greater when teachers use cooperative learning groups with different tasks assigned to each group. In these instances, some group's tasks may take less time than others. Therefore, it is essential that teachers plan lessons in ways that provide additional, relevant challenges for those students and/or groups who complete the primary task early. A way of doing this is to provide students with task-related extension activities.

Earlier in this chapter, I noted the importance of keeping the administrators interested and learning. The challenges discussed in the preceding paragraph are as important when teaching adults as they are when teaching children. The following suggestions are for extension tasks for those individuals or groups who finish the primary tasks in this program early.

Extension 1: Review the teaching by the presenter in this workshop thus far. Write a paragraph for one of your performance standards on which you believe the presenter needs to improve. Be sure you identify the teaching in the language of the performance standard (claim), place a value judgment on the performance, interpret the impact on student learning and provide the evidence that supports these subjective conclusions. Write a recommendation for improvement. Be sure to specifically identify the impact of the recommendation on the administrators in the room.

Extension 2: Think about the recommendation you wrote in extension 1. Write one or more questions you can use in a post-conference that you should ask to be sure you have all the information to make the judgment leading to your recommendation. Remember, you can't read the presenter's mind, so he/she may have a well thought-out reason for the action taken that you don't yet understand.

Extension 3: Write a paragraph about a standard the presenter successfully met. Be sure you identify the teaching in the language of the performance standard, place a value judgment on the performance, identify the impact on student learning and provide the evidence that supports these subjective conclusions.

Extension 4: Go to the section in this book entitled "Where Do I Find the Time For All These Write-ups?" Describe any strategies, not on the list, that your group has used (or you have used) to save time or stay organized without diminishing quality. Your strategies can be added to the list and used to help other supervisors–evaluators in the future.

Extension 5: Put a check next to the performance standards you think are most important. Be prepared to explain why you chose those standards. Compare your answers with those of the other group members who are finished with the assignment. See if you can reach consensus.

Extension 6: Respond to the following statements and questions.

- Identify the ways in which teaching an effective lesson is the same as running an effective staff meeting.
- Identify the ways in which teaching an effective lesson is different from running an effective staff meeting.
- What are some techniques you have used or seen used for running effective staff meetings?

Extension 7: Answer the following questions.

- What is the most significant similarity between running an effective staff meeting and teaching a successful lesson? Why did you choose this similarity?
- What is the most significant difference between running an effective staff meeting and teaching a successful lesson? Why did you choose this difference?

Extension 8: Think about an upcoming staff meeting. Write a "lesson plan" for the meeting that utilizes the practices you identified as effective in the previous extension activities.

Extension 9: While you are waiting for the others, write a definition for the legal concepts of just cause (and/or progressive discipline, duty of fair representation or harassment) in your own words.

Extension 10: Write an improvement plan for the second lowest-performing teacher in your building/department.

Extension 11: Write your own extension activity to go along with one of the preceding lessons or one of the concepts taught in the book.

CHECKING FOR COMPETENCY AND UNDERSTANDING

Chapters 2 and 3 contain various instruments that can used to monitor evaluator competency on the concepts and skills taught in this book. These are structures designed to assist those assessing evaluators' work on the various skills and concepts. Below is an assessment that may be done once or twice a year with the training groups to refresh what has been learned and to identify the concepts that need re-teaching. It is fun, but effective.

"Hot Seat" Open Book Assessment

- Your group has thirty minutes to review the questions on the study guide below.

- After that, your group will be randomly given one of the four questions and have twenty minutes to prepare the answer to present to the class. You may use the book, your notes or any other materials from the workshop to prepare.

- Also in that twenty minutes, you must choose two members of your group (a.k.a. the "presenting pair") to come to the hot seat to present the information and two other group members (a.k.a. the "question answerers") to come to the hot seat after the presentation to answer questions from the trainer and the other groups about your question.

- Each group will be given two "life lines" that their two question answerers may pass to another group member who knows the answer when they are unable to answer one of the questions presented.

Study Guide for Open Book Test 1

1. Supervision and evaluation programs are designed to formatively assist teachers in their continuous improvement as it relates to their districts' educational standards and processes. Supervision and evaluation is also designed to summatively assess teachers' performance as measured against their districts' educational standards and processes.

   a. What educational standards do we use to supervise and evaluate teachers? (Think local, state and national.)

   b. How is supervision and evaluation effectively used by evaluators to assess performance as measured against those standards?

   c. How does your district's evaluation document create a process for this work?

   d. How do you assess your own knowledge of the educational standards and processes?

   e. Where can an evaluator go for additional information and coaching related to your district's educational standards?

2. Supervision and evaluation programs are designed to formatively assist teachers in their continuous improvement as it relates to the districts' educational standards and processes. Supervision and evaluation programs are also designed to summatively assess teachers' performance against required legal standards and processes. It is important that evaluators have adequate knowledge of this body of legal information for all their evaluations. However, when an evaluator is working with a tenured teacher (professional teacher status) who barely meets or does not meet the standards, the typical outcomes are that the teacher improves sufficiently or that the teacher might be disciplined or terminated. These situations often shift the evaluation's context more heavily into the realm of labor law. In these cases, it is important that evaluators have comprehensive knowledge of the legal standards and processes.

   a. Which legal standards and processes are important for an evaluator to be cognizant of during supervision and evaluation? (Think local, state and national.)

   b. Which legal standards and processes must evaluators adhere to in their work with low-performing teachers?

   c. Why is it important for evaluators to be cognizant of the legal standards and processes even when the evaluator is not working with a low performer?

   d. How does your district's evaluation document create a process for following the required legal standards?

   e. Where can an evaluator in your district go for help in following the legal standards and processes, particularly when involved in the evaluation of a low-performing teacher with tenure (professional teacher status)?

3. Supervision and evaluation programs are designed to formatively assist teachers in their continuous improvement as it relates to the district's educational standards. Supervision and evaluation is also designed to summatively assess a teacher's performance as it relates to the various public relations (political) standards and processes so schools can be accountable to the public.

   a. Who are public educators' public relations (political) constituencies? Why is each of these constituencies important?

   b. What are the public relations (political) impacts when a district ineffectively supervises and evaluates teachers?

   c. What are the public relations (political) impacts when a district effectively supervises and evaluates teachers?

   d. What can teachers, building administrators, district administrators and support staff in our public schools do to build public support for public schools?

4. Supervision and evaluation programs are designed to formatively assist teachers in their continuous improvement as it relates to the district's educational standards and processes. Supervision and evaluation programs are impacted significantly by the various social–emotional standards and processes. It is our summative conclusions (particularly those we put in a written observation and/or evaluation) that can complicate and intensify the interpersonal and emotional climate during supervision and evaluation.

   a. In what circumstances does supervision and evaluation cause a strong emotional reaction in a teacher? (Think about average-performing and high-performing teachers as well as low-performing teachers.)

   b. In what circumstances does supervision and evaluation cause difficult interpersonal situations for evaluators?

5. How does supervision and evaluation impact a school's and/or a district's culture? What can an evaluator do maximize the positive impact and minimize the negative impact of supervision and evaluation on the school's/department's culture?

6. Where does an evaluator go for support/coaching/advice when involved in an evaluation that causes difficult emotional reactions in the teacher or the evaluator?

7. Where does an evaluator go for support/coaching/advice when involved in an evaluation that causes difficult social dynamics between the evaluator and the teacher and/or the evaluator and his/her staff?

8. In your group, choose a difficult social–emotional situation related to the supervision and evaluation of a teacher in which one of you was actually involved. Tell the class what skills and/or techniques the evaluator used in handling the situation and what the group learned from the chosen case.

9. How do you as an evaluator gauge the impact of your work as a supervisor and evaluator on the culture in your building/department or district?

CONCLUSION

The activities in this chapter are only a sample of the myriad of teaching strategies that can be used to teach the various concepts and skills in this book to evaluators. However, no amount of excellent teaching (training) ever eliminates the need for coaching, assessing and re-teaching. As illustrated in the cases noted in the Archaeological Dig on page 23, nearly all the impact of even the best training in supervision and evaluation will disappear in a relatively short time if there isn't continual coaching, assessing and re-teaching.

The busy lives of evaluators inevitably make them focus on the "crisis du jour" and not on the time-consuming, emotionally challenging and less immediately compelling activities needed to successfully supervise and evaluate teachers.

Yes, it is hard work for a district with dysfunctional supervision and evaluation to transform its program. Yes, it does require a commitment of evaluators' and central administrators' time and resources to turn a dysfunctional system into a successful system.

Yes, it does take time, vigilance and a skilled central administrator to continuously coach, assess and re-teach, even in districts with successful supervision and evaluation programs.

However, once a district is operating a successful program of supervision and evaluation that attends to the educational, legal, public relations (political) and social–emotional dimensions, you can expect a school culture that provides:

- higher student achievement
- higher teacher morale
- higher public perception of the school's/department's performance.

SOURCES

Garmston, R. (1997). *The presenter's fieldbook: A practical guide.* Norwood, MA: Christopher Gordon Publishers.

Hershey, P. & Blanchard, K. (1982). *Management of organizational behavior: Utilizing human resources.* Englewood Cliffs, NJ: Prentice Hall, Inc.

Saphier, J. & Gower, R. (1997). *The skillful teacher.* Carlisle, MA: Research for Better Teaching.

Stone Soup. Illustrated by Paterson, D. (1993). Troll Associates. ISBN 0-89375-479-1.

Notes

Notes

Notes

Notes

Notes